W9-BHM-556

the Supper Club
BOOK

A Celebration of a Midwest Tradition

DAVE HOEKSTRA

CHICAGO
REVIEW
PRESS

Copyright © 2013 by Dave Hoekstra
Foreword © 2013 by Garrison Keillor
First edition
Published by Chicago Review Press, Incorporated
814 North Franklin Street
Chicago, Illinois 60610

ISBN 978-1-61374-368-3

Interior design: Jonathan Hahn

Library of Congress Cataloging-in-Publication Data
Hoekstra, Dave.
    The supper club book : a celebration of a Midwest tradition / Dave Hoekstra. — First edition.
        pages cm
    Includes index.
    Summary: "The supper club of the Upper Midwest is unmistakably authentic, as unique to the region as great lakes, cheese curds, and Curly Lambeau. The far-flung locations and creative decor give each supper club a unique ambience, but the owners, staff, and regulars give it its personality. Author Dave Hoekstra traveled through farmland, woods, towns, and cities in Wisconsin, Minnesota, Iowa, Michigan, and Illinois, eating at salad bars, drinking old fashioneds, and most of all talking to old-timers, local historians, and newcomers. He discovered that far from going the way of so many small establishments, supper clubs are evolving, combining contemporary ideas such as locavore menus and craft beer with traditional Friday night fish fries and Saturday prime rib. He brings to life the memorable people who have created and continue the tradition, from the blind dishwasher at Smoky's to the Dick Watson Combo playing "Beyond the Sea" at the Lighthouse and the entrepreneurs and hipster crowd behind the Old Fashioned. Corporations have defined mainstream eating habits in America, but characters define supper clubs, and this combination oral history and guide, with more than one hundred photographs, celebrates not only the past and present but the future of the supper club"— Provided by publisher.
    ISBN 978-1-61374-368-3 (hardback)
    1. Restaurants—Middle West. 2. Dinners and dining—Middle West. 3. Middle West—Description and travel. I. Title.

TX907.3.M55H64 2013
647.9577—dc23

2012046446

Printed in the United States of America
5 4 3 2 1

For Mom, a coal miner's daughter from southern Illinois,
and Dad, whose road began in the Union Stockyards of Chicago.

Contents

Foreword

By Garrison Keillor

The Moonlite Bay Supper Club is the swank spot for dining in Lake Wobegon, a little snuggery overlooking the water where candles flicker in maroon globes on the tables, Home of the Generous Ribeye, featuring the keyboard stylings of Ramona Magendanz, where expert mixologists will prepare your favorite cocktail to your complete satisfaction. This is *not* the permanent kaffeklubben and floating cribbage game of the Chatterbox Café, nor is it the hamburger heaven of the Sidetrack Tap, nor is it the Seniors Lunch at Lake Wobegon Lutheran, nor is it Sunday dinner at Cousin Helen's with all the cheery news about her descendants that you've heard before. It is a dining experience where the lights are low and a person can sit in the shadows and enjoy a libation and a good meal and say what you think without Aunt Lois contradicting you at every turn. Aunt Lois isn't here. You didn't invite her to dine with you. This is your right in a free country.

We are not people given to heavy drinking and hearty partying. We are wary of drinkers. They get into their cups and they're liable to drift into long maudlin monologues about the unfairness of life. In Lake Wobegon we say, *Nothing good happens after ten PM*. We say, *Whiskey does not bring out the best in people*. That far-off whooping and caterwauling you hear around midnight—that is not us, nor is it anyone we'd care to know personally. Nonetheless, who can object to an occasional Screwdriver or Bloody Mary or Old-Fashioned if it helps you and the Missus relax and put the cares of the day behind? And that is why people go out to Moonlite Bay. You will sit in the vicinity of nice people like yourself who may nod to you but will not come and plop down next to you and complain about the price of soybeans nor will they sink into a stupor and start singing along with "Rainy Day Woman" on the jukebox. There is no jukebox, just Ramona, and she does not know "Rainy Day Woman." Your waitress LaVerne will bring over the generous condiment tray of carrots, celery, radishes, green onions, and gherkins and the drinks will arrive and you will scan the familiar menu and deliberate your choices, fish, fowl, and beef. And you bask in the confidence that you are about to have a very nice time.

I was introduced to supper clubs by Eugene and Marjorie Guntzel, whose daughter Mary was my fiancée back in my college days. Sunday liquor sales were illegal in Minnesota back then so if they wanted to go out for Sunday dinner, they went to a supper club where you brought your own liquor along and the waitress brought you some ice in a glass. They lived in a little house with an enormous yard in a suburb of Minneapolis and on summer Sundays Gene liked to make himself a double Manhattan and sit in a lawn chair under the big maple tree and take his ease. He didn't talk much about his job—he managed the warehouse of a big ceramic-tile wholesaler—I got the impression it wasn't a lot of fun. He didn't talk much at all—Marj was the talker in the family—and as he swam through the first Manhattan and landed on the second, he mainly just smiled.

Marj was an excellent cook within the parameters of Gene's culinary tastes and she set a lovely table. She had grown up in North Dakota during the dust-storm Thirties and elegance was her trademark. Dinners were served on time on a white tablecloth with good china and silver and were as good as pot roast and potatoes possibly can be. And when she needed a break from cooking, Gene packed up the Scotch and bourbon and sweet vermouth in a canvas bag, and off we went in his Buick Electra in our Sunday clothes, a short skinny man with a big nose carrying the bag, a tall good-looking brunette in her fifties, a tall bearded man in his twenties looking rather aloof, and a lovely young woman faintly embarrassed, and the short man slipped the maître'd a five and asked for a corner table by the window and there we plunked ourselves down. A white tablecloth, cloth napkins folded into bishop's hats, silverware, water glasses. Everything just so. The waitress was stout, wore a starched white outfit and a hairnet, and brought us menus and four glasses with ice. Gene mixed the drinks, a Manhattan for him, Rob Roys for the ladies, straight Scotch for me. The men ordered the twenty-two-ounce prime rib, the women ordered walleye or baked chicken. The relish tray was brought, with raw celery, carrots, green onions, radishes, sweet pickles. Gene raised his glass: *here's to us*.

We clinked. We looked around at each other and smiled. Marj was happy to be freed from her kitchen. Gene felt prosperous and paternal. I was happy to be freed from my good Christian family and their teetotaling meals and the rigid conventions of conversation, especially on the Lord's Day. Mary was happy, I think, that she had snagged a fiancé and thereby proven herself to her parents. We were all happy.

My parents, being Christian separatists at heart, did not care for the word "club," which suggested nightclub, which suggested cigarette smoke and gin fumes and a woman in a low-cut gown singing songs about illicit love. They didn't frequent restaurants. They visited their relatives and ate dinner with them, a constant round of visiting and hosting. Why would you go to a supper club and eat food prepared by someone you didn't know?

Well, there are reasons. Families can get too close and an old bull takes up too much space and a queen mother supervises every aspect of life no matter how small and the ones low down on the pecking order go a little berserk and crave some elbow room and maybe a bump of whiskey along with it, and there's where the supper club comes in. A nice place where decent people can eat good enough food with whomever they like and if they want to have a snort, that's okay, and if they want to talk politics they can do that without Uncle Earl climbing up their back. Freedom of association and of expression were what you needed a supper club for. It certainly wasn't for the meat loaf.

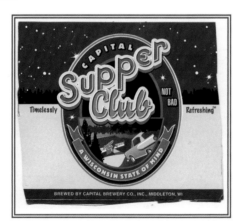

Supper Club
Road Trip Map

CANADA

Lake Superior

MINNESOTA

Ottertail ⚓ The Otter Supper Club
and Lodge

Clitherall ⚓ The Peak Supper Club

94

Fisher's Club ⚓ *Avon*

St. Paul
Jax Café ⚓
Red Stag Supper Club ⚓

94

WISCONSIN

Hayward ⚓ Turk's Inn and
Sultan Room

Sister Bay Bowl
Sister Bay ⚓

The Mill
Sturgeon Bay ⚓

75

Lake
Huron

MICHIGAN

Sullivan's
Supper Club
Trempeleau ⚓

39

⚓ Mr. Ed's Tee Pee
Supper Club
Tomah

90

The Del-Bar ⚓⚓ House of Embers
Ishnala ⚓ *Lake Delton*

43

Lake
Michigan

35

Kavanaugh's Esquire Club ⚓
Smoky's Club ⚓⚓ ✪ *Madison*
The Old Fashioned

IOWA

Ding-A-Ling Supper Club ⚓
Hanover ⚓
Moracco ⚓ Timmerman's
Dubuque Supper Club

Beloit
Racine ⚓ HobNob
⚓ The Butterfly Club

90

✪ *Lansing*

Cliff Bell's ⚓
Detroit

94

Lake
Erie

The Ced-Rel ⚓
*Cedar
Rapids*

⚓ The Lighthouse Inn
and Supper Club

80

*Des
Moines*
✪

Chicago

94

ILLINOIS

Introduction

I live in Chicago, where edible menus, secret eateries, and tickets for restaurants are in vogue with avant-garde foodies.

I am lost.

Then a road map opens up to Midwest supper clubs like a violet in the spring.

I find the essence of place.

Each time I suggest the term *supper club* to people in and out of the supper club circle, I am met with sincere smiles, keen questions, and vivid impressions. Everyone seems to know a Midwest supper club—or they *want* to know a Midwest supper club. It is a place near their heart.

Place consists of four elements: natural, built, cultural, and social. A Midwest supper club covers all four bases. And they are always changing. Supper club—it sounds like a place where the middle class is larger, life is exciting and defined (in sharp black and white), like *Mad Men*, the Playboy Club chain, and Pan Am, all of which enjoyed a pop culture resurrection as I was gathering oral histories for this project.

But the supper club is not a trend. Supper clubs are from an earlier America. Social mores have shifted. I hear supper club operators talk about how customers no longer use the terms *ma'am* and *sir*. Some folks shout, "Hey, you!"

Cultural habits have evolved. People don't spend as much time at "supper," and because of stiff driving laws no one drinks as much alcohol at a supper club as they did during the 1950s and '60s.

Most of the supper clubs in this book were built in the mid-twentieth century. They require attention and upkeep. When you care about a place, what do you restore and what do you get rid of? The world moves at an accelerated pace through technology and tools that didn't exist when supper clubs flourished.

People work from home. People find companions on the computer. This has made the supper club more of an appreciated iconoclast for its organic connections, a rare fruit hanging on a long vine.

Corporations have defined mainstream eating habits in America. Characters define supper clubs. In her 2011 book *A Nation of Outsiders: How the White Middle*

Class Fell in Love with Rebellion in Postwar America, Grace Elizabeth Hale wrote how the need for "self-determination and autonomy" was counterpointed with an internal desire to be "grounded in time and place and a web of human relationships." Such is the comfort zone of a supper club.

While writing this book I was speaking to a friend who owns the Matchbox, a popular Chicago bar, and the adjacent Silver Palm restaurant. He is from Detroit but has not visited his hometown since 1994. Downtown Detroit now breaks his heart. But the place he knows will always exist in his mind.

There is also the natural curve of life. Ed Thompson, the owner of Mr. Ed's Tee Pee Supper Club in Tomah, Wisconsin, died during the year I spent researching this project. He kept watch over his supper club in downtown Tomah because it was a place to spiritually escape the pain of his cancer.

The theme that emerged during my surveys was one of family-operated businesses, people rolling up their sleeves and working long hours to keep the place going. And these muscles were flexed during the summer of 2011, the worst economic period in America since the Great Depression.

I will never forget the people I met on this journey, where place was so important: the blind dishwasher at Smoky's Club in Madison, Wisconsin. The blond hometown girl and her Jamaican husband making a new life for themselves at the Peak Supper Club in central Minnesota. The grandmother who personalizes the matchbooks at Jax Café in Minneapolis. The gentle couples at Fisher's Club in Avon, Minnesota, who share business cards with both the husband's and wife's names. There is the gregarious nature of the folks at the Sister Bay Bowl and Supper Club in Door County and the straightforward meatpacking legacy of the young men who own Timmerman's Supper Club in East Dubuque, Illinois. They all are a team.

Their stories need to be told. Not unlike the oral histories of Negro League baseball players and World War II veterans, the stories of the Midwest supper club need to be chronicled and remembered.

The value of place in a supper club creates a deeper meaning of place. Robert Gard said, "No place is a place until things are remembered." Naturally—Gard was a Wisconsin guy. He joined the faculty of the University of Wisconsin in 1945 and founded the first Wisconsin Arts Foundation and Council.

The beginning of the American supper club is surprising, not unlike asking for cheddar cheese and getting brie. According to the Wisconsin Historical Society, the first American supper club was established in the early 1930s—in Beverly Hills, California, of all places. Milwaukee native Lawrence Frank created an affordable supper club menu of prime rib, mashed potatoes, creamed corn, sweet peas, and Yorkshire pudding. Frank also introduced the doggie bag to an increasingly mobile American clientele.

At the same time in the North Woods of Wisconsin and Minnesota and along the Lincoln Highway in Iowa, some clubs made their mark as Prohibition roadhouses (many with gambling).

The Midwest Supper Club grew into an honest place. It is as unique to the region as great lakes, cheese curds, and Curly Lambeau. The far-flung location (with the exceptions of the Old Fashioned in Madison and the Red Stag in Minneapolis) only feeds the contained little universe quality of the dining experience. It is all about place.

A down-to-earth, real-deal supper club fed off the scenic rolling hills of southern Minnesota, eastern Iowa, and rural Wisconsin. A supper club is to Wisconsin what a roadhouse is to Texas. In his landmark 1949 *Sand County Almanac*, Aldo Leopold wrote of Wisconsin, "Country is the personality of land, the collective harmony of its soil, life and weather. . . . A supper-smoke hangs lazily upon the bay, a fire flickers under drooping boughs. It is a lean, poor land, but rich country."

During the 1950s and '60s supper clubs thrived in that rich country. More than four hundred still exist in Wisconsin, according to Ed Lump, president and CEO of the Wisconsin Restaurant Association.

They are the fork in the road between yesterday and today.

This is what you need to know about the supper club; some of the guardrails I put up while interviewing hundreds of people for this book:

- A good supper club has a dark setting. It is an organically cool place. You can be in a supper club in the middle of the day and it will feel like the middle of the night. Madison's former Supper Club beer brewmaster Kirby Nelson thinks about supper clubs when he quotes the bestselling Dan Jenkins football novel *Semi-Tough*. Miami Bucks footballer Shake Tiller says, "I'd be happy if the whole world was semidark and indoors." Shake would have been at home with the Packers, the Vikings, or even the Iowa Hawkeyes.

- Supper clubs have linen napkins. I got a reaction from all of my interview subjects by mentioning this touch of class—along with relish trays with carrots, radishes, and celery. A few traditionalists told me not to forget about the lazy Susan, which always has a place in a vintage supper club.

- A supper club still has a Friday night fish fry and will serve prime rib on Saturday.

- A supper club is not a club. You don't have to join. So here is a stumper: why are they called supper clubs? During Prohibition some of the oldest supper clubs were literally clubs where customers stored their hooch in small lockers. Today, they are full of social rituals. There is an appointed time of arrival, which is incongruous to the supper club's meandering nature. Supper clubs are simply a place to go—and a place to be seen by friends and neighbors.

  Lump adds, "Supper clubs have the atmosphere of the common man's club. Years ago, more than today, you would find people with supper club jackets just like bar jackets."

- A good supper club is filled with clumsy furniture. Like high-back chairs with lots of Naugahyde. Very important. Many supper clubs have held on to equipment and furniture from the 1960s with heirloom passion. "I was at a Door County supper club that also had banquet-style furniture," Lump says. "A lot of supper clubs had a lot of space so you could divide the area for banquets when the club wasn't busy. That's why you also see chairs with padded backs and metal frames with banquet, high-back chairs."

- Unlike some suspect diners, bars, and cafés, kids are welcome in a supper club with their parents.

- Supper clubs are almost always out in the country—or were out in the country—with a lake and woods view. And out in the country people call dinner "supper." Supper can be served as early as 4:30 PM.

- The waitresses who carry your food are usually called Helen, Sally, or Gloria. They walk and talk in measured steps. The distinct places of Iowa, Wisconsin, and Minnesota can be heard in the inflection of staff members.

- Supper clubs opened as a one-stop destination where gentle folks would spend an entire evening, from cocktail hour to the cool nightclub-style entertainment after supper.

- Beer is never served on tap at a real supper club. During the supper club's peak years of the 1950s and '60s, fancy draught systems did not exist. Real supper clubbers drink brandy old-fashioneds and martinis. Wisconsin residents drink more brandy than people anywhere else in the United States. They call the brandy old-fashioned with a cherry and orange garnish the "brown martini." Lump says, "We have a lot more places licensed to sell alcohol than many states of similar population." I did not know this until I began researching this book. It answered my question on why there are hardly any supper clubs in Illinois or even in Rockford near the Wisconsin border. People in Illinois don't drink so many old-fashioneds. But the minute you cross Wisconsin into Beloit, for example, you can find supper clubs with old-fashioneds.

- Many supper clubs were named after the winding highways they sit along. Lump has been president of the Wisconsin Restaurant Association since 1981 and recalls, "We used to go to Club 93 along Highway 93 in Arcadia, Wisconsin."

- The supper club is about the longing for belonging. No one goes to a supper club alone. It is a community within a community, a place to catch up on local news and events.

When brewmaster Nelson was doing a pilot run of Supper Club Lager, his partners at the Great Dane Brew Pub wanted to call it Kirby's Supper Club. "That kind of embarrassed me," Nelson reflects. "But they said, 'If you think about it, a lot of supper clubs have had the person's name on it—because whenever you were there, that guy was working. He knew you by name, he knew all the customers. A one-on-one connection evolved over time. It didn't have the insanity you see in some places today.'" Lump says the Midwest supper club carried a "customer base that was there all the time."

Scott Faulkner, second-generation owner of the sixty-three-year-old Edgewater Hotel in downtown Madison (a supper club hot spot) concurs. "Somebody from the family is back in the kitchen, someone from the family is out in front. The bar manager usually was the guy who was not from the family. It's a comfort thing. A lot of people can't afford to be a member of a private country club where you go to see people and eat. This takes that place for the blue-collar family. It's their club. No dues."

- A supper club is about self-reliance. President Barack Obama rose to political prominence in Illinois, just south of the teeming Wisconsin–Minnesota supper club corridor. Obama's ascension mirrored the resurrection of the supper club in pop culture. In his bestselling memoir *Dreams from My Father* Obama wrote of the fluidity of identity and the potential of free self-invention in America.

Jim Leary is a Wisconsin folklorist and director of the Center for the Study of Upper Midwestern Culture in Madison. He was born and raised in Rice Lake in northwest Wisconsin. He says, "My folks were one generation removed from being poor laborers and starving ranchers. Breakfast was breakfast, midday you had lunch, and in the evening you had dinner. The word 'supper' wasn't used in my family as a term for a meal, but I would often have friends on farms or working class where the midday meal was 'dinner,' the evening meal was 'supper,' and lunch was a meal you'd have at a card party or a house party, some kind of light thing. So the word 'supper' means a substantial evening meal for rural and working-class people."

And that is the spirit of this book.

A place in time that is not as distant as you might think.

DAVE HOEKSTRA, APRIL 2012

PART I

The Roots

1

Turk's Inn and Sultan Room

11320 North US Highway 63, Hayward, Wisconsin
(716) 634-2597

It is unclear if Turk's Inn and Sultan Room is the oldest supper club in Wisconsin. But it sure feels like it.

Turk's opened in 1934 on the northern outskirts of Hayward (population 2,312), known for the Freshwater Fishing Hall of Fame and Museum and the Moccasin Bar, a tribute to the art of North Woods taxidermy.

You wish Turk's could also be captured in time. So far it has been.

The supper club is a Turkish bath bubbling over in bric-a-brac like stuffed pheasants, collector's plates of almost all US presidents, gold tassels, paintings of all sorts, and black-and-white photographs of famous customers like President John F. Kennedy and Mike Connors from the late 1960s television show *Mannix*. President Kennedy and Senators Robert and Ted Kennedy all visited Turk's. Actor Mickey Rooney came in once, admitting he was lost.

Beatrice "Marge" Gogian was doing her best to keep all this afloat in the early summer of 2011. She wore her black hair in a 1950s pageboy style, and she slowly moved about the tchotchke-filled club recovering from a 2009 fall that broke her hip and a leg. Marge did not disclose her age, but most of those around her put her a few steps past eighty.

Turk's Inn thrives on the outskirts of Hayward, also the home of the Freshwater Fishing Hall of Fame.

Owner Marge Gogain still offers a helping hand in Turk's small kitchen.

A touch of Istanbul—founder George "the Turk" Gogain came to America's heartland from Istanbul, Turkey.

Marge is the daughter of the original owner, George "the Turk" Gogian. She has never been married. Marge has no children. "Still single," she says. "Still lookin'."

Supper clubs are a constellation of family-run establishments. Marge is *the* family at Turk's.

Edward Lump, president and CEO of the Wisconsin Restaurant Association since 1981, calls Turk's Inn "a national treasure." He says that Turk's may be the oldest supper club in Wisconsin.

"The Red Circle Inn [in Nashotah] claims the oldest restaurant in the state, starting in 1848," Lump says. [The Mill in Sturgeon Bay opened in 1930.] "But Turk's is the most unique supper club of any. I've been there quite a few times. Look at the history of the supper club and the founder, who was well connected with all kinds of political figures who stopped in—Egyptian royalty when there was such a thing. I mean he's got a picture of himself on a camel with King Farouk."

George the Turk came from Istanbul and Marge's mother, Isabella, was from Armenia, which borders Turkey. They came to America after an arranged marriage. When George and Isabella opened Turk's on Highway 63, two miles north of the center of Hayward, they played up their heritage.

Each red menu was shaped like a fez, complete with a black cloth tassel that dangled in the nocturnal air. The back of the menu featured a cartoon of "George," "Mom," and "Margie" in traditional Turkish garb. George wore a red fez and baggy pants and Mom and Margie had white pillbox hats with long veils.

George and Isabella had the moxie to create a supper club menu of Turkish delight. For example, a late

1930s menu presents "DOLMA: It is said that George the Turk came over to this country in Noah's Ark, and he brought with him a recipe for a Turkish dish—and what a dish! It's called Dolma. It has a base wrapped in grape leaves, stuffed tomatoes, and green peppers. A superb treat—your palate will be the judge."

George mixed the imagery of mystical Turkey with the Noah's Ark comfort zone of the North Woods. "He tried to teach people here how to eat pilaf, cracked wheat, shish kebab [leg of lamb marinated in wine and seasonings]," Marge recalls.

It was an amazing experiment. In the backwoods of northern Wisconsin you could drink Turkish coffee and nibble on Turkish pickles at Turk's Inn. Pastries included baklava (with honey and chopped nuts; "a delicacy eaten by the harems in the Arabian Nights," according to the menu) and the cheese-filled beorek ("light as air, crisp as paper, and fragile as romance"). The Turkish specialties are still served at the grand old supper club. Appetizers include Turkish pickles and the beorek. Turkish coffee is also on the menu.

"My dad always said he wasn't going to copy everybody else," his daughter relays in firm tones. So while Turk's Inn is known for its steaks, it is one of the few Wisconsin supper clubs to pass on the Friday night fish fry, an oddity since Hayward is so closely identified with fish.

Marge says, "A butcher friend taught him how to be a butcher. He used to age and cut his meat, which we still do. That was his specialty. My mom's specialty was fried and broiled chicken. And we're still famous for our porterhouse and New York steaks. If they want prime rib I talk them into having a porterhouse. Everybody has prime rib. When my dad died we decided we would not change anything. I was the butcher for a long time until I broke my leg and my hip. Now I'm convalescing so my help knows how to do it."

Marge's right-hand man is Tom Shuman, who was once Turk's insurance agent. He is now a Hayward farmer with 180 to 220 head of cattle. Shuman came on the scene after George died on Christmas Day, 1979.

A fez cocktail menu with tassel.

"George had a marvelous personality," Shuman says. "He was about five feet tall. He smiled all the time. He had a mind like an eagle. After he died I saw a need for somebody who had a little extra time to help Marge and her mom along a little bit. We all called George's wife 'Mom.' She cooked all the meat in that kitchen. Today you would have no idea how those people worked. When her mom became ill Marge had the whole responsibility of running the place. I knew the place. My folks took me there from the time I was four or five years old." Shuman was born in 1939.

Marge says, "We don't use Tom's meat though. We get our meat from Swanson's in Minneapolis [a wholesaler who purchases the meat from the packers]. We age it for five weeks in the walk-in cooler until it gets nice and tender. Then we cut it and flavor it. I taught Tom how to cut the meat. And Tom knew how to do everything the way my mom and dad did it."

Victoria "Cookie" Piecuch has assisted Marge on a daily basis since her fall. Marge lives next door to the supper club and comes by to help when there are crowds. Cookie also helps Marge around her house. Cookie started working at Turk's in 1953 when she was twelve years old.

"It was so busy here in the 1950 and '60s," she says while Marge inspects the small kitchen. "I also had my own restaurant, the '63 Inn [now the Aspen Wood Inn], south of Hayward [on Highway 63]." Cookie and her husband, Richard, built the motel and restaurant back when US 63 was a new hip way to get between Minneapolis, to the southwest, and Ashland, Wisconsin. "Richard also helps Marge," she says. "When we're busy I have him come in and tend bar." Cookie and Richard's six children have all worked at the Turk throughout the years.

In the mid-1950s Cookie learned Armenian dances at Turk's Inn. The impromptu instructions would take place at two or three in the morning, after the supper club closed.

"Armenian kids would be working there," Cookie recalls. "There were cousins from Istanbul and Egypt. We had Armenian music on the jukebox. The guys wanted to dance. We would dance in the kitchen, around the kitchen table. It was a sideways step, not like a polka where you go 'round. We went back and forth. It would have been more fun in the dining room because I love to dance. But it was amazing."

George the Turk collected art, memories, and everything else. Marge looks up at a stuffed owl near a bar cluttered with antique liquor bottles and decanters. Many bottles had collected dust. "Oh, yeah, that owl is against the law now," she says.

Customers walk into Turk's Inn and are met with a pseudo–living room setting with an old piano and a Chinese golden pheasant and silver pheasant preserved in full wingspan. There's a partridge, not in a pear tree but on the crowded wall of this Harem Room, which is regarded as the supper club's lounge.

Shuman said the rural setting made Turk's popular with politicians from the state capitol in Madison, a few hours south. "They could kind of let their hair down a little bit," he says.

The Sultan Room (bar area) is across the hallway. The rear ninety-seat Kismet Room (for good luck) affords a tranquil view of the woods with a walkway to the Namekagon River. And off to the side of the Kismet Room is the exclusive Gogian Room, with white tablecloths, green linen napkins, and a portrait of Marge when she was a young woman. The room's bronze Persian rug is from when "Persia was Persia," as Marge puts it.

You could get lost here. That's what George did.

"My dad loved birds," Marge says. "He had cages out there. He kept beautiful peacocks. He planted flowers. He loved being outside."

Marge Gogian's early life was a flight of fancy. She went to Chevy Chase School for Girls in Washington, DC, and New York University. At Chevy Chase was the only time Marge was addressed by her real name of Beatrice. Her father had nicknamed her Marge in tribute to a favorite customer at the supper club.

After college Marge was a stylist for the fashion photographer Gordon Parks in New York City. "I hired the models and got all their accessories," she says. "I went to Saks Fifth Avenue. That's always been my favorite store." It still is, beating out Hi Ho Silver in Hayward.

Through connections made at the supper club, Marge and her father attended President Kennedy's inaugural ball in Washington, DC. She designed her own silk dress inlaid with gold threads. A photograph of the memorable event is prominently displayed in the Kismet Room. And this is why JFK's commemorative plate ranks the highest in her collection. The plate has a special place in a glass case in the Kismet Room.

Marge says, "Jack was running for president and he spoke at Hayward High School. Then he came here. Jackie wasn't here. He ate a steak. That was our specialty. [Late US Justice] Harry Blackmun used to come all the time. He'd stand by the stove with my mother and put his arm around her." Servicemen and public servants who visited Turk's Inn ate free.

The acclaimed Egyptian photographer Dan Leo photographed a young Marge during a visit to Egypt. The photos are on display in the Gogian Room. It becomes clear Marge has carried a sharp sense of style her entire life. Did this influence the supper club?

She answers with snappy Wisconsin wisdom: "I try to be like I should be."

Molly Stoddard is a kindred spirit to Marge in that she has lived her life the way she wanted. The Hayward resident is former lead singer of the popular country band Molly & the Heymakers, who recorded for Warner Brothers in the early 1990s.

The album cover of their 1998 release *Lucky Flame* was shot at Turk's. "Turk's was our spot," Molly says. "Any time we had a producer from Nashville come up or someone we wanted to impress but freak them out at the same time we would take them to Turk's. And everybody got into it. Music business people are quirky and they dug it. Like the Sultan Room, nothing has changed since 1952. Marge does have times when it is difficult to be there. They fight in the kitchen. You hear pans being thrown. Then you're waiting and waiting. We went there once with twelve people. And our food didn't come and it didn't come. You could hear them fighting in the kitchen. We were walking to the bar and mixing our own drinks. By the time our food came we were so trashed. I couldn't even taste my food."

Molly grew up in Ely, Minnesota, north of Hayward. Her father, Bill Otis, sang in the Canadian Opera Company and she went to high school in the Hayward area. She remembered the first time she saw Turk's.

"I went there as a kid and it was rockin'," says Molly, who was born in 1958. "That was in the heyday. All the way down to the river they had exotic birds and plants. The place was a series of places where you would sit to wait to get into the dining room. And it was just packed. You would sit in these little booths to wait to get in. Now they're just filled with junk, stacks of weird magazines. But you would sit out there and have an hors d'oeuvre. That was back in the day when people were drinking serious cocktails. My grandma loved the place. We'd have to get all dressed up. I had three sisters and she would buy us matching outfits and purses. So to this day when I go to Turk's, I still get dressed up and Marge loves that."

Stoddard was Molly Scheer when she led the five-piece Heymakers band. They maintained a studio in Hayward although the record label was in Nashville. Stoddard was raising children of her own at the time and did not want to uproot them. "I'm kind of a hick," explains Stoddard, who plays fiddle, mandolin, and rhythm guitar. "And I'm still here. I like it up here."

George the Turk had a fatal heart attack in 1979. Marge was traveling in Europe. She returned to her roots. "I didn't want to leave my mother alone," Marge says. George and Isabella were married fifty-three years. "I've been here ever since. After he died, my mother never came out here, except to clean the bar or something like that."

The shadows are getting long at Turk's Inn, but Marge still has vivid memories of when the supper club opened in 1934. "I was a little girl," she says. "We lived upstairs. I heard all kinds of racket. It was Memorial Day weekend. I came downstairs to see what all the racket was. They had a three-piece combo playing big band music. No carpeting. There was a dance floor. The women were in long gowns and big hats and the men were in white suits. I thought, 'What's going on here?' Then I thought, I better get back upstairs before I get caught! They never knew I came downstairs. They celebrated for four days about this place. We no longer have dancing here. When they started asking for a tax on places that had dancing, my dad said no. He put in the carpeting."

But for Turk's seventy-fifth anniversary party, Molly Stoddard brought a half-dozen belly dancers to the supper club. "I had a little café [Madeline's] for years in Hayward," Molly explains. "I had a bunch of college girls working there. We had

A good supper club has linen napkins—and a scenic country view.

an open mike night. A young woman came in and belly danced. I thought it was amazing so I hired her to come in and teach everybody that worked there, all ages, how to belly dance."

At one point fifty women were belly dancing in the small town of Hayward. "I was the matriarch of the group," Molly says. "About six of us went out to Turk's to belly dance. We got Marge out with us. She hadn't had anything like that forever. She loved it."

Marge is proud to call her beautiful little dining complex a supper club. "This is a supper club," she says in no uncertain terms. "We have linen napkins and nice table-cloths. We're one of the few that still do that. We have a relish tray if they order it. We used to give it for free. Supper is an old-fashioned name, and dinner is a modern name. That's all I know." From a distance, Cookie shouts, "My grandpa always said Jesus had the last supper, not the last dinner."

People are not apathetic about the eclectic Turkish suppers at Turk's. "People love it or they just don't get it at all," Molly says. "It's a polarized reaction. And it's really expensive. Turk's has big-city prices. It's like my place."

Molly owns the Pavilion wine bar in downtown Hayward. She still plays music in the Danger Band, performing weekends at the small European-influenced bar. "Most locals don't come in and they don't know what's going on," she says. "But the second homeowners appreciate it is something odd and a little different for a small town. Turk's is the same way."

Turk's Inn serves lots of brandy old-fashioneds and has a heady selection of bottled beer: Beck's, Budweiser, Miller Genuine Draft, Miller Lite, O'Doul's, Leinenkeugel's Red Lager and Sunset Wheat, Michelob Ultra, Guinness, and others. Cookie says Miller Lite, Leiny's Red, and Budweiser are the best sellers.

"It's not a bar where you drink and get drunk, stuff like that," Marge says. "We have all kinds of drinks. I learned how to tend bar when I was a young girl. My dad learned how to tend bar and he hired all kinds of college boys to tend bar. We never hired a professional because they drank." She stops and laughs. "My mom and dad never drank. People always wanted to buy my dad a drink. He'd have them pour a bit of Scotch in a tall glass, fill the rest up with water, and when they weren't looking he'd dump it in the sink."

When George "the Turk" Gogian first came to America, he became a chocolatier in Philadelphia. He opened a candy factory.

"He lost everything during the Depression," Marge says. "He lost his business. He didn't know what to do." George found work at a Philadelphia hotel and enjoyed the increased opportunity to meet people. Isabella's mother lived in Saint Paul, so the young couple moved to the Twin Cities, where George got a job at the Hotel Leamington in Minneapolis. While in Minnesota he learned about the rural beauty of Hayward, 145 miles away.

"He fell in love with the Namekagon River, which runs behind our place," Marge says. "He found a job at a small restaurant in Hayward. The highway [63] was built so he decided he wanted to have his own place. The banks would not loan him any money because it was the Depression. His relatives in Philadelphia thought he was crazy to come to Hayward. But my dad didn't like working for anybody."

A regular at the since-razed restaurant in downtown Hayward was an area lumberman who offered to help George build the new supper club on the outskirts of town. "My dad had a great personality," she says. "He loved to talk." His networking ability opened another door to Barney Divine, chief conservation warden for the state of Wisconsin. Divine made frequent visits to Hayward. The two men connected over their love of the Wisconsin land. According to Marge, Divine invited George and the lumberman to his office in Madison, 280 miles south of Hayward.

Divine gave George a $3,500 loan to start Turk's Inn.

"He wrote out a check and said, 'George, take this home, pay off the lumberman, open your business, and when you are able to pay me back you can do so,'" Marge relates. "My dad came home and they finished this building. My dad always loved the river, which is why he picked this land."

The South Central Wisconsin Association of Retired Conservationists (SCWARC) discovered Divine explaining the emerging mid-1930s conservation movement in the state, which corresponds with the earliest appearance of supper clubs. According to SCWARC, in 1938 Divine explained the motivation for becoming a warden this way: "The answer is hard to put into words. It's a matter of deep-seated feelings, a combination of circumstances that makes men forget monetary gain and do a job that they can put their heart and soul into. Maybe it has something to do with love of the outdoors, the woods, the lakes and streams, the creatures of the wilderness. Maybe it takes men who have some sort of feeling for nature's infinite plan and who derive from the natural things that so often surround them a greater inspiration then they might gain from closer contacts with the works of man."

Once George had the place up and running, Divine drove to Hayward to see how the business was going. Divine noticed George was operating without a furnace. "He only had an oil burner," Marge says. "Upstairs we had a pot-bellied stove to keep me warm. I was always cold. That was the second time he saw Mr. Divine. A couple days later we got a wire from his wife saying Mr. Divine died of a heart attack. My dad repaid his wife."

And now Marge is repaying her father.

Turk's Inn remains open year-round, downsizing to a Thursday-through-Sunday evening schedule in northern Wisconsin's rugged winters. "The only time I was closed was when I had a heart attack [in 2007]," Marge says. "I was in the hospital for a long time and I had to close. My dad had five heart attacks. When they told me I had a heart attack I told them I couldn't have had one. I never ate like my dad. Of

Turk's Inn, "An Exotic Oasis in the Northwoods," according to the postcard.

course it was in my genes. When I broke my hip and leg I put the help in charge. I figured they knew everything I knew."

The Wisconsin Restaurant Association's Ed Lump worries about the future of Turk's Inn should no one step up to replace Marge. "It's is a very unique place, not just to Wisconsin, but almost anywhere," he says. "It is too bad when you see these businesses fade into the sunset. It would be hard for somebody to come into that location and do what she is doing. It's such an off-the-cuff thing. The pictures, the artifacts. The recipes are unique, the atmosphere. I imagine when the time comes it will continue as a restaurant of some kind, but not like that. A lot of supper clubs are that way. In fact, if you remodel and put modern conveniences in them you lose a lot of flavor. It's all just special. And Marge is special. A chance to meet Marge, that's what a supper club is: an older person doing all the key jobs and touching the customer in a way they feel special."

Cookie is Marge's confidant. "Right now her spirits are there," Cookie says in an interview in the fall of 2011. "But she has a will where it would go to charities and scholarships. People have wondered why I won't take it over. It would not be the same and her wish is for the restaurant to be done. Once everything is over, the place is gone."

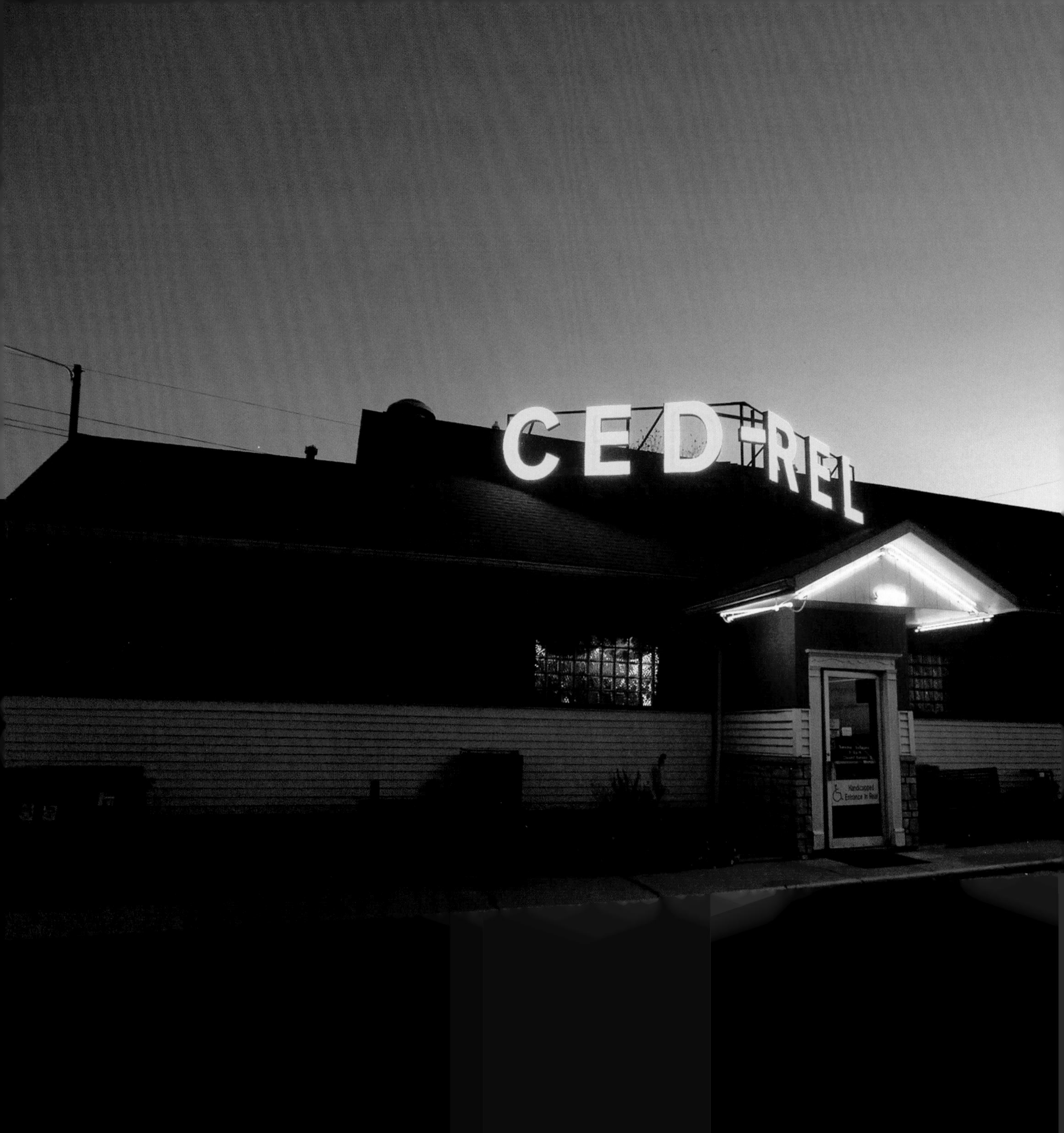
CED-REL

2

The Ced-Rel

11909 16th Avenue/Highway 30, Cedar Rapids, Iowa
(319) 446-7300 • www.cedrelsupperclub.com

Somewhere down a country road in the summer of 2011, winds of more than one hundred miles an hour leveled the volunteer fire station in Garrison, Iowa (population 403). All five fire trucks were buried in the rubble. The town library lost its roof. Volunteer fire chief Steve Meyer estimated that 90 percent of the buildings in town sustained damage.

Grain farmers Dick and Teresa Noe had only their house left standing. They lost most everything else on their farm. The two are regulars at the Ced-Rel Supper Club, twenty-five miles away on the outskirts of Cedar Rapids. They visit the Ced-Rel between fifteen and twenty times a year.

The country road is paved with goodwill.

The Ced-Rel is owned by Jeff Selzer and Mary Jo Dannar. They are young people in the supper club game, but they have traditional values.

"That Sunday I said to Jeff, 'What do you got that we can make and take for food?'" Dannar recalls during a break from prep time at the Ced-Rel. "We're going to the Noes' to see what they need. And you can't go to a farmer's house without taking food."

Dannar knows this because she is a farmer's daughter from Bellevue, twelve miles south of Dubuque.

Ced-Rel's vintage neon can be seen for miles.

American farmers Dick and Teresa Noe.

"They called us before they came and asked if they could do this," Dick Noe says in a separate conversation in the Ced-Rel's party room. "They brought pulled pork, coleslaw, dessert."

Teresa sits next to her husband and speaks in a measured cadence. "They even brought ice cream in a cooler," she says. "It was very much appreciated. We were in a state of shock. We pretty much lost everything. We lost three buildings; most of them were grain bins. We lost our shop where we work on our semis. The garage to our house was damaged." Dick says, "Garrison is a very poor community. It was hard to help your neighbors because they had as much damage as you did. You relied on friends and family."

The Noes raise eight hundred acres of corn and three hundred acres of soybeans on a farm that Dick Noe's parents bought in 1935. Dick graduated in a class of seventeen people from Garrison High School in 1961. He started farming in 1978, just before the farm crisis. He met Teresa when she was working the grain load and payroll at the USDA office in Vinton, near Garrison.

"We've been coming here for thirty years," Dick says. "It's a luxury-type deal. For a while we were coming once a month."

Teresa wears a beautiful gray dress accented by a gold necklace. "The shrimp here is phenomenal," she says. But she does not smile. "We will be glad when this year [2011] is over."

Unlike Wisconsin supper clubs with a scenic lake view, the Ced-Rel is in flat farm country along the old Lincoln Highway west of Cedar Rapids.

The Lincoln Highway was America's first transcontinental highway, connecting the Atlantic and Pacific oceans. It was dedicated on October 31, 1913, predating the more celebrated Route 66 by thirteen years.

An advertisement in the 1916 *Complete Official Road Guide of the Lincoln Highway* pointed out that Cedar Rapids was the largest city in Iowa with "the World's Largest Mills" and "232 trains every day." A newly mobile America was visiting what the ad called "the Model City of the Middle West."

The Ced-Rel has been around since 1917. It was a product of this new connective America. The Ced-Rel began its life as a gas station. Tourist cabins for Lincoln Highway travelers were built in the 1930s before being torn down in the late 1940s. The current Ced-Rel motel next to the supper club was built in the mid-1950s, according to the current owners. The classic Ced-Rel neon sign in front of the motel is over fifty years old.

"During to the mid- to late 1920s this restaurant began as Club Ced-Rel," Selzer explains. "It was a private key club. We still have the original door where you can

Like the best rural supper club, the Ced-Rel was raided during Prohibition. Owners could keep an eye out through the original one-way front door window.

look out but you can't look in. The first person who became a key club member was a Cedar Rapids judge. We don't have his name. To us that's sort of the roots of a supper club; a key club, a speakeasy.

"A lot of people think the name comes from Cedar Rapids. 'Stretch' Sedrel owned it then as a key club. They had a contest to name it. A lady said, 'Why don't you change the *S* to a *C* and hyphenate it?' She got free membership to the key club. A lot of people think the *C-E-D* stands for Cedar Rapids. Make it up as you go along."

Fittingly, it was the escape of the open road that brought Dannar and Selzer together. They are a couple but they are not married. "We were at a motorcycle reunion in 2005," he says. "It was the ABATE of Iowa—District Five [Brotherhood Aimed Toward Education]."

Dannar steps in and clarifies, "I called him for the first date and he said no. Then he called me back because he realized I was asking him out."

Selzer rides a 2001 Heritage Springer. Dannar rides behind him.

"Around here it is so flat," Selzer says. "You go by Mary Jo's hometown [near Dubuque] and there's hills and bluffs." Friends are easier to see in open spaces.

The Ced-Rel seats about seventy friends and neighbors in the back party room and another 135 in the front room facing the Lincoln Highway. Regulars often clamor for the dozen seats around the horseshoe bar.

In the summer of 2010 the couple replaced the supper club's smoke-stained carpeting and repainted the walls gray and the ceiling black. Selzer unlocked a secret to the quintessential supper club mood. "I heard this from our previous owner that supper clubs always had dark ceilings," he says. "She knew what she was talking about. When supper clubs started, people started changing more into the rare side of the meat. People didn't want to see the blood on the plate. That's one reason in the early days supper club had dark ceilings."

Like any good old supper club, the Ced-Rel was raided during Prohibition. Constables found booze and slot machines. During the early 1960s Rat Pack members Dean Martin and Sammy Davis Jr. had dinner at the Ced-Rel minus their leader, Frank Sinatra, who apparently had bigger fish to fry.

The Ced-Rel has had only three sets of owners. After Stretch, Bob and Pat Snyder owned the supper club from 1958 to 2002, when they sold it to Selzer's parents, Ken and Mary Catherine Selzer. During the late 1970s era of the Snyders' successful run, the Ced-Rel's Camelot burgundy and black interior was inspired by one of Pat Snyder's favorite restaurants at Caesar's Palace on the Las Vegas strip.

Ced-Rel owners Mary Jo Dannar and Jeff Selzer, whose orange Crocs pay homage to non–supper club chef Mario Batali.

"On December 19, 1985, a semi came through the northwest corner of the restaurant," Selzer recalls. "The guy fell asleep at the wheel. This was when it was a two-lane highway. Now it is a four-laner. The place wasn't open, but they were doing prep work in the kitchen. . . . They ran out to see what hit the building."

The main beam of the dining room kept the truck from destroying the entire restaurant. The armored knight that used to stand by the front sign was lying on top of the truck's cab. Observers first thought someone was seriously injured. "It was Christmastime; they called up some friends and sealed the corner up with plastic," he says. "They were open that night but everyone had to eat in the back party room."

Jeff Selzer bought out his parents in July 2010. Kenneth Selzer ran a successful family construction business in Fairfax, seven miles away from the Ced-Rel. "When it became one hundred years old none of us kids wanted the construction business," says Jeff, who was born in 1968. "So he closed the books on it. But he's always been in business. I've always loved to cook and always liked to eat. He said business was business no matter what business you are in. You run a business the same way whether it is a restaurant or building houses."

But why buy into a dusty dream off the beaten path?

"This is a very established supper club," Selzer answers. "We bought the clientele that came with it. It was a no-brainer. Or do you start a place no one has heard of and take a crapshoot? This is still taking a crapshoot. But the odds are in our favor.

"In 2002 the economy was better than it is now. But our bread-and-butter clientele is the farmers. We have a lot of Cedar Rapids people who come out but the people who come out every week or every other week, that's the farmers. You have to have real good food because you can't pass anything by the farmers. A city person might think it's a good steak, but you can't pull the wool over a farmer's eyes."

In the late 1950s a thick-cut Iowa chop was featured on the menu at $9.60, when the supper club's motto was "Serving food for particular people." The current motto is "The taste you will remember." That motto did not come from a farmer. Selzer says, "A few years ago our bug man came out to spray and we got to talking about different restaurants in Cedar Rapids. Then he said of our place, 'You go out there and it's just that taste you remember.' I went, 'Hey, can I use that?' We were just chewing the fat."

Between 2007 and 2011 the Ced-Rel won the "People's Choice" award for best steak house in the area in a contest sponsored by Cedar Rapids television station KCRG (Channel 9). Selzer doesn't season the meat because he figures there is no reason to season a quality cut of beef. "We have salt and pepper if they want it," he says.

Dannar and Selzer buy their meat from local vendors. "Any beef you eat here came from no more than ninety minutes north, south, east, or west of us," Selzer says. "They know our criteria. I know on the East Coast they're all about grass-fed cattle. Keep that on the East Coast. You want corn fed. Grass fed will be more stringy and the flavor won't be there like it is for corn fed. On one of her shows Rachael Ray said grass-fed cattle was the way to go. Maybe she has friends who raised grass-fed cattle. That week we had five to seven phone calls asking if we had grass-fed cattle. I never had a phone call about it before that."

Dannar's mother, Rosemary, still raises one hundred head of cattle—alone. She was born in the early 1930s. "Her biggest thing is that they can run out on the pastures until six weeks before they're ready to be sold," Dannar explains. "They come in and get corn fed only in third-crop hay, which is your better hay, too. And she's top seller at the sale barn [in Monticello, Iowa]. It's more solid and more pleasing. Sometimes grass fed has that more bitter taste, like if you take iceberg lettuce and compare it to romaine.

"I think farmers and supper clubs go together. Growing up on a dairy farm, that was our treat. For every one of our birthdays and Mom and Dad's anniversary we went to the Moracco [in Dubuque]. A supper club meant you were going somewhere nice. You dressed up in your Sunday clothes. It's kind of amazing the dress has become casual. They used to bartend and hostess here in high heels and a long skirt. I'd be falling all over the place. But we still wear black dress pants and a shirt.

"You use respect in a supper club. You weren't a squirming kid in a chair. You actually got along with your brothers and sisters, otherwise you wouldn't get to go the next time. Not rushed in and out. There's people there you're always going to know. You're always going to know that same bartender behind the bar."

Growing up on a farm, Dannar quickly learned that the rural community calls dinner "supper." She says, "I never changed that lingo until I got in the military. Dinner? Dinner was at lunch."

Dannar and Selzer know the rules of the supper club road. Dannar says, "One thing about a supper club is you can't change anything on the menu. It's amazing. Jeff's tried some wonderful dishes [shrimp alfredo pasta] but they come out here for the same thing. We had two orders of shrimp go out and people loved it. But two orders don't keep it on the menu. The 'Oh My Shrimp' is his creation and absolutely wonderful. It is one of our top sellers."

Selzer begins with sixteen- to twenty-count shrimp. They are butterflied before being stuffed with cream cheese, garlic, crabmeat, and chives. The shrimp is drizzled on top with homemade eel sauce (soy, mirin marinade, sugar) and "Yum Yum" sauce (mayonnaise, dash of water, garlic powder, paprika, butter, pinch of cayenne pepper, and tomato paste).

"It's a crab rangoon on steroids," he says. "It's too good to be called crab-stuffed shrimp. That's too blah. Ninety-seven percent of the people, with the first bite they took, they said, 'Oh my!' They didn't expect that flavor. Finally that's what we named it."

On the flipside, the Ced-Rel does incorporate legacy recipes. Some have been handed down on faded white three-by-five file cards. Others have arrived as oral histories. "I hate measuring stuff," Selzer says. "I'm the same way Pat [Snyder, former Ced-Rel owner] and my grandpa were. My mom was a measuring fool. All the salad dressings were handed down on recipe cards. Mary Jo came up with a couple. We're known for our cottage cheese dip on our relish tray. That was handed down from Pat [Snyder]. We've had a lot of people try to copy it. Around here no one does a cottage cheese dip. They may do a side of cottage cheese instead of a vegetable or potato, but no one has heard of a cottage cheese dip."

The notorious Ced-Rel cottage cheese dip has seven secret ingredients. People guess four of them: cottage cheese, cream cheese, salt, and onion. Selzer smiles slyly and recalls, "Shortly after the folks and I bought this place, I'm in Atkins, one of the small towns west of here. A church is having a garage sale. I see a cookbook. I'm always intrigued by cookbooks. I'm flipping through and something catches my

Server Tasha Schrage loaded up with chicken livers, onion rings, homemade meatballs, carrots, celery, radishes, and, yes, the Ced-Rel cottage cheese dip with crackers. She got a good tip.

eye: Ced-Rel Cottage Cheese Dip. The lady selling the cookbook for the church was probably in her mid-seventies. She didn't know me. I asked, 'Where did you get this recipe?' She said, 'Son, you just have to know people.' I bought the cookbook, turned to the Ced-Rel page, and handed her my business card. I said, 'By the way, your recipe is only off by four ingredients.' Her faced turned more white . . ." than cottage cheese.

The Ced-Rel has also always had a bean pie. "It's like a security blanket," Selzer says. "Whether you eat or not, you have to say, 'There's the bean pie.'" The bean pie had featured pinto beans but Selzer changed the recipe to Great Northern beans. "You're going to have your pinto beans in Texas and New Mexico," he says. "But up here, no."

But some other standards are missing. "Friday night is the only night we do catfish. They never had prime rib here until we came into play. That kind of died out. We were doing it on Tuesdays only but we took it off the menu."

The food is accompanied by the supper club cocktail standards, old-fashioneds and Manhattans. "When we first took over I asked one of the old-timers, 'Why is an old-fashioned an old-fashioned, how did it become?'" Selzer says. "He told me that years ago you couldn't get good whiskey and this is what you had to do to be able to drink the old-fashioned: the older people would put sugar, bitters, and soda water in the whiskey to sweeten them and make them drinkable."

During late morning of a late summer visit, the Ced-Rel is ready to roll. Dannar and Selzer have been at the restaurant since 8:30 AM. The supper club does not open until 5:00 PM (closed Sunday and Monday). Selzer is the chef. During the morning hours he orders and preps the food and cuts the meat. Dannar is the housekeeper, bookkeeper, and bartender. She makes the relish trays on Tuesday, Wednesday, Friday, and Saturday. "She's what makes us look good," Selzer says while Dannar is away in the kitchen.

The Ced-Rel is a stage awaiting its actors. Utensils sparkle, the dark, burgundy leather chairs from the 1960s are empty, and white linen napkins are crisp and neatly folded.

"Supper clubs always have linen napkins," Dannar declares. Selzer adds, "Linen napkins are more expensive. We don't do our own laundry linen out here because we have a septic system. It couldn't handle it. So all our linens are taken out, washed, and brought back. Does it cost more? Yes. But it looks a lot nicer. If you're going to spend $29 on a steak meal are you going to want a paper napkin? We have a strong two hundred [linen napkins] rolled up and ready to go for backup. That way we're not rolling at night during the meals. Each night when we're done, then the waitresses will roll up. So we have about 350, ready to go and rolled up."

One regular customer has his own carpeting business in Iowa City, about twenty miles south of Cedar Rapids. He lives in Dubuque, about ninety minutes to the east. Dannar says, "During the week when he has jobs to do, he'll stay at the motel. I'll go, 'Kingsley! Get in the coat room and wrap the napkins.' He goes, 'OK.' It's a weeknight and we'll have locals sitting at the bar. We don't have a busser on weekdays. So the regulars will take it upon themselves; they'll go in the kitchen, grab a cart, and start bussing tables. We don't have customers. We have family."

One customer bequeathed the Ced-Rel a cool Art Deco-ish clock filled with clock and spoon symbols. For decades the restaurant had generic outdoorsy paintings that looked more like Wisconsin and the Hamms beer murals of Minnesota than rural Iowa. Selzer says, "All the pictures we have now are farm photos from farmers who come out once a week. If you don't want your name on it, take a picture without your name. It means something to us, to have your picture."

It also means ownership, investing in a memory.

"Last year one of our friends got a good deal on carpeting," Dannar says. "He asked if we wanted to recarpet this place. So we redid everything. We took the booths out. We repainted the walls. We started at midnight on a Saturday, we quit at three in the morning and by seven the next morning we were back here painting. All day long people kept coming in, grabbing a paint brush for however long they could be here. My sister Nancy had her sewing machine set up in the back room sewing the new curtains. These are actually the original maroon curtains. My sister took apart the original curtains and made new curtains out of them. We did the entire room in three days with family and friends. That's good friends. And we only met them through here."

Richard and Dianne Pickart are good Ced-Rel friends who have been dining at the supper club since 1964, a year after they were married. "My parents came here a lot," Dianne says over a Friday night shrimp dinner with relish tray. "They were livestock and corn and wheat farmers by Van Horne. This place has always been popular with farmers."

The Pickarts are family farmers about seven miles from Garrison, Iowa. They farm about four thousand acres of corn and wheat. "No livestock anymore," Richard

Ced-Rel fans Dick and Dianne Pickart from Keystone, Iowa. They have been coming to the supper club since 1964.

says. "Just grain. We know the Noes. Farmers help farmers. We also got hit by the winds in the summer, although not as bad as others."

Dianne says, "Jeff and Mary Jo brought food to us. They brought us slices of prime rib, a chocolate cake, pecan pie. It really helped us for the next few days. We just made it. Rather than worrying about what we were going to eat, it was right there for us. A supper club is like a home away from home atmosphere."

The spirit of the Ced-Rel uplifted the Pickarts. Dianne explains, "After the storm they [Remington Seed] told us they were going to abandon our seed corn crop. He [Richard] was sort of down. He wanted to come out here and I wasn't too sure about that because he was down. What was interesting is that even the town people were very interested in what happened to us. We met a couple from Iowa City who had no idea how the damage affected us."

The area farmers help maintain quality control at the Ced-Rel. Dianne says, "The farmer knows good quality because we process our own. We didn't do it ourselves, but we took our own livestock to market. We know good quality beef when we get it. And we've been places where we can say we didn't get that, but here it is pretty consistent."

Traditional homemade relish trays with radishes, carrots, and pickles are featured at the Ced-Rel. Selzer says, "When we first bought it at least thirty people said, 'Can't get rid of the relish tray.' They think, 'Somebody new is buying it, they're gonna change something.' So after about the thirtieth person I said, 'Give me your name and number and when I get rid of it you can help me board up the front door.'"

The Ced-Rel relish tray is unique in that it features chicken livers. "It's something you don't hear of any more," Dannar says. "We have people who eat them as a meal. I can't believe that. We could not take them off the menu."

A supper club flourishes in the air of such rituals. "We have people who have been married fifty years," Selzer says. He looks at an empty table across from the bar and adds, "And he proposed to her at that table. Let's say the place is 80 percent full and maybe there are six other open tables. But his table is taken. They'll sit up here at the bar and have a couple of drinks and wait for that table. Because that's where he proposed to her."

Previous Ced-Rel owners did not have a children's menu, but Selzer changed that. "We all gotta die," Selzer says. "I'd like to have the next generation bring their kids here." The "Little People" (under ten years old) menu features cheeseburgers, homemade corndogs, and macaroni and cheese.

About twenty-seven people work at the Ced-Rel, including seven waitresses. There are no waiters. Dannar and Selzer did not change the kitchen when they bought the supper club. "It's a small kitchen but it is designed for organized chaos," Selzer says.

Friday night kitchen staff (left to right): Jeff Selzer, Nicole Harding, Darlene Kilpatrick, Hannah Schulte, and Collin Osby.

The rear party room is anchored by a green bridge mural that seems to move back and forth when a guest slowly walks by. It is an optical illusion and not a test to see how many old-fashioneds a guest has consumed. Selzer does not know the origins of the painting. Like a good supper club story, it came with the property.

The twenty-four-unit, one-level motel west of the supper club rents rooms by the night ($45 in 2011), by the week ($200), and even by the month ($600). Since the motel is in Linn County, there is no motel tax. Contractors and blue-collar workers stay at the Ced-Rel motel. The motel is rural, dated, and it can be lonely. The Ced-Rel motel carries the sixty-watt-bulb aura that illuminates a Sam Shepard short story.

When supper-clubbing at the Ced-Rel, take a close look at the pictures behind the bar. The rustic images form a string of memories. You see a collage anchored by Selzer's grandfather Ralph Tines, who died in 1987. Tines taught Selzer how to cook. Near the collage is Dannar's mother and father and the family on the farm. Brothers and sisters. And Mary Jo and Jeff. Family.

Selzer looks around the modest supper club on a sleepy country road. He says, "When you can find a job where you're on vacation every day, you've found paradise. I might be working nine hours a day, fifteen, eighteen hours a day during Christmas, but I enjoy doing it. It's a passion. I am blessed because I enjoy it that much day in and day out."

3

Sullivan's Supper Club

W25709 Sullivan Road, Trempealeau, Wisconsin
(608) 534-7775 • www.sullivanssupperclub.com

Sullivan's Supper Club is nestled along the Mississippi River north of tiny Trempealeau, settled in 1854 by French explorers near La Crosse, Wisconsin. The fur traders discovered a big bluff surrounded by water and named the area "mountain in the water."

The supper club is next to Perrot State Park, and its founder was Ed Sullivan, no relation to the man who introduced the Topo Gigio mouse puppet to American television audiences. The club offers a serene view of the mighty Mississippi with Winona, Minnesota, on the other side. The batter-fried walleye filet is very good, and the bottled beer is cold. A modern green and brown decor leans toward a 1980s Houlihan's restaurant.

Sullivan's offers a typical supper club experience in upper Middle America—until you meet the Sullivan's longtime chef, Dennis Clements, aka the Mouse. The restaurant suddenly becomes a big fuzzy memory. Clements comes out of the kitchen and extends a hand. This is not like meeting Paul Prudhomme or even Guy Fieri. Clements is four-foot-eleven and weighs ninety-five pounds.

He smiles. Each of his ears slowly extends and appears to wiggle. You do not need to ask why he is called the Mouse.

The Beatles never appeared on the stage of Ed Sullivan's Supper Club.

All aboard for Trempealeau—"mountain in the water," according to French explorers.

"I was born thin . . . two pounds, seven ounces. And I never grew up," says Clements, who was born in 1954. "I got the nickname walking down the stairs during eighth grade at Winona [Minnesota] Junior High."

Clements has been cooking at Sullivan's since 1984. It is his second tour of duty at the supper club, which the colorful and playful Ed and Sally Sullivan opened in 1968. Clements was born in the southern Driftless Region of Wisconsin and grew up in Winona. He started cooking in Elbow Lake, Minnesota, hoboed to Texas for a couple of years, and "came back up, cooked at the Golden Horn in Utica, the Hillside Fish House, here, went to another place for a couple of years, came back here, and *staaaaayed*."

Mystery authors Stephen King and Peter Straub have channeled Clements. "I'm a character in King's [2001] book *Black House*," Clements says. "I don't know how that happened. It's about little Centerville, where he bases some of his book."

Sullivan's chef Dennis "the Mouse" Clements, also featured in a Stephen King novel.

King's coauthor Peter Straub is from Wisconsin. *Black House* is set in the world of King's Dark Tower series and features the roadside attraction "the world's largest six-pack," six enormous tanks of beer that, like the Mouse, also actually exist about twenty miles down the road in La Crosse as a tribute to Old Style beer.

"The *Black House* story features the fictionalized town of French Landing, which is actually Trempealeau. French Landing's most famous dive establishment is the 'Sand Bar,' where you will find 'the Mouse,'" Clements says. "I'm a character shooting pool and riding my Harley. I've never met Stephen King."

There is work to do on this midsummer Saturday afternoon at Sullivan's Supper Club and Bar. Clements is prepping, cutting tenderloins into tips and making cheesy potato and ham soup. "We have prime rib every night and a Friday night fish fry," he says. "We sell a lot of pan-fried pike. Shrimp and [beef tenderloin] tips is our mainstay."

On a parallel Saturday, before taking the stage with his Jim Bee Three band in La Crosse, Ed Sullivan nods his head and says, "Dennis may have been a character in a lot of books. I hired him from a newspaper ad. He'd always been in the food business around here. That's the thing about small-town people. When they say 'good morning,' you don't have to look out and see if the sun is up. They're the real deal." Sally Sullivan adds, "One time we had a Halloween party and Dennis came dressed as Spider-Man. He had to go to the children's department to get the costume. He's been with the restaurant a long time."

Sulllivan's is a midsized supper club on a narrow road to and from the state park. The dining room seats 130 including a twenty-two-seat bar that is part of the original restaurant Ed and Sally opened. Chris and Lisa Colombo have owned Sullivan's since 2001. (They did not want to be interviewed for this book.) They are the fifth owners of Sullivan's, which dates back to the 1940s as Charley Karn's Pheasant Inn, where the proprietor kept live pheasants—for food and pleasure.

Ed and Sally bought the former Jackson's Riverview, a sportsman's club operated by licensed guide Frank "Jackson" Grupa. He would take customers hunting and fishing around the Mississippi River and the state park. The Sullivans had never been in the restaurant business before buying the fifty-eight-seat club.

"The fishermen and card players were not happy when we bought the place," Sally says. "They opened at eight AM."

The kitchen had a small grill with two small fryers. Batter-fried chicken was the number one seller at $1.50 for a half chicken with salad bar, potato, and beverage. Ed had an uncle who was an executive chef from Youngstown, Ohio, who gave them some business tips.

The celebrity television name didn't hurt, either. "Of course Ed Sullivan was still alive then," Ed says matter-of-factly. "A lot of people read into that, 'Oh, I didn't know he had a franchise.' Well, it's not Wendy's. We were the one and only Ed Sullivan's."

The one and only Ed Sullivan's Supper Club had one of the first fancy salad bars in the La Crosse area. "We had over thirty-five items on our salad bar," Sally says. "If we would ever take off beets or our noodle salad—we made all our own dressings on-site—people would get upset. We had homemade bread and homemade Irish brown bread. Homemade soup. Garlic toast and muffins."

Ed looks at his wife and says, "Our theory was that you don't buy or run a supper club. You marry one."

Ed and Sally are sweethearts from Aquinas High School in La Crosse. "Class of '55 and '56," Sally says. "Born and raised in La Crosse. We got married in 1960. I had to get that in there."

Ed's father, Edwin J. Sullivan, was a meat salesman, and Sally's father, Jim Christie, was a La Crosse police officer. "Our whole life we've done whatever Ed says and it's been a success," Sally says.

In 1967, Ed was on the road playing middle-of-the-road music in a yearlong tour with what was then the Jim Bee Four. Ed and Sally had set up a modest home in Mishawaka, Indiana, where Sally and the drummer's wife were substitute teachers.

Sally recalls, "He comes to Indiana and says, 'Sal, we bought a restaurant.' I said, 'I beg your pardon?' He took me to a liquor store parking lot. I thought he was going to ask for a divorce. That's where he told me. You know what I said to him? First thing: 'Where did we get the money?' Then I said, 'Fine, if you think we can do it, we're going to do it.'"

Ed had saved some money from his full-time gig as a crane operator in La Crosse. He will never forget the date he made the move to open a supper club: June 10, 1968.

Ironically, Sally's favorite song from the Jim Bee songbook is "Fools Rush In."

Ed and Sally packed up their stuff in Indiana and drove to Trempealeau on a Sunday afternoon. They took over the restaurant at five o'clock the next day.

Sally says, "The guy that owned it before gave us a dollar bill and said, 'Here, kill yourself.'"

Ed and Sally Sullivan lived a high life when they owned the supper club. It was a really big show. They resided in an apartment at the supper club with their three daughters. Their daughter Kathy was a hostess who later married head chef Alan Van Vleet. He set up the kitchen at age sixteen and wound up mentoring the Mouse.

Ed says, "It was the whole package. Our kids were involved. Kathy was six when we bought it, Sara was four, and Paula wasn't even born yet. We lived at the restaurant and at night the kids would open the door and look out. Our customers would see these two little heads peeking out so they'd come out and sit with the customers. It was truly a family thing. We had customers to die for. We were on the river. We had people come in pontoons, airplanes, and boats. They walked in from the state park. You go from Saint Paul to Saint Louis and there aren't that many places on the river that you can do what we did."

Sally continues Ed's stream of thought as she has done for more than fifty years: "We'd show customers the Mississippi River and ask them if it runs north or south or east and west. We'd win every time. It runs east and west in front of our restaurant. We had our own boat dock. We didn't boat, but we'd go down and pick them up."

One time the Jim Bee Four were performing at a morticians convention in La Crosse. "There were a sea of caskets," Ed says. "Custom made for the Packers, fishing, hunting. We played at this one booth and they asked if I had ever been to a place with this great food called Ed Sullivan's. I said, 'Yeah, I have,' and I was jerking him around. I pulled out a business card." The Sullivan convention fans ran a hearse and limousine service in Milwaukee. They wound up selling Ed and Sally a gold and black pallbearers' limousine with six doors.

It made for a convenient last supper club angle. "We'd pick people up at the marina and take them to the restaurant in the limousine," Ed says. "When we'd pull up to the marina their jaws would drop."

Ed and Sally had a ball. They were never worried about the remote location in small Trempealeau along the Mississippi. Even today visitors make their way up a hill past the brick ruins and caves of the Melchoir Hotel and Brewery, built in 1857. "We're twenty minutes from LaCrosse, twenty minutes from Winona [Minnesota]," he says. "People are looking for a little spot like that."

The previous Jackson's consisted of only five tables and a gambling machine. It was smaller than a slot nickel. Ed says, "In 1983 we put an addition on to make a little more room and we played there now and then. One night early on a guy came in and gave us a plaque that read 'May you be in heaven a half hour before the devil knows you're dead.' The lights came on and we decided to do the Irish supper club thing. I tended bar and Sally did the food. Eventually we got busier and busier where we had to get more help."

Sally even opened up her Emerald Isle Gift Shop with $25,000 worth of trinkets she brought back from a trip to Martin Standun in Spiddal, a village northwest of Galway, Ireland. Today the gift shop serves as a wine cellar.

A nine-foot-high stained glass window still keeps an eye on the salad bar. The 1895 window was salvaged from a razed Catholic church in Caledonia, Minnesota. The saint's painted face, hands, and feet were crafted in a detailed technique that is no longer used in America.

Under Ed and Sally, the supper club served green pies and Irish coffee. Every guest received a "green" shamrock white chocolate as they left Sullivan's. Sally smiles and says, "We have been to Ireland four times. When you look out the windows of Ed Sullivan's Supper Club it's just like looking at the Lakes of Killarney."

In 1974, at the age of thirty-seven, Ed bought a new green and white Cessna Cardinal and learned how to fly. The supper club's name and a shamrock were painted on the tail for good luck. He sold the plane in 1984 when the Sullivans built the addition to the restaurant.

Why did they sell the supper club in 2001? "We just hit the wall," Ed answers. "We ran out of gas, buddy. We got tired." Sally adds, "So many people that own a restaurant have people running it for them. We never missed a day. If somebody came and said they'd like a fried-egg sandwich—which they did—we went into the house, got eggs, and made them a fried-egg sandwich. I hostessed with my daughter Kathy. We both believed when we knew somebody, we'd give them a hug and a kiss before we'd seat them. From both of us. We knew what people ate, our bartenders would have their drinks with the napkins ready when they came in. You need service."

Sally likes to mention the "Service" seminars she would do for friends. She stops as if she were waiting for a drum roll, then begins: "*S* is for smile," she says with a smile. "*E* is enthusiasm. *R* is respect for not only your customers but people that work for you. *V* is vitality— always love your job because if you don't love what you're doing you're dead before you die. *I* is integrity. If you overhear a conversation at a table you *never* repeat that. *C* is courtesy to workers and customers, and *E* is for effort."

Ed says, "A customer would walk in the door and you use their name and say, 'Hey, how have you been?' Then you give them a good product at a competitive price. And when they leave you say, 'When am I going to see you again, buddy?' It's so basic but people have lost the concept of that."

Ed enjoys retirement, at least as much as a former supper club owner, airplane pilot, and crane operator can. He still plays bass on the keyboards in the Jim Bee Three, which formed in 1963 under the guidance of guitarist Jim Bielefeldt. Ed is the rhythm guitarist and banjo player. They have monthly gigs along the La Crosse riverfront, not far from Ed and Sally's home in Onalaska.

Ed and Sally still host their "Blarney Party" radio show mash-up of big band and easy listening music they started in 1983. At the beginning they would broadcast live from the basement of their house in Trempealeau. In 1989, they moved the operation to the La Crosse Radio Group in Onalaska. Kathy works as a salesperson at the radio station. From 1992 to 2008 the "Blarney Party" raised $1.5 million for the Children's Miracle Network through radio and television appearances. Ed and Sally spin classic country every Friday and kick off the "Blarney Party" on Saturday mornings.

"You'll hear everything from [Dave Brubeck's] 'Take Five' to 'The Beer Barrel Polka,'" Ed says. "We take a lot of requests and talk about things going on in our life. We just talk like we're talking now." Ed has fifty-eight thousand songs on his laptop computer. He says, "Music has pretty much been my life outside the restaurant."

Sally says, "He never plans a thing. We just go to the studio and we roll."

Erik Pyka is the manager at Sullivan's now. He began working at Sullivan's at the age of sixteen and is twenty-two on this sleepy afternoon in the summer of 2011. He started as a dishwasher and moved on up through bussing and cooking.

Sullivan's general manager, Erik Pyka, loves the supper club view of the Mississippi River.

"Right when I turned eighteen I started bartending," he says. "Because in Wisconsin you do that."

Pyka grew up in Trempealeau, where his father, Al, is an engineer on the BNSF (Burlington Northern and Santa Fe) railroad that runs past the restaurant. He blows the horn when he rolls through. A Green Bay food critic once wrote that Ed

Sullivan's pork chops were so tender that the meat fell off the bone when the train rolled by.

"The experience here is awesome," Pyka says. "The sun sets on the other side of the trees across the Mississippi and it is crazy how beautiful it is. It lights up everything. If it is right and you get a shot of the bluff it turns pink. Just for [owners] Chris and Lisa to trust me with their restaurant is something. They could hire a manager so they don't have to be here all the time. When ownership changed, a lot of people who had ties to Ed and Sally stopped coming. But we're noticing a few more coming in from town. The best compliment we get is that it has stayed consistent. Everything is as good as they remember twenty, thirty years ago."

Sullivan's ambience is as dark as a distant secret. The club has held on to the age-old tradition of linen napkins. "It's classy," Pyka says.

In a separate conversation, Ed Sullivan adds, "In 1983 we had a customer come up to us and said everything was wonderful about the place, but, 'You need to have linen napkins.' Before that we had green paper napkins because of our ribs. But we thought, 'By golly, you're right,' and we started the linen napkins." The wooden chairs are also from the Sullivan's beginnings in 1968, but then other furniture is from the 1980s.

It's perfect supper club motif. "It's mixed up," Pyka admits. Pyka does not find many of his peers at the supper club where he works. "A supper club is part of that old-time mentality," he says. "The things that haven't changed here probably will never change because of that mentality. We get an older crowd, but we also get it passed down. 'My grandparents used to take me here,' 'My parents came all the time,' that sort of thing. That's the only reason a supper club can keep going. The food is unbelievable and the view is incredible, but it is going to be an older crowd. It is a tradition. You look at all your criteria, you'll say, 'How is this a restaurant?' It's a supper club. The hours have never changed. We're open five until what we call close, dark almost, nine or nine thirty. We don't get a lot of people traveling at night out here. Sundays we're open eleven thirty until about nine at night. It shortens up a little bit in the winter because it gets darker earlier."

But Ed and Sally stay bright all year long. Sally is watching her Hawaiian shirt–clad husband play keyboards in the Jim Bee Three in a newfangled downtown La Crosse nightspot. She is looking back on the supper club, the Mouse, and plainspoken hard work.

"Music or food, you have to create the atmosphere yourself," she says. "People can go anywhere and eat; they can bag their own groceries and pump their own gas. But when they come to a nice supper club they need to feel welcome and pampered."

PART II

Supper Clubs
with Shtick

4

Jax Café

1928 University Avenue NE, Minneapolis, Minnesota
(612) 789-7297 • www.jaxcafe.com

Good things come Cozy Cossette's way when she's working the small coatroom at Jax Café and supper club in Minneapolis. Happy Anniversary. Best Wishes. Happy Birthday. All in one day.

Cossette not only will take your coat during a cold Minnesota night, she will make a match for a warm memory. She manually typesets Jax matchbooks for dinner guests. It's a unique touch that started in the late 1960s. Smoking in restaurants may be against the law, but you cannot legislate tradition.

Cossette has monogrammed hundreds of thousands of sentimental matchbooks in her lifetime. She thinks of their little destinies. "I wonder how everything is going to be," she says while setting type in the workspace she describes as her little house. "Especially when we get requests for 'I Love You,' 'Will You Marry Me?' I also get the fella who will come in here with the ring and say, 'Will you hold on to this for me?'" And Cossette does.

Welcome to Jax. Cossette started here in 1959 as a twenty-nine-year-old waitress and hostess. She jumped into a family business, working for Joseph Kozlak Sr., the grandfather of current owner Bill Kozlak Jr. Bill's father, Bill Senior, owned the supper club between 1979 and 2001. His promotional-minded brother, Joe Kozlak Jr., came up with the personalized matchbook idea. A match salesman—yes, there were match salesmen—convinced the family the monogrammed match-

(*top*) Jax, circa 1933, with unknown entrepreneurs in front.
(*boittom*) Bright lights, big city—Jax today.

Cozy Cossette manually typesets matchbooks for guests at Jax Supper Club from her office in the club's coatroom.

books would be a way customers could "see their name in lights," according to Bill Senior. At its peak, Jax monogrammed one million matchbooks a year. "Now it's twenty thousand, thirty thousand a year," he says.

Cossette is a native of Granite Falls, Minnesota, about one hundred miles from the South Dakota border. Her integrity and no-nonsense approach hint that she may have been a cowgirl in a previous life.

"My husband and I had been here to eat," Cossette recalls. "I liked this the first time I walked in. When Bill Junior and [his brother] Jack bought the place from his dad [in 2001], it wasn't as nice as it is now. They built up everything, cleaned the place up. Enlarged stuff. It was a complete success."

Cossette retired from Jax in 1975 and helped her daughter raise five boys. Cossette's husband, Bo, was a government welder in Minneapolis. He died in 1983, and she returned to Jax. In this big world, this is Cossette's little domain. She works on a manual Franklin Manufacturing embossing machine that is more than twenty years old.

Cossette is very picky about her tiny metal letters in black, gold, silver, green, and red. "You have to have a system," she says. "I put the letters in and they heat up. When I put the first one in, I have to wait a while. After that is taken out, then they're cooling and I'm putting the others in. By the time they are finished and put away, I go to the next batch."

When Cossette is done with a personalized matchbook, she crosses it off her list with a pencil. Her work is all done by hand. There are no computers. She looks away and presses down on her machine. She mumbles to herself, "There you go, 'Happy Birthday,'" looks at it and says, 'Oh, I forgot the *H*.' She frowns. Once she adds the *H* she smiles again. "We do little [monogrammed] notepads too," she says. "But they're not a big seller. People want the matches because they can't buy matches in stores. It's the one thing customers really like. It's the personal touch."

The "personal touch" lives at Jax Café because it has remained in the same family since its building went up in 1910. Patriarch Stanley Kozlak was a native of Rapka, Poland, who came to America in 1887. He was seventeen years old and found work as a laborer in a sawmill along the Mississippi River in Minneapolis. He next opened a butcher shop and furniture store before breaking ground at 20th and University for what was to become Jax. The brick building housed his hardware, furniture, and funeral service businesses. Build it and they will come. And go.

"He became the ambassador to the Poles that came into this town," Bill Junior says. "This is an Eastern European neighborhood with some Italians. It was very industrial early on. A lot of people worked in the industries around here. It is almost like a Chicago neighborhood. There is a church on every other block and a bar on every other block. My great-grandfather knew everybody."

The General Mills and Pillsbury factories are still within two miles of Jax Café, as is the Twin Cities iconic Grain Belt Brewery building. (The brewery closed in 1976 and the beer is now made in New Ulm, Minnesota.) Stanley died in 1916 at the age of forty-six. His son Joe was only twenty and elected to grow a North Woods moustache to look old enough to run a funeral business.

Joe and his brothers built a new mortuary building adjacent to the Kozlak complex. When the mortuary was moved from the original location in 1933, that location was leased to Jack Dusenka. "So the name 'Jax' comes from Jack Dusenka," Bill Junior continues with a grin. "The signmaker told him that he was a cheap Pole and that 'Jax' would be less letters in neon."

In 1933 Jax had the second liquor license issued in the city of Minneapolis, but Bill Junior hints that the hooch was flowing during Prohibition. "My grandfather might have done a little bootlegging," he says. "One day my uncle Joe's son asked him why after church on Sundays he always needed Uncle Bill or somebody to count the Saturday night money with him. It was because he didn't want to drink alone."

A Jax neighbor made the sixteen-foot-long lighted panorama of Snow White and the Seven Dwarfs; no one knows why.

The original Jax encompassed about one-eighth of the ten-thousand-square-foot building as it stands today. Bill Junior looks around the bar and says, "This was the original restaurant. The bar was originally called Jax Aquarium Bar." An aquarium with tropical fish was the front of the bar fixture. Later it was moved to a wall above the wooden booths. One night, between closing and opening, the glass burst and pieces flew and stuck into the opposite wall. "Thank goodness nobody was here," Bill Junior says.

The legendary aquarium was replaced in 1941 by a sixteen-foot-long green and white lighted panorama of Snow White and the Seven Dwarfs, made by an artist neighbor. "He sold it to my grandfather for $300," Bill Junior said. "All handcrafted. No copyright. We've had some big offers over the years from people who want that. We've had animation people come in to have their picture taken in front of it. People are freaked out about it and don't know why. It's really out of place for a bar or supper club."

Today's coat check room/matchmaking booth was the original kitchen. There was a pool hall. Upstairs there was a dance hall and living quarters. "In 1943 my grandfather bought the bar from the gentleman he was leasing it to [the second owner, Jim Harris]," Bill Junior says.

Jax is just six blocks from the Mississippi River. "There were twelve, thirteen restaurants around here when my grandfather started," says Bill Junior. "This a rural area, a no-man's-land until 1945. We've always called dinner 'supper' in this area. Even on *The Waltons*. It's a rural thing.

"Over the years a lot of the real good restaurants in this neighborhood died off or were sold. The suburbs sprouted. In the early years maybe downtown had ten restaurants. Now there's forty. It's hard to survive twenty years in a restaurant. You have to remake yourself. We've been fortunate. We haven't had to close to remake ourselves, but we've put a lot of money into it. Since 2006 there has been a resurgence in the neighborhood with younger people. Some of the old dive bars became fancier. There's a popular tiki bar nearby [Psycho Suzi's Motor Lodge]. Buildings that were manufacturing became artists' quarters."

Young Twin Cities people began flocking to Jax for its retro supper club feel. At the beginning of the hit television series *Mad Men* about the sauced-up advertising world of the early 1960s, season premiere parties were held at Jax. "I didn't know what to expect the first time we hosted one of those," Bill Junior says. "It was at nine o'clock on a Sunday night. Everybody was dressed to a T. People drank like it was that era. I dropped in with my wife to see what was going on and ended up tending bar for three and a half hours. The second year was even better. Since then we've had fifteen parties booked with the *Mad Men* theme. People are wanting to drink the old cocktails again. They grew up on martinis and then drink straight gin or vodka and their eyes get crooked in a hurry.

"In reality people perceive this as a steak house and/or a supper club. Absolutely. There's times 'supper club' rubs me the wrong way because people think nothing but blue hairs and hearty food. But at the end of the day, all that we do fits the criteria of a supper club. When someone orders an appetizer platter or a birthday cake, we serve it on a lazy Susan. We still have linen napkins. Some of that

The rural view from Jax's urban veranda.

Someday this supper club customer will have bigger fish to fry. He is catching his own trout at Jax's.

expensive stuff we could cut out, like making the matchbooks, too. But then you're cutting out part of the soul of what you've done for seventy-five, eighty years."

Supper club dining didn't hit the Twin Cities scene until 1954. Life was good. The Minneapolis Lakers were NBA champions. Bill Haley had his first hit with "Shake, Rattle and Roll."

The main supper club dining room was paneled in rich Indiana walnut. New gold and red carpeting, formica tables, and gold upholstered chairs were added to create a three-hundred-seat dining room. The room was lined with red-flocked wallpaper because red sells. The Olde World Garden and sixty-seat patio were added. Jax had the first outdoor dining in Minneapolis.

"They used to raise their own chickens back there," Bill Junior says. "It was an area where people waited for a table. Then they put in the trout stream. Again, it was my uncle [Joe Junior] and my grandfather [Joseph Senior]. They were in Colorado where they saw somebody doing that with trout and thought it was so cool. It wasn't being done in Minneapolis. They hired an architect and drew it up. It had its own well to bring in the water. It's only a foot deep or so, so rainbow trout could live in that climate. In this town people would probably eat walleye, but we can't stock it with walleye. So a lot of people who never had trout or don't like it have had trout here because of the thrill. And you don't need a fishing license either."

Customers can have their picture taken while catching the fish. After dinner they are presented with a complimentary photo folder that says "I caught my limit at Jax."

When the trout stream with the fisherman's net debuted, the two Joes imported live flamingos to wander about the stream. However, because of their tropical nature, the flamingos could not adjust to the cold spring water and were replaced by heartier African crown cranes. The exotic birds wintered in the Saint Paul Zoo before the tradition ended in the 1960s. But to this day, thg trout stream is drained after November and refilled again in mid-April, weather permitting.

During the season, Jax orders between 150 and 200 rainbow trout at a time every two weeks. "On Easter and Mother's Day we need an adult supervisor out here," Bill Junior says in the tranquil garden. "It's usually when the tulips are up and some kids think it's a park and they run through the place. I know at least two of my sisters' and six of my friends' kids who have fallen in."

During the 1960s and '70s, Jax was a popular spot for sportsmen of all sorts. Minnesota Twins legends Harmon Killebrew and Tony Oliva came by the supper club, as did Vikings scrambling quarterback Fran Tarkenton. "We have sports booster lunches, so Bobby Knight has been here," Bill Junior says. "When the Final Four was in Minneapolis in 1992, [North Carolina State basketball coach] Jim Valvano did a chalk talk for a corporate party for 7-Up. Athletes were part of the community back then. A lot more than they are today."

A large portrait behind the main bar honors Curt Karls, who for years worked at the Schmitt Music Company in downtown Minneapolis. He was a Jax regular. When he retired his coworkers commissioned an artist to paint his portrait. "All the people in the painting are his coworkers," Bill Junior says. "They surprised him with that painting. In the caption they say, 'A career is a collection of the people you have known.' That went up in the early 2000s."

The stools lining the bar are mismatched, another classic supper club trait. "That's where my mom came into play, when we started remodeling in the late 1980s. Although we still have some of our old furniture, because we have customers who have to have the backside. People have an attachment to them. They bring back memories. Some of the bar stools go back to 1966. They've been rebuilt at least six times. For years all the Chicago people have said how this reminds them of the old Berghoff bar. And a little bit of Gene and Georgetti."

Down toward the end of the bar, a fancy walk-in phone booth has been decommissioned. It is for display only, harking back to the days when you could reach out and touch someone.

Ray Mlinal and Joyce Zanzlski are having prime rib sandwiches on the patio by the trout stream. A retired insurance executive and native of northeast Minneapo-

The dashing Ray Mlinal and Joyce Zanzlski. Ray has been coming to Jax since 1965.

lis, Mlinal has been coming to Jax since 1965. "Jax Café is the best supper club in the Twin Cities," he declares. "A supper club provides seafood, steaks, chicken, pasta. It is a place that will welcome families. And it is a place that makes one feel very comfortable. Linen napkins. Most of the servers have been here a long time."

Zanzlski, a Minneapolis resident, adds, "And the server's dress is black and white. Very professional. The matchbooks are a very nice touch."

"When I started in 1959 it was steaks, potatoes, and salad," says Cozy Cossette. "No desserts of any kind. After-dinner drinks. People came out for a full evening. [When it changed] a lot of that had to do with MADD and legislation but it worked out well for everybody. People still come in for an entire evening, but they don't have the drinks they had before. They wait for the desserts. We have a nice dessert tray."

Has Cossette ever had a grasshopper—the ice cream drink—at Jax? "Yes," she answers in a whisper. "I've always liked grasshoppers. I'm not a big drinker. Well, maybe when I was younger I had a few drinks. I'm not a pushover. I usually bring my grandkids in here on their birthdays."

Bill Junior adds, "Even through the mid-1980s people drank before dinner, they had dinner, then they drank after dinner. It was the night out. You didn't have dinner and go see a movie. Friday afternoon the bar business would be better than the Friday night might be today. Drinking is obviously different. We still sell a lot of ice cream drinks. When I started bartending you made lots of Smith & Kearns [brandy and white crème de menthe served in a lowball on the rocks] and stingers [Kahlua, cream, and soda water in a lowball over ice], but if you order one now, a bartender goes, 'Whoa, what's that?'

"We never had to be involved with the wine list because diners weren't that educated. When I got out of college [Saint John's in Collegeville, Minnesota] that was one of my first assignments. The writing was on the wall. People weren't drinking three Manhattans or martinis or sidecars before dinner. We had to find a way to make money somewhere else and that was the wine list."

Knockout drinks like Smith & Kearns and stingers were phased out in 1985, the same year Jax hired its first full-time pastry chef to produce creative desserts to replace the after-dinner drinks. Bill Junior isn't afraid to say that "back in the day" there was an "unoffical" men-only everyday lunch.

The businessmen had the same waitress every day. "They would only call if they weren't coming in," he says. "Mostly men were working. Women weren't working. One of the best stories a customer told me [was from a man who] worked for Honeywell. Honeywell was one of the first companies to go 'no drinking' at lunch. All the Honeywell guys would have a 'Honeywell martini.' I go, 'What's that?' He said they would serve the martini in a coffee mug in case the boss came in. He looked around the room and everyone had a beer or a cocktail and the four Honeywell guys had coffee mugs."

And beer is never served on tap at a supper club. "Until we redid the bar in '91 we had two tap lines—and wine on tap," Bill Junior says. "We did give in on that. For the longest time we had only local beers on tap. We had three of James Page beers. Summit [out of Saint Paul] and Gluek [pronounced *Glick,* phased out in 2010 after a 150-year run].

"It's funny," he continues with a sly smile. "In Wisconsin, they drink beer out of a can. And brandy slushes are another Wisconsin thing. Here, we serve bourbon old-fashioneds. When

Ice cream drinks are still popular at Jax, with pastries to absorb the alcohol.

Wisconsin people come to town, you know when they say old-fashioned, it's going to be brandy."

The free parking lot across the street from Jax has large signposts so supper clubbers won't forget where they parked. Even the signs' themes have a midcentury supper club touch: Burgundy Boulevard, Lobster Lane, Pheasant Run. Bill Junior says, "They do scavenger hunts throughout the city and one of the things is to find Burgundy Boulevard."

Jax's second level consists of a small stage and swirling dance floor that is used for weddings and private parties. There is a full kitchen and the Cavalier Bar, with red leather, no-back bar stools from the late 1930s. "Every supper club has to have more than one bar," Bill Junior jokes. "And the men's room has to be in the bar." A second coat check is also upstairs.

In 2004 the neighboring Saint Anthony Athletic Club installed its Hall of Fame in Jax's second floor, and inductions are held on a yearly basis. Club honorees include Minneapolis Lakers NBA pioneer George Mikan (who graduated from DePaul University in Chicago), American Football League legend Gino Cappelletti, and University of Minnesota football player Vern Gagne, who went on to become a famous wrestler. "You'd be surprised," Bill Junior says. "There's people who eat here for ten, fifteen years not knowing there's an upstairs."

Remembrances are as thick as the shtick at Jax. "Absolutely for sure my earliest memory is coming down on Sundays after church," Bill Junior says. "We were closed and my dad would count the tills from the night before. My sisters and I could run ragged and eat croutons, the five-cent mints that were behind the bar, and drink as many Cokes as we could get our hands on. Early dining I remember sitting on the old phone book. There were no booster chairs back then. And all I ate were bacon sandwiches for five years."

Bill Junior and his wife, Dana, have three children: Isabella, born in 1999; Billy, born in 2002; and Ava, born in 2007. "They love coming here," he says. "My son asked me the other day when we were going to shut the stream down and who is going to pull the coins out. My daughter has been eating prime rib since she was three. We went to pick her up at preschool and the teacher had to show me something. The kids were quizzed on their favorite foods—macaroni and cheese, chicken wings, pizza. My daughter said, 'Prime rib, prime rib.' She was four years old."

Bill Junior, born in 1969, is third generation in the business, fourth in the Jax building. He worked his way up through Jax from busboy to maintenance to bartender. "I never cooked," he admits. "I love to cook now." He has four older sisters and a younger brother. None are in the business.

Third-generation supper club owner Bill Kozlak Jr.

"They were in the business in high school and college," he says. "Then they wised up and got out. Third generation is absolutely the toughest. I have friends in prominent companies in Minneapolis and the plan is it gets sold off before the third generation. The first one, the value keeps going but they need the money to retire. It's hard to make as much money as the previous generation and pay down more debt than they paid down. From my dad on down they said, 'You'll never survive after your dad's friends die.' It's been a struggle at times. There's no doubt we have an older clientele but we have baptisms, first Communions, a ton of prom business, and college graduations. It has gotten younger the past six, seven years. Our market is literally five years old to ninety, and they come from Wisconsin, Iowa, and northern Minnesota.

"On Gopher [football] game days we have people who drive down from Duluth and Saint Cloud, up from Rochester. We send a shuttle to the game. Years ago we filled both floors, five hundred people, before every game. Back then they were the only game in town and all the games were at one thirty. We'd premix eight gallon jugs of martinis the night before. People would walk out in top hats and top coats, a drink in each hand, to drive three miles. All that has changed. If you had a dress code, you would be empty."

With live trout, vintage matchbooks, and hearty Minnesota food, the stories are well fitted at Jax.

5

Sister Bay Bowl

10640 N. Bay Shore Drive, Sister Bay, Wisconsin
(920) 854-2841 • www.sisterbaybowl.com

Earl "the Pearl" Willems wasn't out to strike it rich. He just loved bowling. During the 1950s, bowling and Wisconsin went together like cheese and curds. Everyone bowled. Bowling television shows were sponsored by Schlitz beer. Miller beer funded huge PBA (Professional Bowling Association) tours in the mid-1960s. The twelve-lane bowling alley at the American Serb Hall in Milwaukee (still known for its Friday night fish fry) was the original location of the popular Wisconsin television show *Bowling with the Champs*. Harvey Kuenn, baseball's 1952 American League Rookie of the Year, bowled in the off-season to stay in shape. Imagine that. Kuenn, of course, was from West Allis, just outside of Milwaukee.

So in 1958 Earl tore down the iconic dance hall at the Sister Bay Hotel on the four-corner downtown of Sister Bay in Door County. In its place Earl built a $75,000 six-lane bowling alley with beautiful maple lanes right in the back of his hotel and bar. He loved bowling almost as much as he loved his wife, Rita.

Earl had previously bowled at Congress Lanes down Highway 42 in Sturgeon Bay, but now he had an orbit of his own. People laughed at Earl. At the time no more than three hundred people lived in Sister Bay. But then, three hundred is a perfect score.

Today the Sister Bay Bowl and Supper Club has an enduring niche as one of the most unusual supper clubs in America. People roll through the supper club

Sister Bay Bowl, summer 2011.

Celebrating the first three hundred game at the Sister Bay Bowl and Supper Club in 1967, left to right: George Arle, Dicek Weisgerber, Emery Larson (who bowled the historic game), Dick Wilke, and Ron Daubner.

Dressed for bowling success in 1965: top, left to right: Leo Daubner, Ron Daubner. Bottom, left to right: Howard Luther, Dick Kostka, Glen Sitte.

rituals of having a couple cocktails at the knotty-pine-trimmed bar area. They move into the 130-seat dining room with a northerly view of Sister Bay. The walls are lined with historic black-and-white bowling photographs, including Earl's first Halloween bowling party, circa 1959. Pictured are teams of dressed-up locals from Irene's Beauty shop, Master Freeze (a now-defunct locker and freezer manufacturer), and Casperson's Deadbeats. Casperson's was a Sister Bay funeral home. After supper amid the walls of fame, it's not uncommon to go bowling in the adjacent alley. Score is still kept by hand with pencils on broad sheets of paper.

Earl died in 2008, the fiftieth year since the supper club added the bowling alley. He was eighty-seven years old. His daughter Sharon Daubner and her siblings had assumed control of the operation in 1983 after Earl and Rita retired. Sharon honored her father's memory by having a new outdoor high-density foam sign installed that says EARL'S SISTER BAY BOWL.

Sharon's husband, Dick Daubner, is the affable bartender who has worked at the Bowl, as we will call it, since 1977. Dick and Sharon got married in 1971. He is a member of the Door County Bowling Association Hall of Fame.

"Bowling has fallen off the map," Sharon Daubner says during a conversation in the bar. "There are too many entertainment options. But he was ahead of his time. Putting up a bowling alley in 1958 was huge."

Earl hired local boys to manually load and drop the bowling pins by yanking on a string. Dick Daubner was one of those boys. Earl turned to mechanics in 1961, salvaging Brunswick Company pin setters from a bowling alley that was going out of business near Green Bay.

A bowling alley was an unlikely turn for the remote, small-town location.

Sister Bay gets its name from the Sister Islands that flank the harbor leading to Sister Bay. The original Sister Bay Hotel burned down in 1912 in a downtown fire that destroyed six buildings. The hotel was rebuilt in 1918 as one the earliest stagecoach destinations in Door County. Sharon's grandfather Louie Willems came to Namur, Wisconsin, from Belgium in 1935. Namur (population 1,112) is a Belgian community between Green Bay and Sturgeon Bay. Louie built the Rock nightclub (now Alexander's restaurant) near Fish Creek in the town of Gibraltar on Highway 42 south of Sister Bay.

Sharon says, "In 1942 my grandfather was doing well and the Sister Bay Hotel came up for sale. He invested in the hotel, and in 1950 my father took over running this place. Actually my father had just gone to college for seven years in Iowa and Saint Louis to become a chiropractor. He graduated from Logan College in Carterville, Illinois. He ended up being a bartender and making what the Sister Bay Bowl is now."

Earl and Rita met at Casey's Supper Club in Egg Harbor. Rita was a waitress at the Alpine Golf Resort in Egg Harbor. She stopped in for a drink at Casey's after work and found Earl as a customer.

Earl and Rita inherited a bar, dance hall, thirteen rooms, and three bathrooms, predating the now popular Door County bed-and-breakfast tradition of waiting in line to use the bathroom. "I grew up dancing in the dance hall," says Sharon, who was born in 1951.

A baseball diamond was set behind the dance hall. Locals played afternoon games in a small field surrounded by young birch, cedar, and maple trees. Those trees are now old and tall. After the games fans and players would adjourn to the hotel and bar.

No computerized scoring in Sister Bay, Wisconsin.

The Sister Bay Bowl women's bowling team 1959, left to right: Frannie Casper, June Overby, Snooky Hanson, Rita Willems (owner of the Sister Bay Bowl), and Barb Schneider.

Sister Bay Hotel, future bowl and supper club—in 1917 (left) and 1957 (right).

A Green Bay Packers season ticket holder since Lambeau Field opened in 1957, Earl promoted the Bowl in the sports community, and its visibility grew in the burgeoning Door County tourist scene.

"Earl's father charged him $100 a month rent," Dick Daubner recalls. "The next month his father was at the supper club and Earl pulled in with a brand-new Chrysler. His father goes, 'Brand-new car, huh?' Earl says, 'Business is really good.' So his dad says, 'OK, I'll charge you $200 a month.' Earl loved people. He always had a wad of money in his pocket."

Earl got his nickname, the Pearl (before basketball star Earl Monroe), because it rhymed and he was a "gem of a guy" according to longtime Door County residents.

At the height of the supper club movement in 1964, Earl and Rita purchased the home and dentist's office adjacent to the hotel. They converted the house into a 130-seat supper club. "It became the Sister Bay Bowl and Supper Club, which it is known as today," Sharon says proudly.

The Bowl remains the anchor of the modest four-corner downtown "district." The former Bunda's department and drugstore is across the street, as is a third-generation hardware store. Husby's bar has been across the street from the hotel/bowling alley/supper club for one hundred years.

In 1958 the Sister Bay Bowl pinned its hopes on the future.

Like most traditional supper club owners, the family lived on the property. Earl, Rita, Sharon, and her siblings Gary, Steve, and Penny made for a formidable bowling team.

Three generations of Willems men have now tended to the Sister Bay maple bowling lanes. All of the supper club's bartenders need to know how to undo a jam on a bowling machine.

Many stores and restaurants in Door County are seasonal, but the Bowl is open year-round. "We watch everyone else close," Sharon says with a tired tone in her voice. "But we've been here for local people bowling. For ten years we've been struggling if we should stay open in the winter. We have a steady clientele but we also have new young people coming in and saying, 'Is this really a bowling alley?' You get these funny questions. They're amazed when they look in there, because it's the older-style bowling alley with the wooden lanes."

The Sister Bay Bowl supper club always puts its best foot forward.

Dick says, "It's amazing how many people our age bowl and come up and ask how to keep score. Because in the cities it's done by machines."

Even in today's high-tech world the Bowl hosts three nights of leagues that begin in September and run through April. Dick recalls, "When I started tending bar there would be a single shift on Monday, a double shift on Tuesday and Wednesday, a single shift on Thursday, and a double shift on Friday—all for bowlers. That was in the 1960s when there was a lot of agriculture and cherry growers here. They had nothing to do in Sister Bay. And nobody traveled in the wintertime."

Sharon Doersching is a Willems cousin who has been a waitress and hostess at the Bowl since 1979. She says, "Back then people wouldn't even go to Sturgeon Bay [about thirty miles south of Sister Bay]."

During bowling's renaissance period, the Bowl would host a regular Sunday afternoon tournament. Dick says, "The place would be packed with people just watching the tournament. In that bowling alley my father-in-law had a bar at the far end. It was the Pickers Bar. He wouldn't allow Hispanics and blacks who harvested the cherries into the main bar. They'd come with their paychecks on Friday night. They never hung around for the apples [picking] because it got too cold and they wanted to get back to Texas. Cherries were quick money. Local people had to pick the apples."

Sharon Daubner says, "That was a different time. They'd come here by the truckloads; we called them the Cherry Pickers. For six weeks [July to mid-August] this town was a different color." Sharon Doersching added, "Now we have multicultural people here, of course not as many as the city."

As far back as the early 1920s the cherry industry in Door County covered ten thousand acres, according to the Wisconsin Cherry Growers association. In 1959 Door County was known as Cherryland USA and grew 95 percent of the tart cherry crop in the United States. During the 1960s between twelve thousand and fifteen thousand hand pickers would migrate to Door County to harvest cherries.

Two things happened: mechanical harvesters worked faster than the migrants, shaking seven thousand cherries off an average tree in about seven seconds. That's sixty to a hundred trees per hour with enough cherries to make twenty-eight cherry pies.

Also, the value of Door County real estate became so high, farmers gave up cherries to sell the land. The family-owned Seaquist cherry orchard remains within three miles of Sister Bay. Sharon Doersching says, "Fortunately we have a couple cherry growers that have taken it over like conglomerate cherry orchards."

The cherry pies are still popular at the Bowl, although Sharon Daubner smiles and says, "I picked cherries and ate so many of them I like cherry nothing to this day."

Born in 1941, Sharon Doersching was an English teacher at Marquette College and Gibraltar High School near Fish Creek during the fall and winter seasons and worked at the Bowl during cherry happy summers. "Unfortunately we have customers where we're starting to read their obituaries," she says. "A lot. Every summer when I hostess I get two or three fantastic stories, one this summer where an elderly lady told me she spent her honeymoon in one of the [hotel] rooms here. She brought her grandchildren. There were traveling salesmen who slept here. Sharon and I host the majority of the time. If we don't know their name, we know their face. When someone new comes in we introduce ourselves right away. Because customers become family."

Dick Daubner is the perfect guy to meet behind the bar of a Wisconsin supper club. He is built like a 1960s Packers lineman and his name could be Fuzzy or Max. He smiles all the time and he speaks in a deep rural Wisconsin drift. It is impossible to not get caught up in Dick Daubner's world.

Sharon Doersching says, "The personality of the person at the bar is a huge draw that you don't get in some other restaurant. People come here to have a drink with the bartender and that's part of the supper club experience." Dick shrugs his shoulders and reasons, "Well, you got to know them because they stayed all night.

You got to know about their kids and where they worked. They were here five or six hours. What are you going to do? Sit and not talk to them?"

Notable Bowl customers over the years have included Green Bay Packers announcer Kevin Harlan, who has plugged the Bowl and its bowling on telecasts. Late Chicago radio personality Bob Collins was a regular, as was longtime *Chicago Sun-Times* food critic Pat Bruno. Chicago Blackhawks Hall of Fame goalie Tony Esposito, who bought a summer home in Door County during the 1990s, comes in often. Door County is about a five-hour drive from Chicago.

"When I was playing I wanted somewhere to go to get away from it all," Esposito said in a winter 2011 interview from his home in Saint Petersburg, Florida. "Everybody kept telling me about Door County. So the first time was '79 or '80. We're driving through Sturgeon Bay, going north, and I said to my wife, 'Geez, this is so much like back home in Canada.' With the pristine trees and all that stuff. We had supper clubs in Canada. It was a laid-back family-type place and a supper club brings back fond memories."

Esposito promptly found a sense of place at the Sister Bay Bowl. The perch hit home. "I'm from Sault Sainte Marie so I was used to perch growing up," explained Esposito, whose father, Pat, worked scrap recovery in the Sault Sainte Marie steel mills. "Everybody kept telling me to go to the Bowl, go to the Bowl. My wife and I loved it and we eventually bought a place there. I spend my summers there and go to the Bowl at least two times a week. After I got done playing I'd go up there every New Year's Eve. My wife and I would go up a day or two early. Their perch is the best but they also have great chicken and I like their sirloin steak."

Esposito doesn't mind rubbing shoulders with the supper club locals. "They can take pictures, I don't mind that at all," he said. "I'll sign anything they want. It's fun. Lots of Chicagoans come up there and Chicago—that's my place."

The Esposito family became such good friends with the Bowl family, he invited them to his Florida home. "The Bowl is a throwback," he said. "The Wirtz [Chicago Blackhawk owners] family has been there. Bill Wirtz came up in the late '80s. His family went to Door County when he was young. We've all bowled, but we're no good. I've brought Phil [his hockey-playing brother] and we've bowled. But you don't expect a bowling alley, you know what I'm saying? When they told me 'Sister Bay Bowl,' I asked, 'What do you mean 'Bowl'? I can eat at a bowling alley?"

The Sister Bay Bowl and Supper Club is indeed known for its lightly battered broasted lake perch. Dick Daubner was born in 1947 in Ellison Bay, about four miles north of Sister Bay. His chiseled face is as Wisconsin rugged as the limestone deposits that enrich the county's fruit trees. In no uncertain terms Dick remembers the glory days of commercial perch fishing along the bays of Door County. "You could put the perch on the bar in baskets and give it away, it was so plentiful," he says. "You could go down to the dock here with a rod and reel and catch a bucket of perch in a half hour." Sharon Doersching says most of the community's fathers were commercial fishermen.

Clyde Casperson was the owner of the local funeral parlor. He liked to have its Halloween parties at the Bowl. Clyde loved the Friday perch so much all he wanted when he ordered was a double order of perch and nothing else. No potatoes, coleslaw, or even bread. "It was called 'the Clyde,'" Dick recalls. "And if you ask our waitresses today for a Clyde they will know what to give you.

"When the supper club started nobody knew how many perch they would sell. Ten orders? The record here is 775 orders on a Friday night. The records were six to seven tons of perch a year in the late 1990s. Now we serve about five tons a year. We always got them from Maricques [a commercial fishing family that dates back to 1934] in Green Bay, almost 100 percent. There was a time we got some from Sturgeon Bay. Every supper club had a Friday night fish fry. If they didn't have a big kitchen they would pan-fry them."

Over the years alewives became predators to the perch. Dick says, "Fishermen tell me the reproduction of perch is critical within the first two weeks of when they hatch. Not only with water temperature, but how rough the water is." The perch have not come back to the bay of Green Bay. Starting in the mid-2000s, commercial fishermen weren't allowed to fish out the perch because the perch supply was dying.

Dick continues, "The state of Wisconsin said, 'We'll knock it off for at least two years.' Restaurants were fine with that if that's what it took to bring it back. Well, it hasn't come back like they thought it was going to come back. Now it comes from

Breakfast is rarely served at a Door County supper club.

Lake Erie, Lake Superior, Canada, wherever. So the price has gone up." Dick looks at a framed archived menu and says, "On the wall over there we started at $1.75 for a Friday night fish fry. We are now paying $12 a pound."

The perch now appears on the Bowl menu at "market price," just like lobster.

The perch is flown in fresh weekly. The Bowl uses its own broasting machine. "Most people use oil for everything they're going to fry," Sharon Daubner explains. "But Sister Bay Bowl's perch has its own machine. Kind of a combination pressure cooker and deep fry."

The killer cheese curds are locally sourced from Renard's Cheese in Sturgeon Bay. The curds are delicately breaded, lightly floured, and deep fried. The supper club also serves homemade potato salad, coleslaw, and breads.

"We still have relish trays for larger parties and banquets," Sharon Daubner says. "We took it off the regular menu for cost. We had linens for banquets but not for everyday suppers. Years ago you had breakfast, dinner, and supper. In the old days you had dinner at lunchtime.

"And a supper club opened its doors at four o'clock. It was only the evening meals. It was always a salad, entree, the relish tray. You'd get a cocktail, your Manhattan. Years ago we had nightly entertainment in the summer."

Years ago the Bowl offered regular entertainment on a stage near the front door. "We had the Birminghams country-western band from Sturgeon Bay that charged $175," Dick recalls. "They packed this place every Saturday. The lead singer [Donny Birmingham] died. It was unbelievable. The Village Mule, which is this little motel down the street, would get on the phone and say, 'Will you shut your windows? Our customers can't go to sleep.'"

Now live entertainment is offered about once a month with Door County favorites like the Mullet Hunters, Stone Sober, and Southern rockers Whiskey Ditch, who played before a packed house on New Year's Eve 2011, when customers walked back and forth across the street between the Bowl and Husby's bar.

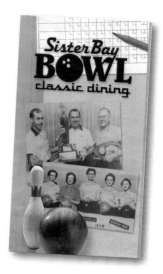

Classic dining and a classic menu design.

The old-fashioned supper club drink stirs up year-round debate at the Sister Bay Bowl. Sharon Doersching says, "I was in Chicago and my friends forgot to warn me, 'You can't order an old-fashioned here.' I got a Manhattan. It was terrible."

Dick says, "Why [the Wisconsin old-fashioned] is brandy, I don't know. I do know you go to Las Vegas and order a brandy old-fashioned, they will say, 'What part of Wisconsin are you from?' Old-fashioneds are made with two lumps of sugar, a dash of bitters, you put your orange down at the bottom, and muddle and muddle. Then you put your ice in, your brandy, soda, and water. Old-fashioneds are always a standard at Sister Bay."

Doersching then reasons, "Possibly some of the nationalities that settled in Wisconsin came with brandy, even though you think of whiskey being heavily Scandinavian and German in the northern peninsula here. It may have something to do with the fishermen, the early lighthouse keepers. The early lumbermen. It was a men's culture here. They literally had to bring wives in here at one time. Shot of brandy and a beer. That's Wisconsin. The brandy drinks came from that, when women wanted something fancier—quite frankly. Or something a little fruitier."

A couple visitors leave the table for the bar.

Dick continues, "You go to every other state and order a Manhattan and it is made with whiskey or bourbon. You go to Wisconsin and order a Manhattan and if you don't make it with brandy you will be told you made it wrong. It became a conflict. We have a big tourist trade from Chicago and they'd order a martini or Manhattan on the rocks and I would make it with brandy. They would say, 'This isn't right.' Now a guy comes from Madison, Wisconsin, orders the same thing, I make it with brandy and they say, 'This is great!' How do you know?"

Sipping cocktails went hand in hand with the meandering nature of a 1960s supper club.

"The drinking laws changed that," Sharon Daubner says. "I remember coming here when this was your only stop for the night. You weren't going to be running around to a bunch of places or going right home after you ate. This was your night out. That was the logic for live music Friday and Saturday nights. And everybody danced. Life is still like that in a microcosm, we still have that on special occasions."

Dick adds, "Everybody wanted a grasshopper [drink] after dinner. And you'd have rock-hard ice cream to work with as a bartender." Sharon Daubner says, "My mom and dad made a lot of money off the bar. The drinking laws, the no-smoking laws, the economy. All those things are hitting all restaurants. Right now is a hard time to be running a supper club. We just can't raise our prices as fast as [the cost of] food is going up."

But there is a younger core audience interested in 1960s supper club culture, just as television viewers flocked to the loosey-goosey advertising world depicted in *Mad Men*.

Sharon Doersching reasons, "Supper clubs were prior to the huge communication age of 'instant everything,' the Internet, cell phones, Facebook. Television not in every home, but in every room? Before you had to go out for your social life."

Summer always served up the most special memories at the Sister Bay Bowl. The small town swelled with tourists, the sun set late at night, and families bonded throughout the day.

Sharon Daubner's older brother, Gary, suffered severe brain damage in a 1971 automobile accident when he was eighteen years old. "He was in the hospital five months," she says on a sunny day as she watches Gary rake leaves outside the Bowl's northerly window. "Intensive care. He never was the same. This is what he does. He is our maintenance man and I don't know what we would do without him."

For the past forty years Gary has also run between five and ten miles a day, earning the nickname the Sister Bay Jogger. Sharon continues looking at her brother and says, "He can't really work in the Bowl as far as service. But he can work hard. We love him to death."

Sharon Doersching says, "At one time we had eight mother-daughter teams here and some grandmother-mother-daughter teams. When my daughter was in college she worked her way through school at the Bowl. They always have to add summer staff. My son cooked. There's five of us mothers still working here who worked with their daughters."

Dick and Sharon Daubner hope that the Bowl stays in the family.

Dick and Sharon Daubner, New Year's Eve 2011, listening to the not-so-mellow sounds of the Green Bay rock band Whiskey Ditch.

"The third generation usually is the end of the family business," Sharon Daubner concedes. "When it is this much of a hands-on business, and it doesn't matter if it is a hardware store, a supper club, or a grocery store, there's something about the work that the grandparents and parents put into it—and young people want it as good as instantly. They're not going to make the salaries at their age they saw their grandparents and even their parents make after years and years of work. There were weeks of the year where they worked 24/7, literally on duty all the time."

Dick and Sharon Daubner have three children. Jason is a PGA golf pro at Peninsula Park Golf Course in Door County; Michelle is a fifth-grade schoolteacher in Sister Bay; and her twin brother, Michael, is the supper club's general manager. The twins were born in April 1976. Sharon Daubner says, "There's nieces and nephews, but none of them want this as their business. Michael is the last one."

But then, on November 11, 2010, Earl's then–thirty-seven-year-old grandson Jason took to the lanes after supper. He bowled his first three hundred game at the Sister Bay Bowl.

A cabin in the woods.

6

Ishnala

S2011 Ishnala Road, Lake Delton, Wisconsin
(608) 253-1771 • www.ishnala.com

They come to bid a summer farewell at Mirror Lake.

There is not a cloud in the blue velvet sky and the air is still, creating not even a ripple in the water. Barbara Schmock says this stillness is why they call it Mirror Lake. She knows because she has been part of this first Sunday in October ritual several times.

Ishnala Supper Club is in the middle of the 2,220-acre Mirror Lake State Park, west of the Wisconsin Dells. It is the only supper club located in a Wisconsin state park. The restaurant closes on the first weekend of October and reopens every May, when Wisconsinites emerge, shaking off the snow and rust of another winter in a triumph of character.

Schmock has brought her eighty-four-year-old mother, Janet, to supper for this informal farewell. A friend, Nancy Henry, walks between Janet and Barbara. Henry is a middle-aged woman from Middleton, Wisconsin. She just returned from a cabaret weekend in Manhattan. She speaks of Kitty Carlisle and a sophistication that is hard to find these days. She should be wearing a pill box hat and smoking a cigarette through a silver holder. But smoking is no longer allowed in Wisconsin supper clubs.

Several minutes before the three women sit down for supper, Barbara Schmock adjourns from the table. She walks downstairs and takes a stroll along the lake. Bar-

Ishnala is the only supper club in a Wisconsin state park.

(Left to right): Nancy Henry, Barbara Schmock, and her mother, Janet—a supper club road trip from Madison.

bara sees reflections. She thinks about when she was young, when her mother and late father, "Smoky" Schmock, would get away from Madison, about forty-five miles south of Ishnala.

Her father was the beloved owner of Smoky's, a popular steak house/supper club in Madison. He died in the spring of 2001 at the age of eighty-five.

In the language of the native Ho Chunk, Ishnala means "By Itself Alone," and that is Barbara's purpose for these several moments.

Ishnala once was a ceremonial grounds. Two red pine trees, each fifty feet tall, grow through the roof of the restaurant. Guests walk through the front door and see a long arrowhead-shaped bar that hangs like a teardrop over Mirror Lake and sandstone bluffs. Like any good supper club, kids are welcome at Ishnala, and here they even receive souvenir arrowheads.

Ishnala doesn't take reservations, but that doesn't matter. Time is tempered by kayaking or canoeing on the lake in vintage log canoes.

Ishnala is not easy to find. Once you exit I-94 you have to negotiate dizzy turnarounds and head a couple miles down dirt roads flanked by hemlock, white oak, and white pine trees. A 1950s-era canopy that spells out I-S-H-N-A-L-A and a kitschy tepee are the signals you have arrived. The supper club is like a campground. Meals are prepped in a log cabin kitchen and wheeled in a shopping cart to the restaurant, where they are served.

The supper club was opened by the Hoffman House chain, which started in Madison, Wisconsin. Hoffman House owned one hundred acres of land, which it sold to the Department of National Resources (DNR) in 1999. Ishnala now maintains five acres inside the park along with 630 feet of shoreline. The lake is stocked with bass, walleye, and bluegill. A wooden walking bridge leads guests to the park campsites on trails from the restaurant.

The state park is open year-round. One of the old cottages of the Ishnala compound has been turned into a warming house for cross-country skiers. The DNR bought the extra acres to expand its trail system.

Steve Kincaid has been making this trek for dinner since he was six, when his parents first brought him to Ishnala. He is forty-four on this final night before the supper club closes for the season. Kincaid and his wife, Melissa, open and close Ishnala every year.

"I love the setting," says Kincaid, a chiropractor from rural Baraboo, about ten miles away from the supper club. "My earliest memory here is all the trees coming up through the floor. We've been to the House on the Rock, which has a similar thing going on with trees coming up from the floor to the roof. There's the mannequin of the Native American. I have a picture of myself standing in front of the cement tepee on the edge of the building."

Who needs Disney World?

The supper club lifestyle is in Kincaid's blood. His grandparents owned the Fireside Supper Club in Fort Atkinson, Wisconsin, and the Sandy Beach Resort in Round Lake, Wisconsin.

Steve and Melissa come to Ishnala two or three times a month. Many times they bring their daughter, Rowan, ten, and son, Declan, eight. Steve says the sup-

Welcome families are a characteristic of a good supper club.

An old-school arch greets visitors at the Ishnala.

per club has the same Frank Sinatra music, the same colors, and the same woodsy smell as it did when he first arrived on the scene in 1973.

"The Dells have a lot of good restaurants. But we sit here an hour and half before dinner and just relax. When I walk in here they all know my name. I always order the same meal. New York strip, extra rare, three butterfly prawns."

Ishnala is on Steve's mind even in the dead of winter. "We ice fish here so we come by and check on it," and he gives a fatherly nod to the back porch. "Then we say we can't wait until they open again. We reflect on it."

During the late 1800s, the fertile grounds were home for a Native American trading operation. A log cabin trading post was built in 1909 and later purchased as a private residence. The current entrance, staircase, and stone fireplace in the lounge area are part of the original log cabin. The Hoffman brothers bought the residence in 1953 and opened the second restaurant of their chain, which began in 1945.

The brothers got to work. They added the Arrowhead Bar, a Tepee Bar (that has become a Tiki Bar with two outdoor decks), a Pow-Wow banquet room, and a dining wing with one hundred tons of flagstone rock from a nearby quarry.

"They built everything around the trees," says owner Bob Prosser, who also owns the Hoffman House in the Rockford Holiday Inn. The Arrowhead bar seats about 30 people, and the dining room seats 170. The Tiki Bar holds about forty. Most of the faded red supper club chairs are from the 1960s, reclaimed from old Hoffman Houses.

During the 1960s, female Ishnala servers wore feathered Pocahontas-inspired outfits. Susan B. Anthony (real name) is a Milwaukee attorney who wore one of those getups in the summer of 1975. "I didn't love the costumes," Anthony said during a phone interview. "The cocktail waitress wore a short fringed thing with a headband. Dinner servers did not have to wear that. We did have to wear the headband. I wasn't crazy about it, but it was a good job. It was the summer before I started law school and I needed money. We made real good tips."

Prosser says, "We'll probably bring back the Pocahontas thing. I'm trying to get someone to make them for me."

Prosser was familiar with Ishnala when he came on board in 1985 as part of the Hoffman House family. In 1977 Hoffman House sold its restaurants (which peaked at seventeen stores including Elk Grove Village) to the Jolly Green Giant Corporation, which in turn was bought out by Pillsbury. Prosser, fifty-two, started working for Hoffman House as a sixteen-year-old busboy in Wausau, Wisconsin. Prosser now visits other supper clubs and will implement ideas at Ishnala.

"Blink Bonnie's does everything on sizzlers," he says. "We tried that. The Gun Club in Beloit [since burned down] serves a bone-in rib eye and we're serving it for a special."

Steve Kincaid has been dining at the Ishnala since he was six years old.

Another supper club staple is huge main portions, and Ishnala fits the bill. There's a sixteen-ounce New York strip steak and a twenty-ounce prime rib. "People call and ask if we have vegetarian," he says. "To be honest I don't care. You're not coming here for that. Come on, knock it off. We're meat and potatoes."

Prosser also operates Hoffman House Catering in suburban Batavia, which serves about three thousand Meals on Wheels daily. "People are so happy we haven't changed anything over the years. The structure, the tables are all the same. It's all about the memories."

PART III

Wacky-Named Supper Clubs

7

HobNob

277 Sheridan Road, Racine, Wisconsin
(262) 552-8008 • www.thehobnob.com

The slow good-bye to the warmest of seasons comes from the signals of state fairs, a chorus of cicadas, and not wearing white pants after Labor Day. But summer always leaves in the dead of the night. Suddenly, like a one-night stand in a cheap motel.

You know summer is a fleeting fancy because you are from the Midwest. August 1954 demands a quick road trip.

The two-lane Sheridan Road/Wisconsin Highway 32 connects Chicago with Milwaukee. Beautiful midday views of Lake Michigan are in sight as you cross the Illinois-Wisconsin border. Joe Adcock is hitting home runs for the Milwaukee Braves. The Crew Cuts hit "Sh-Boom" comes on the radio. Life could be a dream.

There is a new restaurant on Sheridan Road between Racine and Kenosha, Wisconsin. Higgins HobNob is a supper club with live music on the roof. That is wild.

The supper club has linear architecture reminiscent of Frank Lloyd Wright, who designed the administration building and great workroom of the S. C. Johnson company up the road. You see the restaurant and you stop. Seagulls are dipping across sandbars and waves. Most Wisconsin supper clubs have woods views, but the HobNob has to be the only one that is built on Lake Michigan. The elite real estate is in step with the cool restaurant name.

Higgins HobNob, summer of 1955.

Higgins HobNob classic menu.

"'Hobnob' is to rub elbows with the ones in the know," HobNob owner Michael Aletto says in the summer of 2011.

The Aletto family is only the second owner of the HobNob. Michael's father, a longtime Chicago area restaurateur, bought the HobNob in 1990. Aletto was thirty-two then. He had quit his job as a banquet captain at the Four Seasons Hotel in Seattle and had plans to backpack through China and Japan. Instead he went straight to work at the HobNob. In 2000, Aletto and his wife, Anne Glowacki, bought the HobNob from his father.

Life could be a dream.

Guests always tell Aletto about his supper club's great location.

"When people say I have a great location, I say no, I have a beautiful location," Alletto says before a Saturday night rush. "A great location would be out by the interstate."

Aletto has a thing about I-94, which sits ten minutes west of the HobNob. Just two years after the HobNob opened, construction began on the interstate that linked traffic from the Wisconsin state line to the Edens Expressway portal into Chicago. The road trips on Sheridan Road would leave, in the dead of the night.

The HobNob began its life in 1937, away from the lake at 516 Sixth Street in downtown Racine. Color picture postcards promoted it as "Wisconsin's Swanky Cocktail Lounge and Bar." And it had AIR-CONDITIONING, and it was where you could "wine and dine."

"We had people in there like Walt Disney because comic books and the Little Golden Book series were published by Whitman Publishing in Racine," says William

Higgins Jr., the son of founder William "Bill" Higgins Sr., over the phone from Florida. "Walt would come to Racine every two or three months on business. He would eat at the HobNob. Frank Lloyd Wright was another big customer. He would be in there with the Johnsons [of the wax company] and often would draw pictures on the tablecloths. A waitress might scold him and he would say, 'Don't worry, it will come out in the wash.' I wish we had saved them."

Higgins Junior was born in 1929. His father rented the original HobNob and then sold it. Higgins Senior then became manager of the Racine Country Club until he opened the present-day HobNob.

HobNob owner-operator Michael Aletto.

Higgins Junior grew up in the business, working in the original non–air-conditioned basement kitchen as a teenager. "I'd put relishes, olives, carrot sticks, and celery into the dishes," he says. His father built the current HobNob as a country hideaway where people eat and listen to music, and he once conducted basement gambling in the tradition of old-school Wisconsin supper clubs. Stories grow over time.

Big Bill Senior began digging the hole for the HobNob in 1953. "We opened exactly 365 days later," he says proudly as if looking at a watch. "My father died in 1963. I ran it from 1963 to 1990."

Why did Higgins Junior stick with the family business?

"I had no choice," he answers bluntly in the spring of 2012. "It cost him a lot of money. It cost $450,000 to build the HobNob. You couldn't do it today for less than a couple million. And we got that lakefront property for a song. I put up the sign, STOP, LAKE MICHIGAN, and put up the curbing so no car could possibly go over that."

Rooftop cocktails that no longer exist at the HobNob due to high winds from Lake Michigan.

As in a traditional supper club, Higgins Junior, his father, his mother—the ornately named Belle Murphy Higgins—and his brother lived on the premises, in a large apartment upstairs from the restaurant. "I was there all the time. Of course after I got married I moved out," he recalls. "We had dancing on the roof with a five-piece band for many years. It got to be a chore and people wanted to start serving food. What if it started to rain? We never served food upstairs."

A huge oil portrait of a fancy-dressed Higgins Senior hangs at the front door of the HobNob. "He played semipro ball in Racine; he raced outboard motor boats in

Detroit," Aletto says. "He was a character." Aletto speaks in a wistful tone as if characters are an endangered species.

"Around 1990 my father and mother were traveling up this way because they belong to an Italian club in Round Lake [Illinois]," Aletto says. "They heard things about Kenosha and how it was growing. They were driving along Sheridan Road. My father likes water. He was a sailor. He came in here and fell in love with this place. He asked the bartender if it was for sale."

It was.

It is a piece of heaven.

Michael Aletto hasn't made many changes at the HobNob since 1990.

He installed new carpeting. People don't use pay phones anymore so the dual phone booths have been turned into intimate wine cellars. In 1996 Aletto added an extra 120-seat dining room with a view of Lake Michigan and the lush shrubs, river birch, and willows that surround the supper club.

The restaurant's red vinyl chairs are part of the original HobNob, but Aletto brought in new purple chairs

Classic HobNob neon in Racine, Wisconsin.

from the Meadowbrook Country Club in Racine. (Fun fact: one of the country club owners is the father of NFL quarterback Tony Romo.) "They are probably fifty years old," Aletto says while spinning and turning toward the chairs. "I had lime green ones before." Mismatched furniture is a wonderful characteristic of a supper club.

Dave and Mary Lewis of Racine celebrating a birthday at the HobNob.

As different as the rambling appointments can be, supper club regulars are all about ritual. Dave and Mary Lewis have been married twenty years. They've been coming to the HobNob for a little more than ten years. They live about a quarter-mile south of the restaurant. He is director of operations for the Kenosha water utility. His late father, Ken, was a craftsman who painted churches in southern Wisconsin. Mary Lewis is recently retired from Modine Manufacturing (established 1916) in Racine.

On this particular summer night they are celebrating Mary's birthday. He is having steak. She is having lobster. Their cocktail glasses are filled with brandy alexanders. The clink of the glasses drowns out cicadas that signal the passage of time.

"We know the bartender, Randy," Dave says. Randy keeps a pair of binoculars behind the bar to watch distant vistas. Dave continues, "We always request Roz as our waitress. Teresa is the hostess. Michael feels free to sit down and talk to you while you're eating. He talked to us fifteen, twenty minutes about his kids and the things going on their lives. All those little things mean a lot to us." Mary adds, "You're rushed through a lot of places. Here they don't rush you at all."

Dave and Mary dine at the HobNob at least once a month. Dave looks at his bride. He then looks out at the lake from across the bar and says, "We always sit in one of these two booths in the bar. Absolutely. They know it's our favorite spot. You can't get a better view. The area is a little different. It's a state highway but there's all these cool houses along the lake. This is more than just a restaurant to us."

Out on the lakefront veranda, Geoff and Jaynie Rench are having post-supper drinks. They have been a couple since 1978 and are regular guests at the HobNob. They appear to be an impeccable pair, Geoff in a sharp white coat and Jaynie with white pearls around her neck and powerful Sally Jessy Raphael talk show glasses.

Geoff chooses his words carefully and with elegance. "There is a chorus here," says the long-time native of Racine. "Eclectic isn't good enough, you know? Somehow it works. Little side rooms. And rooms behind those side rooms. It looks like the whole thing was assembled out of parts from somewhere else. And Michael hasn't changed the look much from when Bill Higgins had it. He's only changed what's hanging here and there. He inherited all this.

Geoff and Jaynie Rench, eternal HobNob hipsters.

"Higgins lived upstairs. He got divorced. Bill Senior had passed on. Bill Junior's younger brother Jim was a priest. He'd be around every now and then and hold court in the first booth just inside of this room by the lake. Jim did some changing of the decor but he didn't depart from whatever scene you could put to it. But Bill Junior had two Dobermans which he let out on the roof. I remember walking out of here one night going toward my car . . . " And Geoff starts barking and growling very loudly. He smiles and continues, "That was Bill saying, 'Don't come back now.'"

Geoff knows his supper club turf. He takes a sip of Scotch and says, "The farther west and north you go in Wisconsin, the more distinctive the 'supper club' term is. A supper club, as I understand it, is a restaurant that has tablecloths. Linen napkins. Usually there's music and it's decades past—a mighty Wurlitzer of some kind. I don't know if there's any of those left. A broad menu. And no color pictures of what our foods look like!"

Janie works in advertising and design out of Milwaukee. She designed the present-day, gently retrofitted HobNob logo. "I was thinking of the lake," she says. "The sailboats. The beautiful trees. I wanted the logo face to be modern but stand the test of time."

Lillian Gildenstern is softly playing "Moon River" on a full-sized Kurzweil eighty-eight-key piano in the supper club lounge, just a few ripples away from Dave and Mary. She is eighty-one years old on this summer night in 2011.

Gildenstern only appears at the HobNob between seven PM and one AM on Saturdays, and her repertoire is only between the 1930s and the 1970s. "This is a relaxing place to play, along the lake," she says during a break. "Then the moon comes up and I start with the moon stuff like 'Moon River.' When there's a full moon, that's quite a thing. Especially for people who are here for the first time with all the windows."

Gildenstern is a musical fixture around Racine. She started playing when she was five years old in her parents' farmhouse in Kenosha County. She began her professional career playing music in 1965 in an Elks club in downtown Racine. For the next eleven years she appeared at the now-defunct Valley Supper Club on Sheridan Road in neighboring Kenosha.

She began her regular HobNob gigs in 1997. "I wanted to give something extra to the guests," Aletto says. "Music was virtually dead in this area. Music had been in this supper club in the past. We knew her from town, from working at another restaurant." Gildenstern had been filling in playing polka and big band music with the Brass Ball Bangers.

Aletto explains, "There were powerful musicians that came out of the area. Kenosha and Racine had a lot of drum and bugle corps and would win national competitions. Lillian doesn't play by note. She plays by memory. She sings all the songs you would hear in the '40s, '50s, and '60s, when people would sit around the piano bar singing until two in the morning and have their cocktails. Sometimes the younger people don't get her, but people in their fifties and sixties do, because it's something their parents brought them to. So they remember it."

Gildenstern has raised five children. They are all in Kenosha except for one son in Plano, Texas. She was married forty-two years to Harold, a home builder in the area. He died of cancer in 1992. "I never traveled with my music because I was a homemaker and a mother too," Gildenstern says. "I always played the Kenosha-Racine circuit. My husband would drop me off when I'd play, then he'd come pick me up. We'd go to breakfast. Back then you would play until one in the morning."

Kenosha mayor Keith Bosman is her cousin. "My brother's son was in the big leagues," she says with a note of pride. "He came in last time he was in town. Dick Bosman [who pitched for the Washington Senators] is my nephew. He sat by me at the piano last Thanksgiving. He works for Tampa Bay [in the minor league system]."

A Kenosha native born in 1944, Bosman is the only pitcher in major league history to miss a perfect game due to his own fielding error.

"We're a close family," Gildenstern says. "I'm a big baseball fan. I played organ at the Kenosha Twins [Midwest League] games in the 1980s. I demonstrated for Hammond Organ. They said I sold more organs than anyone because I made it look so easy. I play mostly by ear."

Gildenstern has met other celebrities who weren't related. When she was appearing at the Valley Supper Club she met vampire-horror actor Vincent Price. "He was also an artist and he had a showing at Carthage College," she recalls of Price, who was also an accomplished chef who once showed Johnny Carson how to poach a fish in a dishwasher. "I shook hands with him and he autographed something for me. He was real tall, gaunt and thin."

He needed a supper club.

Restaurants are in Michael Aletto's blood. His father, Dante, ran Aletto's Cottage Inn from 1955 to 1963, during the wide-open honky-tonk days and nights of Lyons, Illinois, near Chicago. Like father, like son, Dante took over the Cottage Inn from his father, Ed. Dante later operated the Carousel restaurant and piano bar in west suburban Warrenville, Illinois, from 1963 to 1974.

Michael Aletto began his career as a host at the Carousel. Ed Cella, Michael's maternal grandfather, owned the Montecristo restaurant, 645 Saint Claire Street, during the height of the 1933 Chicago World's Fair. He also ran the popular twenty-four-hour Glass Hat on Rush Street in Chicago. Ed Cella canned ravioli and was a finance guy for the Archdiocese of Chicago.

Although Aletto has been around restaurants all his life, he wasn't clear on the whole supper club thing. "I didn't know the definition of a supper club," he says, as Gildenstern deals "Satin Doll." He "had been to a lot of them as a kid. Supper clubs are generally just open for dinner. They were all independent restaurants. Each supper club was an identity of the person who owned it. That's how it became a club. The bartender could be the owner, and everybody was coming in to see the owner. Remember, part of that word 'club' is loyalty. You had the same people, they sat at the same table and had the same meal. The bartender knew your drink when you sat down, whether it would be sweet, sour, or a dash of this. There is no loyalty in today's world.

"Supper clubs used to serve relish trays, bean caddies, things like that. That's been gone probably thirty years here. But we still serve choice of salad, choice of potato, with the entree. We have the Friday night fish fry and the prime rib on Saturday. We still have linen napkins."

The front room is empty around five PM on this particular Saturday. Aletto is wearing a silk tie, knotted to the neck, and a blue suit. He is loyal to values of the past. "The first ten years I was here we were gangbusters," he says. "Manufacturing in the area was going strong. There was only one franchise in town. That was the Olive Garden. Most restaurants were independent. As you got closer to the interstate there were more fast-food franchises. At the same time I wondered why more independent restaurants didn't come into this area. I was doing three hundred people on a Saturday night. Now I do 150, which is more controlled and easier on me.

"Everybody is blown away when they are in here. It is, 'Where am I?' the blast from the past. I call it giving people 'warm fuzzies from yesteryear'; the times when they were with their parents, when they were small with their grandparents, and it was a special occasion. Everybody would get dressed up. People wore suits and ties."

Aletto talks of his life at the HobNob in measured, chronological tones. When he gets to the year 2000 his voice drops like the fall of a curtain. "A lot of things happened in 2000," he says. "The disappearing of manufacturing. Internet telecommunications. Stock market crash. That took a lot of wealth away from people.

"We had road construction for eight years. We're like the old Route 66 except we have a lake view. This was the throughway between Milwaukee and Chicago. Then we had the housing boom and discretionary income went to paying the credit cards. Then the housing bust, the financial bust. And that's where we are now."

Racine is built on manufacturing that developed along the banks of the Root River. Much of that manufacturing is gone now. Besides S. C. Johnson & Son, Racine was a car manufacturing center in the late 1800s, and the Pennington Victoria tricycle was created in Racine. It used to be a big union town. Malted milk was invented in Racine in 1887.

Aletto came up through working-class ranks, attending hotel and restaurant school at Washington State University. He worked at hotels in Chicago, Houston, and Seattle. He understands the supper club has a niche audience. "Think about it," he says. "People in their thirties and forties are starting a family. They're going to go to an Applebee's and get in and out in thirty minutes. They can't afford coming here for the big, long dinner. That's why we have an older crowd. The kids are out of the house. The husband and wife come out to dinner with their friends. And in the old days when people went out they had fun. They had three or four drinks and all they wanted was a big steak and a big potato.

"In today's world, everybody is an expert. You're an expert on wine. You're an expert on gourmet food. The ironic part is they've forgotten how to communicate with each other. We have on our menu that it takes an hour and a half for a steak. We put that on there because everybody is so used to getting fed and out in forty-five minutes because corporations are turn, turn, turn. We can't do that, not with our staff and what we do. When they start thinking about how it's taking a long time, instead of looking at their watch, talk with who you are with. Look at the atmosphere of the room. Take it all in.

"When people come in this restaurant they take a tour. How many people come in a restaurant and take a tour?"

Like a silver line cast to the lake, the HobNob menu tries to depart from the predictable. The 2011 menu included an appetizer of Thai-style duck rolls served with orange sauce and coconut curry sauce and a grilled applejack pork chop topped with applejack brandy sauce and sautéed apples.

"When people come to a restaurant like this, they have to understand this is what it is," Aletto says. "We do have a vegetarian meal on the menu. We do have chicken on the menu. For eighteen years I tried to push all kinds of food here. I had ten different seafood specials. Finally I realized no matter what I do, people always perceived us as a steak house. Prime rib is our number one. Why am I fighting it? We still have seafood on the menu. I have halibut all the time, East Coast fish, all kinds of salmon. Wiener schnitzel is still on the menu the old-fashioned way. Most restaurants deep-fry Wiener schnitzel." The German specialty is pan-sautéed in clarified butter at the HobNob.

Aletto continues, "And duck. You don't find duck anymore."

But like every Wisconsin supper club, you do find the old-fashioned cocktail. "My father was in the restaurant business all his life in Illinois," Aletto says. "He wanted to help me here. He was sixty-seven. We were rockin'. He was bartending. He hadn't bartended since 1975. People are ordering these big tub [twelve to sixteen ounces] drinks. He goes, 'Mike, what is that?' It was the god-damned old-fashioned. He was used to drinks in three- and four-ounce glasses. He was blown away. If I were to open up another restaurant, that would be the drink I would highlight."

In the summer of 2011 Aletto and his wife live in Sarasota, Florida, with their daughters Czesia, twelve; Kinga, eleven; and son, Dante, nine. (He has daughters Regina, twenty-five, and Michelle, twenty-seven, from a previous marriage.) Alleto returns to Racine about once a month and lives in the vintage Higgins apartment above the HobNob.

"By living away and then coming back I have a new understanding again," he says. "My eyes are not worn. It really is a beautiful place. I can see why people want to look around. I can't do this forever. My goal is to pass the baton on to somebody who can carry it further than when I had it. You want people to be more successful than you were. A restaurant is easy to buy but it's hard to sell."

Good dreams never come at a discount.

8

The Otter Supper Club and Lodge

306 N. Highway 70, Ottertail, Minnesota
(218) 367-2525 • www.ottersupperclub.com

The casual nature of the supper club fosters community. It is one of the earliest social networks. When you spend five to six hours at a Minnesota supper club you hear local gossip, talk about religion, and utter mutterings on the Vikings. The Otter Supper Club and Lodge is one of those places.

The supper club is a short crawl from uptown Ottertail (population 572) in northwest Minnesota, about ninety-five miles from Fargo, North Dakota. This is a city that's "Otter-the-Ordinary" according to the Ottertail Business Person's Association (OTBA).

Some cities have remarkable statues of presidents or war heroes that define their downtowns. Ottertail has a giant metal otter. Minnesota scrap metal artist Ken Nyberg made the twelve-foot-tall, fifteen-foot-wide otter out of discarded lawnmower blades. (But the "World's Largest Otter" is in nearby Fergus Falls.) The otter is a mammal whose family includes polecats, weasels, and the badger that made neighboring Wisconsin famous. But it also begs the question: if a town were named Polecat Tail, would there be a Polecat Tail's Supper Club? That sounds like a gentleman's club in Chicago.

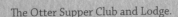
The Otter Supper Club and Lodge.

An otter in downtown Ottertail, just so you know where you are.

The Otter Supper Club and Lodge is one of the most diverse family-run operations in northwest Minnesota. The two-hundred-seat supper club is lined with rustic knotty pine that matches the log cabin exterior.

The Otter is known for its Parmesan-crusted walleye and prime rib on Friday and Saturday nights, but there's also a fifteen-room lodge with a rustic wooden exterior adjacent to the supper club. The supper club hosts live rock and country and western music on summer weekends. And in these parts, there is a difference between country and country and western. As you drive off into the Dakotas, Chris LeDoux and George Strait take a front seat over Kenny Chesney and Brad Paisley.

The Otter has an off-sale (you have to take the liquor off the premises) liquor store for setups—and an on-sale (you can drink on the premises) bar that complements lunch, dinner, and late-night menus. Popular in the South, setups are where customers bring in a bottle of liquor and are "set up" with their mixer of choice. Beer is generally the only alcohol served in these establishments. In the summer of 2011 the Otter offered promotions that just wouldn't be possible in bigger cities: happy hour beer was priced on the day of the month, so if you visited on June 1, the beer was only a penny. Pull tabs? Step right up. The charity game is operated by the Ottertail Lions Club.

The Otter Supper Club opened in 1968 on Highway 78 on the outskirts of town. The rambling Otter Tail Lake is across the highway. The lake is stocked with walleye, sunfish, and crappie. It is the eighth largest lake in the state.

Cathy Mueller was a bartender at the supper club from 1975 to 1995. "Back then it was like a metal storage building and people just threw their money on the bar," says Mueller, who now owns Boll Realty Company in Ottertail. (Mueller's maiden name was Boll.) Her company has sold the Otter three times. "They had Polka fests every Sunday with quarter beers and hot dogs. When I left the Otter I came to work for my mother and when she passed away I took over the real estate business."

Ottertail is a very small town. Mueller knows the Otter history better than present-day staff. "[The late] Chuck Minge put in the hotel and the off-sale," Mueller says. "Four Winds Hospitality Suites put in the log cabin woodwork in the early 2000s. The Otter has always been known for great food, but it's always locals and people staying at resorts. You don't get people driving sixty miles just to eat there."

Deep Minnesota blue en route to the Otter.

Tourism is an economic engine in Ottertail. Like pepper on a steak, the area is sprinkled with thousands of streams and lakes. Snowmobiling is popular on rural trails in the region, and there's the time-honored Minnesota pastime of ice fishing. The supper club is open year-round.

The Thumper Ponds Resort and golf course is walking distance from the Otter Supper Club. In June 2008 O. J. Simpson played a round of golf there and lore has it that he had supper at the Otter. He told the locals he claimed to be a seven handicap.

During the peak of the 1870s tourism season, Ottertail (population then 1,200) had five hotels and twenty-seven taverns. The present-day Saint Paul House gift shop was a stagecoach stop, brothel, and bar. A railroad had been planned for Ottertail and railroad workers were attracted to the village. The July 1880 edition of the *Empire Reporter* said, "Hurdy-gurdy houses and pool halls were just part of the activity in Otter Tail City during the boom." The railroad wound up being built several miles away, passing through Bluffton and Detroit Lakes, Minnesota. The old taverns and hurdy-gurdy houses opened the door for the current Otter.

"The Otter has been the hot spot in Ottertail," veteran supper club office manager Patty Wambach said in the summer of 2011. "It's known all over. We have people who come from Canada and Iowa for fishing. We have guide services that provide fishing so they get a reduced rate on their room. They like the Otter because we have a little bit of everything."

Wambach has been at the Otter since 2007. She moved to Ottertail from Fargo. "I had heard of this supper club," she says. "Because this is in the heart of the lakes. And it is a hangout for locals."

In July 2011 ownership of the supper club was transitioning to Dan Hurder, who had just purchased the Otter with his father, David, a chemical engineer. They bought it cold turkey. Hurder was the general manager of the Hilton Garden Inn in Fargo.

Hurder, born in 1981, had never been to Ottertail until he visited the supper club in March 2011. "I liked everything about it," says Hurder, a native of Cleveland, Ohio. "It's old but it still has some charm. It's never been totally gutted and redone. None of the previous owners made you feel like you were sitting in a bar in Minneapolis because that's not what people are looking for around here. A lot of people have gone modern, but this was true to the region. It had rural character. It was a fit for the way I wanted to take my career.

"The other piece of it was that it had such a local following and people were very invested in making sure it would be here for years to come. That's what convinced me to buy this. It was coming with a loyal following. Sometimes when you buy a new business you're fighting an uphill battle to regain a customer base that left for whatever reason."

Hurder tweaked the menu with more seafood offerings, such as mahimahi, and added wraps. He has left tradition alone. Wambach points out, "Traditional linen napkins are something we feel strongly about. You still need to have that fine dining atmosphere, yet relaxed atmosphere. It's not over the top. You can dance in here. There are fresh flowers in a small vase on the tables in the evenings."

"A supper club to me was dining and dancing," says Wambach, who was born in 1958. "It wasn't a chain restaurant. It always had a hometown, home-cooking feel. That's what we frequented growing up in [Fargo and Morehead]. I grew up on a dairy and grain farm in Georgetown [Minnesota]. We ran a grocery store at the same time. I came from a family of ten. We were used to eating meat, potatoes, and vegetables and to me that's a supper club thing."

She then asked if I had been to the creamery. If I had been fishing, drinking penny beer, or just zooming down Highway 78 I might have missed the Ottertail Creamery. It is a beautifully restored dark gray and red brick creamery building from 1921 and is now the home of Firestarters Ministries.

During the early twentieth century, creameries were even bigger than corn in northwest Minnesota. The Ottertail Farmers Co-Operative Creamery Association formed on July 18, 1906. "The company sold shares for $25 and incorporated with a capitalization of $4,000," according to a report in the *Fergus Falls Journal*.

In the 1920s the state of Minnesota encouraged co-ops to construct modern buildings. The Ottertail Farmers Co-Op dedicated its new creamery building with a sterling interior of red clay tile in Ottertail on September 21, 1921.

The September 29, 1921, edition of the *Henning Advocate* newspaper wrote that eight hundred farmers and their families had braved bad roads and "came long distances to inspect the beautiful new building." The Ottertail Creamery began sourcing area diners, restaurants, and supper clubs.

Today it is a worship center/concert venue/gift shop/coffee shop.

Pete Thiel and his wife, Pam, are the founders of the nondenominational Firestarters Ministry. The group gets its name from the Bible's Mark 16: "To start fires, to fuel and fan the flames of revival and renewal wherever God leads us." The Firestarters restored the creamery between fall 2008 and spring 2009. In its most recent incarnation, the creamery had been a used tire store from 1972 through the

The historic Ottertail Creamery, built in 1921.

The Ottertail Creamery once sourced supper clubs in the region.

1990s. The Firestarters removed between four and five thousand old tires. Some were Firestones.

The Firestarters replaced the roof and added a prayer tower. The exterior's original red Saint Louis brick was in good shape. The group removed plaster from ten thousand pieces of interior brick to expose the original red clay tile. The creamery's second floor and one-time slaughterhouse became a recording studio and performance space. The Firestarters congregation numbers around one hundred, including poets, musicians, and writers.

Sunday evening services incorporate folk and rock music, poetry, and interpretive dance. "Area musicians used to play there going back as far as the 1940s," Peter Thiel says. In the summer of 2012, Firestarters opened the Old Creamery coffee shop on the first floor, and there are plans for a wood-fired pizza oven.

They brought in everything but a supper club. Ottertail doesn't have much, but they already have the Otter Supper Club.

Peter Thiel is from Battle Lake, Minnesota, about fifteen miles from Ottertail. He grew up in the area. During the early 1990s Peter and Pam Thiel were associate pastors on the Kenai peninsula, south of Anchorage, Alaska.

"Around here a supper club means fine dining and a real good meal," says Peter, who was born in 1956. "We go to the Otter a lot. They have awesome hamburgers." The supper club's hamburgers are charbroiled and served on a toasted bun. A Western Burger is served with barbecue sauce, bell peppers, grilled onions, and American cheese. Thiel says, "You see a lot of the baby boomers' kids at the Otter. And the supper club gets more crowded as a summer attraction with the eleven hundred lakes in our county."

Ohio-born owner Hurder wasn't hip to the term "supper club" even after spending three years with Hilton in Fargo. "I first thought it was a regional term for restaurants," he says. "As I dove into it, I realized it was more of a small-town thing that truly was supper and a club. It served the purpose of fine dining but also served the purpose of entertainment. But fine dining is going by the wayside in any market, but especially out where we are. There's not as much demand to sit down and have a thirty dollar plate of food as there used to be. We're doing smaller portions. Half sandwiches at lunch."

The walleye sandwich is the popular lunch item at the supper club. The ample-sized fish is breaded on-site and served on a whole wheat bun. "One time I had a request for a hamburger with ham on it," says bartender and waitress Joy Perala. "I never heard that before." She did not smile at such nonsense.

Perala has worked at the Otter since 1990, after having been a bartender in Neeska, Wisconsin. Perala has a straight, no-chaser nature, which is evident when visitors begin debating the difference between a Wisconsin supper club and a Minnesota supper club. "Very rarely do I serve a brandy old-fashioned here," says Perala, a native of Minneapolis. "In Wisconsin, they drink those all the time. When someone goes to Las Vegas and orders an old-fashioned, the bartender says, 'You must be from Wisconsin.' Here people drink beer, Miller Lite, Coors Lite. We have Leinenkugel's seasonal beers, whiskey, and Bloody Marys."

Perala also works the Friday Night Meat Raffle, held weekly between six and eight PM. The Lions Club sets up a table with thirty numbers. Customers can purchase a number for a dollar, which entitles them to a spin of a wheel. "If the wheel lands on the number you picked, you can pick whatever type of meat [pork, shrimp,

Even in midsummer, it is never too early to plan for a supper club Octoberfest.

hamburger, and so on] you want," Perala says. "It's often standing room only for that. We serve hors d'oeuvres during the raffle." The meat is locally sourced, including from the supermarket [Carr's] down the street. The pork comes from Amor Pork, across the lake in Ottertail.

Hurder adds, "Basically for one dollar you have a chance to win $18 worth of meat. You can choose cash or meat, but it is a good value." The median income in Ottertail from 2000 to 2009 was $32,926, compared to a statewide median income of $55,616, according to city-data.com.

Thiel understands the community's needs from the ministry down the road. "So much has changed even since I grew up," Thiel says. "We knew every house in town and everybody who lived in every house in town. It's not like that today. For one, there are very few children in Ottertail and very few young adults. Everybody pretty much left when the family farm started to go under. It became quite desolate. Ottertail is basically a drive-through town, a town you drive through to get where you're going."

He laughs, but there are wistful tones in his laughter. "We're taking on the responsibility of restoring downtown Ottertail so it can be a gathering place for people again," he says. "We have hundreds of visitors who go through the creamery building. They like to look around upstairs. There are other buildings in town we want to renovate and remodel. We have about thirty young adults who have moved to Ottertail to become part of the ministry. And now our kids are getting married and having babies. It's exciting to watch.

"The town is coming back. There's the supper club, a new Irish pub. The golf course, but if it had been my golf course, O. J. Simpson wouldn't have played on it. No way."

Some values don't change in a supper club community.

9

Mr. Ed's Tee Pee Supper Club

812 Superior Avenue, Tomah, Wisconsin
(608) 372-0888 • www.teepeesupperclub.com

Allan "Ed" Thompson looked everyone in the eye and thanked them for coming. It is what you do when you say good-bye.

Ed was hosting a July 16, 2011, fund-raiser in the banquet hall of his beloved Mr. Ed's Tee Pee Supper Club in Tomah, Wisconsin. The headliners were an Elvis Presley and Patsy Cline tribute act. The Elvis guy covered "Don't Be Cruel" and "Blue Suede Shoes," songs that were recorded in 1956 when supper clubs were gold. The Elvis guy worked the soundboard when his Patsy sang "Walkin' After Midnight."

Ed sat off in a dark corner, shaking hands and taking donations.

More than three hundred area residents turned out on a warm summer night, making the dinner and show event a success. Ed wore a natty gray suit with a maroon tie neatly knotted at the neck. He wanted to look nice. This was a supper club event. At one point he grimaced and held his left side after walking around the room selling raffle tickets.

Ed had pancreatic cancer. Born on Christmas Day 1944, he died on October 23, 2011. He was sixty-six years old. Ed's life was a full plate. He was a boxer, a prison cook, and the brother of Tommy Thompson, former US Secretary of Health and Human Services and four-time Wisconsin governor.

Mr. Ed's Tee Pee Supper Club, Tomah, Wisconsin.

The late Ed Thompson and his sister Juliann.

"I have nothing but good memories of the place," Tommy Thompson said in the spring of 2012 as he was running in a failed bid for the US Senate. "Every time you go to the Tee Pee there is good food, good friendship, and a lot of joking back and forth. It is a destination point. When I was governor, people would come up and say, 'I stopped at the Tee-Pee to have a meal.' I'm around the state campaigning right now and everybody is bringing up my brother and their friendship. I actually think he touched more lives than I did."

Ed was also mayor of Tomah from 2000 to 2002 and from 2008 to 2010. In 2002, he ran for governor as a Libertarian, garnering 11 percent of the vote. He made an unsuccessful bid for state senate in 2010, which is when he was diagnosed. He stopped his campaign.

"I said I didn't have time for surgery," Ed explained during a conversation at the Tee Pee in June 2011. "I had to march in a parade. Little did I know I had already walked my last parade."

He was given six months to live. That was in September 2010.

Ed beat the odds.

On that June afternoon Ed said something out of left field, which he was known to do around Tomah (population 8,400). After all, his maverick nature used to bring up Billy Carter, the unorthodox brother of President Jimmy Carter. Ed once told the *Chicago Tribune*, "Well, I don't think Tommy resembles Billy at all."

Ed asked if I wanted to buy Mr. Ed's Tee Pee Supper Club. Or if I knew anyone who would be interested in keeping the place alive. Of all of Ed's colorful identities, his role as the owner of the Tee Pee seemed closest to his heart. But Ed's children were not interested in taking over the business.

Ed and his older sister, Juliann, bought the supper club out of bankruptcy in 1990. As Ed fought his illness, Juliann commuted from her home in southern California to take care of her brother and the supper club. She was a retired nutrition and child development professor. She will continue to keep the Tee Pee going until a suitable buyer is found.

Ed and Juliann were the fourth owners of the establishment, which started in 1890 as a livery stable. With the advent of the automobile in 1920 the space became the popular Tomah Theater, with a dark make-out balcony. The theater closed in 1958 and was turned into a supper club.

Perched on the roof of the Tee Pee banquet hall is a vintage Native American princess cooking over a campfire. The roadside art is made of tin and neon.

"That's been here since 1960," Ed said. "We never changed it. That's a big part of the Tee Pee." The Native American signpost celebrates Tomah's heritage. The city gets its name from the majestic Menominee Indian Chief Tomah (1752–1818). "The high school team was the Tomah Indians," Ed recalled. "In 1960 a group of men opened a restaurant here and named it the Tee Pee. It boomed."

Ed knew this because he spent his entire life in central Wisconsin. He was born in Mauston and spent his early years in Elroy, where his parents operated Thompson's Grocery Store.

"We grew up in that grocery store," Ed said. "It was my father's [Allan Edward]. My mother [Julia Ellen] was a first-grade schoolteacher. She was a cook extraordinaire. She baked rolls and biscuits. Everybody thinks their mother was a good cook, but my mother really was the best. Nobody was making money during the Depression but my dad was making money. But he would work from six in the morning until ten, twelve at night. Seven days a week. He built his house himself. Just a hardworking man.

"They were very dedicated to us and wanted us to be successful; I went to the University of Wisconsin for one year. My memories of Tomah go back to when we visited my aunt who lived here. I was grade school age."

Ed and his family would shop at the Tomah Cash Store, a department store that had been uptown for more than one hundred years. Ed smiled and said, "That was a big trip from Elroy [twenty-six miles] to Tomah. They had stop and go lights and everything."

An iconic Native American princess blesses downtown Tomah from atop the Tee Pee.

The Tee Pee logo is deployed right down to cocktail napkins.

Tomah still has an Amtrak station, not far from the Tee Pee. Tomah is also one of the biggest cranberry exporters in the United States, with twenty-five hundred acres of cranberry marshes. "The interstate [90 and 94] divides here so we have a little more tourist trade," he said. "Minneapolis, Chicago, Milwaukee, it all converges right here. Lots of stuff passes through. It changed in the 1960s.

"Until then Highway 12 was the way to Minnesota, bumper to bumper to bumper. You couldn't get across main street [Superior Avenue] here. When the interstate came a whole new community developed out there," said Ed, nodding to a place east of town where the grass grew tall every spring with the promise of a suburban American dream.

Barb and John Cram were at the Elvis and Patsy show in July 2011. The significance of the event was not lost on them.

"I'd say 90 percent of the people in this room are from Tomah," Barb said as she looked around the crowded banquet hall. She and John have lived in Tomah all their lives. They were married in 1971.

Barb's father, Clyde, was a fill-in cook at the Tee Pee. John was a retired cop from the Monroe County sheriff's department who also spent four years on the Tomah city council. They had just completed their first trip to the Graceland Mansion in Memphis in the summer of 2010.

Although he was a tough Wisconsin cop, John's favorite Elvis song will always be "Love Me Tender."

Barb said, "People here come together in any type of hardship. Look at the bowl over there that's full [of money] for the Tomah Area Cancer Society. Everybody gives willingly of their time and what money they can. Ed is pretty community minded. It's going to be very hard to replace him."

Before opening Mr. Ed's Tee Pee, Ed owned Mr. Ed's Bar, a shot and beer joint in Elroy. "I had a lot of fun with the TV show [with the talking horse of course]," he said in June 2011. "But Elroy was going nowhere. We had fifteen hundred people and five taverns. I had the best business in town but there wasn't enough there. This was an opportunity. I didn't have any experience in a supper club.

Mr. Ed's Tee Pee is a supper club—make no mistake about it.

"When we grew up, dinner would be around noon and supper would be the evening meal. We never had lunch. We had breakfast, dinner, and supper. Dinner was really lunch. We had chicken every Sunday. That was our Sunday dinner. Pot roast every Saturday. Usually it was the last pork chop left in the store on Thursday that Dad didn't sell. We had no choice in that dinner."

Juliann added, "That seems Midwest. In California, we don't have supper. We go out to dinner."

Ed continued, "The people we bought this place from opened at four o'clock and I think that's where the idea of a supper club came from, an evening meal place and a place for cocktails. I started opening at noon. We have a Friday night fish fry for ten dollars and prime rib on Saturday. It has to be a tradition. We knew we had to do it. We have tap beer like [Leinenkeugel's] Honey Weiss, Michelob, New Glarus Spotted Cow. In a small town like Tomah, downtown you have to have tap beer. We also make the best brandy old-fashioned in the world."

I had my first-ever brandy old-fashioned at Mr. Ed's Tee Pee. It was very sweet. "We have our own touch," he said with a satisfied smile. "We put a cinnamon stick in it. Most people don't. It's a unique drink. It has bitters in it. Lumps of sugar that you usually muddle and then hit it with a touch of seltzer and the brandy. It's my recipe. I learned it in 1963 from an old bartender, Harvey Leverenz in Elroy. We're known all over for our old-fashioned. The old-fashioned is a staple of the supper club."

Ed had worked in a kitchen before taking over the Tee Pee. He cooked for one thousand inmates in the federal prison in Oxford, Wisconsin, in the mid-1980s. But the captive audience didn't eat as well as customers at the Tee Pee.

The supper club is known for its steak and ribs. The meat is slow roasted for twenty-four hours and basted with a garlic salt seasoning.

"My favorites are the walleye and the prime rib," Tommy Thompson said. "I've had many fund-raisers there. Ed always wanted me to bring more in but I had to remind him they had to be all over the state. I have a farm in Elroy and when people want to meet with me I tell them we will meet at the Tee Pee. Governor [Scott] Walker has been there many times. Senator Ron Johnson goes there. Congressman Ron Kind [3rd District near LaCrosse and Eau Claire]. Politicians of both political parties."

Ed was always proud of the potato cheese soup appetizer. Juliann said, "I've been here fourteen years and never seen a stick of margarine in this place."

Ed was married eighteen years to his high school sweetheart, but he was a hard guy to pin down. They were divorced in 1988 and remained friends. All of their children are accomplished: Joshua Paul Thompson is an attorney in Sacramento; Kristin Ashford is a professor at the University of Kentucky; Ann Marie Greene is a grade school principal in Richmond, Virginia; and Allan "Ed" Thompson III is a mathematics teacher in Tomah.

Elvis and Patsy party attendee Eric Carlson has lived in Tomah for sixty-six of his seventy years. His father, Casper, owned and operated Cap's Vending & Wholesale Co. in Tomah. Carlson worked there until the family sold the music and game company in 1992. Cap's serviced most of the supper clubs in the Tomah-Sparta-Wisconsin Dells region.

"We grew up on supper clubs in Tomah," Carlson said. "On Friday and Saturday nights you couldn't get into any of them. They were packed. People ate, drank, and socialized. You didn't have the Internet. Tomah streets would be packed. You'd meet anybody new who came into town. The farmers came into town. You couldn't get into the door of the Tee Pee. It was a way to get to know people."

The Tee Pee is now the biggest restaurant in town, seating about one hundred people in the dimly lit main dining room, accented by a long bar that seems to wander to Minnesota. Another hundred people can sit in the adjacent Carpeting Room, as it is called, generally used for meetings. During my June visit, a group of Good Sams RVers were having a "Samboree" dinner.

Jean Goosen, Wisconsin state director for the Good Sam Club, said, "We have a Samboree. It's like a jamboree. Everybody who has a camping unit comes. The Tee Pee is a tradition with us. We've been here many years and they treat us well. They have a room big enough for us. We all ordered off the menu and no orders were mixed up. Supper clubs are family friendly. That's what we look for."

Ed added the supper club's cherry pine log cabin exterior when the banquet hall opened on New Year's Eve 1997. Mr. Ed's Tee Pee Supper Club grew in stature.

It had to be the only supper club–bar–indoor golf simulator–banquet hall in the Midwest. Tommy Thompson used the banquet hall for fund-raisers. The banquet hall was important to Ed. It symbolized resurrection, a way back from anywhere.

Ed remembered a 1992 Thanksgiving dinner made up of leftovers from the neighbors—with his German shepherd, Ace. Times were beyond tough. The deal he'd cut to lease his supper club had fallen through. He had to evict his tenants. "I was in financial straits," Ed said over walleye pike at the Tee Pee. "I was dusted. I was down in the cloth. I reestablished the Tee Pee in 1993. By the fall we straightened out the debt. I was so grateful to the people of Tomah I wanted to give a free Thanksgiving dinner. I told Ace that would be the last Thanksgiving we would eat alone."

The free 1993 Thanksgiving dinner attracted three hundred needy Tomah residents. That number grew to twelve hundred in 2010. "Everybody helps," Ed said. "The Boy Scouts, Girl Scouts, Rotary, the Lions club." Churches bake pies. And it all happens in the Tee Pee banquet hall. Community is a staple of a supper club.

After all, everybody in the small town knew about the poker machines Ed had kept in the supper club in 1997. A raid on the supper club ended when five video poker machines were seized by the county district attorney. John Cram, the Elvis fan, helped carry them out. "That's why this supper club doesn't have the [landscape] view of other supper clubs," Cram said. No panoramic windows for the Tee Pee—just a couple small windows with blinds that are easily closed. But Ed beat the rap and was elected mayor.

Ed was a fighter. In 1999 he jumped out of an airplane on a $10 bet. He broke his leg. Ed broke the other leg when he tumbled off his crutches. He liked to tell people he won the bet, but out-of-pocket medical expenses exceeded $15,000.

An amateur boxer who fought in the Golden Gloves, Ed learned boxing as an eighteen-year-old from former 156-pound NCAA champion Jerry Turner at the University of Wisconsin. Ed fought in Rockford, Illinois, and boxed in the navy. He started at middleweight and ended at heavyweight (over 175 pounds).

"I had my last fight when I was forty years old," he said. "I was in a Toughman fight in Superior, Wisconsin."

In a Toughman tournament about thirty-two fighters box over a two-night period resulting in one winner. Boxers from La Crosse, Madison, and other corners of the dairy state sign up to fight for a cash prize. "I promoted one at my old bar," he said. "My brother Tommy was the announcer."

Tommy laughed and recalled, "I was not an impartial announcer because I was saying, 'Hit 'em, Eddie! Hit 'em, Eddie!' which the opponent doesn't want to hear."

Ed said, "Around '81 or '82 I brought a kid named Robert Garro in who had won the Toughman tournament a year earlier in Milwaukee. Young black guy who was really a good fighter. Well, I don't know how good a fighter he was. He robbed a bank the next day and went to prison. Anyway, it was a good fight."

Ed liked telling these stories. They were part of the Tee Pee motif.

"My coach Jim Meckstroth and I drove up to a Toughman fight," Ed continued. "He was always in my corner. I fought this Adonis. He wasn't the greatest fighter, but he caught me a couple of good ones. I won the fight, but after the fight Jim said,

'How are you doing?' I said I was OK. He held up a hand and asked how many fingers he had. I couldn't see his hand. He said, 'That was your last fight.'"

Of course Ed learned life lessons in sports. "You never quit," he said. "No matter how tough it gets, you never quit. Because anybody can quit. Our whole family is that way. With Tommy, it may be, 'It don't look good, don't run for this,' but you just don't believe it. You know your own capabilities and don't quit."

Ed was applying those life lessons as he fought cancer. "What are you going to do?" he asked. "You don't quit. Sometimes you get down. What am I going to do? Sit around and feel sorry for myself?"

On May 21, 2011, Senator Herb Kohl asked Ed to speak at the annual convention of the Coalition of Wisconsin Aging Groups conference at the Sheraton Hotel in Madison. It was sort of a farewell speech, after which Ed was surprised to receive their Humanitarian of the Year award.

"I told them that most of all we have to learn to think together," he said. "Not as Republicans, not as Democrats, not as Catholics or Protestants, but as human beings. We all have the same liver, the same hearts, the same eyes. Rich or poor, we all know sorrow. Why can't we work together? We've been killing each other in wars for ten thousand years and what good has it done? The money we have spent on war we could have eliminated all these diseases.

"I asked, 'How can we continue to be so self-orientated and go down this trail until you face your own demise?' I know that in a short time I won't be here. And when I meet that god that lives in all of us, is he going to ask if you are a Catholic, or a Hindu, or a Muslim? Or is he going to ask, 'What have you done for your fellow man?'

"What really have you done?"

Ed looked ahead with the pride of a boxer and the sizzle of a prison cook.

I saw the answer in his eyes that never strayed far from Tomah, but touched thousands of lives.

10

House of Embers

935 Wisconsin Dells Parkway (Highway 12), Wisconsin Dells, Wisconsin
(608) 253-6411 • www.houseofembers.com

The warmth of an old supper club can suggest the wonderment of a new experience. Implied promise is found in romantic lighting, linen napkins, and gentle demeanor. The House of Embers is one of those places.

I'm sitting in the fifty-some-year-old Wisconsin Dells supper club in search of a good martini. I am surrounded by classic Wisconsin sandstone, the late 1950s building material that mimicked the rectangular geometry of modern art. The stone is native to the Dells. I love the fuzzy feeling it creates.

I see colorful touches that adorn the seven-thousand-square-foot supper club like flowers on a dress. Originally a broom closet, the Omar Sharif Room—a romantic love shack—seats two. The room has mauve-colored walls and is adorned with sweeping leopard-print curtains. Photos of Sharif from his best movie roles hang throughout the space. The concept comes from Sharif's appearance in *Funny Girl*, when he takes Barbra Streisand to dinner in a private room. Nearly four hundred marriage proposals have been made in the Sharif Room since it opened in 1976.

I call an ex-girlfriend in Los Angeles who is dating Sharif. She says he is in Madrid for the holidays and is unable to comment on his room. Despite their thirty-one-year age difference, she says Sharif kisses like he's in the movies: he holds you close, but leans back from the head only. Then, he holds your face from

Christmas trees and martinis at Wally's House of Embers.

The perfect Wisconsin supper club setting, accented by a two-way limestone fireplace.

underneath. She claims Sharif would never put his hand on the side of a woman's face because it would block the camera view. That's supper club style.

The supper club's cocktail lounge is a mishmash of decorating ideas—Martha Stewart meets Emeril Lagasse. A ceiling lamp has a pineapple motif. Framed black-and-white photographs of Clark Gable and Elizabeth Taylor hang behind the bar as if the House of Embers were Musso and Frank in Hollywood.

The back bar and ceiling are illuminated by leaded stained-glass windows salvaged from a Wisconsin church, while a disco ball hangs near singer Billy Anderson, who plays a Hammond B-3 organ. A fan of B-3 greats like Jimmy Smith and Groove Holmes, Anderson has been playing the Dells since 1966. The remainder of the lounge's ceiling is covered in leopard-print swagged fabric. The bar serves twenty-one martinis, including the Margatini—rocker Sammy Hagar's Cabo Wabo tequila mixed with triple sec and lemon and lime juice, served with a salted rim. Old-fashioneds are also very popular at Wally's.

Nearly four hundred marriage proposals have been made in the Omar Sharif Room since it opened in 1976. Wally's wife, Barbara Obois, and her mother decorated the room.

Wally's back bar with stars.

The supper club also has a Humphrey Bogart Room (for two to four people) and a Rudolph Valentino Room (for four to eight people).

And it also has Wally. Wally and Barbara Obois opened the House of Embers in 1959, back when Highway 12 was a two-laner. The supper club's history begins in the 1940s when it was a roadside beer joint named Hilldot's.

The place was owned by Hilda and Dot Zorky, who liked to tip a few, according to locals. Hilldot's was popular with workers at the Badger Army Ammunition Plant in nearby Baraboo. Built in 1942 and closed in 1997, the plant made propellants used in World War II, the Korean War, and Vietnam.

Hilda and Dot sold out to Jake Baton and Joe Jensen, who renamed the joint B & J's. As 1950s suburbia developed across the Midwest, the neighborhood became known as Dells Manor. And Dells Manor became the next name of the emerging supper club. Ray's BBQ was open for a brief time in the same spot in 1958 before Wally and Barbara took over and created the House of Embers.

Girls' night out with legendary Wisconsin supper club entertainer Billy Anderson at Wally's. Ringleader Ellen Weiss of Baraboo gives Billy a peck on the cheek.

The house of blue lights at Wally's House of Embers.

Wally had moved to the Dells in 1954 from Queens to check out the Midwest's wide open spaces. Wally was born in 1927; he is retired and in failing health in the summer of 2012. Barbara died in November 2011.

Wally is humble about how the supper club got its wacky name. "Something burning with charcoal," he tells me during a 2003 stop at the club. "When we started, we cooked with live coal—burning embers." The supper club has used gas since the restaurant was rebuilt in 1976 behind the original Embers. Tables and chairs were carried by hand from the old supper club, now a parking lot, into the new supper club. Wally rebuilt the dining room with beams from a razed barn that were piled in a nearby field.

The House of Embers is known for its tender ribs, smoked over hot hickory logs (they don't use chips, which can create cold smoke). The supper club makes its own barbecue sauce, which is thin and vinegary. You can taste the flavor of the meat under the sauce.

Cinnamon rolls are served before dinner. Yikes! That concept works because the rolls are airy and not heavy. Barbara created the recipe for the cinnamon rolls, which have been featured in *Bon Appétit* magazine. She was always circumspect about revealing the recipe, outside of saying the secret is in how she mixes the dough.

Bartender/chef Mike Obois, son of founder Wally Obois.

The kitchen has a couple of three-ring notebooks filled with legacy recipes from Barbara. The recipes are still used today. Most of the recipes are typed out, double-spaced. "Us kids didn't type in those days," Mike says while looking at a classic cheddar dressing recipe page (tarragon, vinegar, garlic, horseradish, onions, cheddar cheese, cream cheese—*both* cheeses whipped creamy smooth first—sour cream, Wesson oil, and so on). The frail page is stained by grease and the passage of time. "We still make the dressings the same way," he says. "I've made this many times. I think of my mother when I look at this."

Chefs Mark and Mike Obois, along with their sister Debbie, purchased the restaurant from their parents in 1999. Mark and Mike are graduates of the Culinary Institute of America in Hyde Park, New York. Mark left in 2011 but Mike remains as a chef, host, and sometimes bartender. Debbie is bookkeeper and part-time hostess.

Don Koehler, "the World's Tallest Man," was a House of Embers guest.

Wally and Barbara Obois in the bar of the earlier version of the House of Embers, where there was also a Red Room and a Green Room. The menus have changed about every two years, and they figure the hot items on the '68 menu were the ribs and the T-bone steak.

Besides the ribs, the supper club is famous for steaks, Austrian veal (flambéed with brandy and finished with cream, brown sauce, and Swiss cheese), and the supper club staple of fish, in this case breaded haddock (with caper tartar sauce), served on the Friday night fish fry.

"Clientele is much smarter now," Mike says. "They want more flavors. Their budgets are tighter than they were years ago. They want more splash, but we still sell more ribs and steaks than anything. But 2011 was our best summer ever by far, despite the economy. After we did our outdoor addition, everybody wants to sit outside. Even though it's a supper club, outside means more casual. It brings more people in the door."

The House of Embers seats 180, with capacity bumping up to 250 in the summer when al fresco dining is offered adjacent to an outdoor bar. A majority of the good weather clientele comes from Chicago.

The supper club also caters to stars performing at the Crystal Grand Music Theatre, down the road at 430 Munroe Avenue. Crystal Grand guests Willie Nelson and Bill Cosby have feasted on House of Embers chicken and ribs. Late Wisconsin Dells entrepreneur Tommy Bartlett was a House of Embers regular.

Wally had friends from all walks of life. Don Koehler, "the World's Tallest Man," was a House of Embers visitor in the early 1960s. Koehler was eight feet, two inches tall. He did promotions for the now-defunct Big Joe's manufacturing plant in the Dells. A picture of Wally and Koehler greet customers in the front lobby of the supper club. Wally is five-foot-five.

Koehler died in 1981 in Chicago from heart failure, by which time he was estimated to be about seven-foot-ten. He was fifty-five years old. "Dad always says he had a big heart," Mike recalls. "Don had a specially fit car. In the summer he would drive real slow downtown and put his hand out the window to make it look like he was pushing the car. He had quite a few brothers and sisters. He has relatives from Racine who come in because we have the picture on the wall."

Wally's bartender Ian Biney in the spring of 2012.

Before water parks and high-tech pastimes, Doug Alii and his Tahitian Drum Dancers were one of the most popular mid-1960s acts at the Tommy Bartlett Show on Lake Delton in the Dells. The revue featured fire knives, hypnotic drumming, and women in Tahitian dress. The Samoan-born Alii was also a great golfer and the best limbo dancer in Wisconsin. "We'd do a luau at the end of every summer," Mike says. "They'd come in and dig the pit and show us how to smoke the pig. We'd supply the pig. Everyone had a party."

Mike was born in 1960. He looks around the dimly lit bar. The lounge and dining room are filled with antiques that Barbara collected. Mike says, "This is still kind

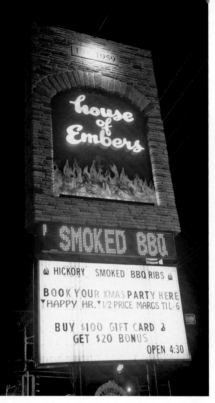

Wally's House of Embers has some of the best neon in the Wisconsin Dells.

of that old funky retro look. People go, 'Wow, this is what it was,'" and he looks at jet black dashes throughout the bar. "My dad's motto was 'Everything in black,'" he says with a smile. "You can tape it or paint it and no one can tell if it is falling apart. Even parts on the outside of the building. People are amazed we're still surviving.

"As a kid we used to walk across the street and swim in the pool at the Mayflower Motel. We didn't have to look both ways. I remember when they widened the highway to four lanes. A lot of the old hotels have changed, but what's changed tremendously is the water parks. That's been very helpful to us with people spending their money in the community."

Wally and Barbara had five children and all of them worked at the supper club at one time or another. One of Wally's favorite motivational tactics was to scatter small change across the restaurant floor to make sure Mike swept up the restaurant with care. Co-owner Debbie was born in 1957; Linda, born in 1955, is a hostess/ waitress; former co-owner Mark is involved with another area restaurant; and a third sister, Mary, works in marketing on the West Coast.

"To me, that's what a supper club is," Mike says. "It's a family. Their blood, sweat, and tears are behind it. You can see their effort. Not that big companies don't care, but this is our livelihood. Right here. If I don't make it here with my ideas, my work, and my staff . . . I've got family to support. People go into a supper club and they know you're going to see the owner, daughter, cousin, or all of them. It's a lot of fun. People say, 'You work all the time.' But you're goofing off, too."

The youngest generation gets the supper club concept in the Dells. Congenial bartender Ian Biney was born in 1987. His favorite Billy Anderson song is the popular calypso ballad "Yellow Bird," a rare call for a man this young. "My friends mostly understand all this," Ian says while mixing, yes, an old-fashioned. "I say I work at a supper club. They ask when we are open and I tell them just for dinner. They're surprised there's no lunch. It's dinnertime, but we still call it a supper club. 'Cause, well, dinner club doesn't sound right."

For most of their lives Wally, Barbara, and their family lived in a modest home behind the supper club. The Obois clan is as tightly knit as a Green Bay Packers ski cap. Up until 2003 Barbara's mother, Lou Stettin, played baby grand piano every Sunday night in the lounge. Her warm-up routine included one whiskey old-fashioned and a cup of soup. She retired at age ninety-five and died in June 2005 at the age of ninety-eight.

Lou and Barbara gave the Omar Sharif room its name in 1976. Mike smiles and says, "My mother, besides loving my dad, loved Omar Sharif. She and my grandma decorated the room together."

Lou Stettin was born on St. Patrick's Day in 1907, in Chicago. She first came to the Dells in 1917. The trip took nine days in a horse-drawn carriage. Her daughter, Barbara, grew up near 57th and Halsted. Lou's husband was a Teamster who ran a trucking company.

Mike and Mark polished their cooking skills under the watch of their grandmother Lou. She attended baking school in Chicago and presented her grandchildren with a birthday cake for each of their birthdays. As they became restaurateurs, Mike and Mark returned the favor and made the cake for her: white cake flour, two pounds of butter, twenty-two egg yolks, and buttercream icing. (Sift the flour three times.)

Now *that* says Wisconsin.

Barbara arrived in the Dells in 1958 and got a job at the legendary Del-Bar (named because it is the halfway point between the Dells and Baraboo, Wisconsin) supper club, across the street from the House of Embers.

Mike says, "We're competitors, but I do yoga twice a week with Jane, the Del-Bar owner. It's a good relationship. If we run out of something we call them; if they need a box of taters, they call us."

Midwest supper clubs look out for each other.

"Walter was a bartender there," Barbara told me in 2003. "That's how I met him. He was supposed to be hip. These girls used to come in with motorcycle clothes on and go, 'Is Walter around?' I thought, 'I better stay away from this guy.' Then he asked me if he could drive me home. He knew I didn't have a car. He had a long, pointy cream Cadillac. I figured he had money." Wally and Barbara got married six months after their first date. Within a year of their marriage Wally and a partner bought the Embers, a nondescript restaurant and bar on Highway 12. The partner dropped out within six months and Barbara stepped in.

They made the new house their home.

Wally was born in Austria, where he lived until 1936. His parents didn't have the money to bring him to America until he was ten. After that, he was reared by his uncle Tony Baldasti in Queens, New York. As a teenager, Wally worked as an apprentice electrician on the battleship *Missouri* in the Brooklyn navy yard.

Uncle Tony had his legs blown off below the knee on the Russian front during World War II. "His buddies were going to leave him," Mark says, sitting in the restaurant's enclosed veranda. "They thought he was going to die anyway. So he pulled out his Luger and said, 'You better take me, or I'm going to take you.' And he lived into his mid-eighties. Whenever his mom would go to Europe, she would take back six bottles of Slivovitz, Uncle Tony's homemade plum brandy, in her trench coat.

And when we'd go to New York, we'd bring some back. I have some here, if you'd like a sip."

We re-adjourn to the lounge. Billy Anderson is singing Louis Armstrong's "(What a) Wonderful World." Someone reaches across the bar for one of those 1960s cartoon cocktail napkins with the quote "Happiness is finding two olives in your martini when you're hungry" by Johnny Carson. A stranger suggests a toast, which is a good idea.

You are among new friends in a dark room that is illuminated by the spirit of tomorrow.

You are happy.

11

The Del-Bar

800 Wisconsin Dells Parkway, Lake Delton, Wisconsin
(608) 253-1861 • www.del-bar.com

One sure sign of a supper club is the linear Frank Lloyd Wright–inspired architecture that blends like butter into the Wisconsin timberland.

The Frank Lloyd Wright visitor center at the Taliesin Fellowship in Spring Green, Wisconsin, was the site of the Bridge Lunch café and gas station. The old Highway 23 bridge used to abut the restaurant. Wright liked the angle. He also liked the Bridge's homemade pie. Wright's son-in-law William Wesley Peters would eat three pieces of pie and four Cokes at one sitting, according to Indira Berndtson of the Frank Lloyd Wright Archives in Scottsdale, Arizona.

In 1947 a truck missed the highway curve, slammed into the Bridge Lunch, and cracked its foundation. Wright purchased the site and planned to build a new restaurant. He never completed the project, however, because he began work on the Guggenheim Museum and the Marin County Civic Center.

At the same time that Wright was pondering a rural supper club, James Dresser was studying organic architecture under Wright at the Taliesin Fellowship. After leaving Taliesin, Dresser designed the New York World's Fair pavilion, the Lake Geneva Public Library, and the original Tommy Bartlett's Robot World in the Wisconsin Dells, just an hour from Spring Green. Dresser also designed Field's at the Wilderness supper club and steak house.

Suggestive signage points a traveler straight into one of Wisconsin's most beautiful supper clubs.

The Del-Bar exterior, spring 2012.

Jeff and Jane Wimmer, owners of the Del-Bar.

But the Del-Bar—halfway between Lake Delton and Baraboo, thus the name—was his pride and joy.

Dresser started dining at the Del-Bar in 1953 with a couple of his buddies. The Del-Bar was owned by Jimmy Wimmer, a quarterback in 1930 at the University of Wisconsin in Madison.

"James Dresser said, 'Jimmy, I'm going to do a little something for you,'" recalls Jane Wimmer, who now operates the supper club with her husband, Jeff Wimmer. "And he worked on the Del-Bar until January 2011 when he died. He did every bit of work. Any addition or remodeling came from him. You could sit anywhere and feel you are in the heart of the building. It is ever present. You can see three or four dining rooms at one time."

Touches of Dresser and Wright are all over the three-hundred-seat supper club. The ceiling near the Terrace, a room that abuts Highway 12 (a continuation of Lake Shore Drive to Chicago) is six feet, seven inches high. Wright was only five-foot-eight. The architect liked to compress the space in his buildings so that when a person left, the space expanded and seemed much more elaborate—like the rolling Dells. The Terrace incorporates dark mahogany and rosewood, which absorb the Wisconsin surroundings.

The Patio is a narrow dining area with a fireplace flanked with flagstone. The Patio sits between the Terrace and the relaxed midcentury bar that seats about fifty people. Dresser's first add-on at the Del-Bar was the Patio, and he incorporated the small steps that were a Wright trademark. Form followed function.

Folks have gathered 'round the Del-Bar bar since a 1963 renovation.

"People would come in through the Patio, walk up steps to the host, and go to the bar and get hammered," Jim Junior recalled. "All the tables were at different levels. When they drank their six Manhattans they'd come back out here [the Patio] and fall up the steps or down the steps. My father called the builder back and said, 'Level it.' In those years people got hammered. It was so rural here in the Dells the cops would pick them up and drive them home."

You always have one foot outside at the Del-Bar. Soothing mahogany and oak is deployed in the interior of the supper club. Olive green carpeting throughout the

The geometric shapes at the Del-Bar were designed by James Dresser, who studied under Frank Lloyd Wright at the Taliesin Fellowship in Spring Green, Wisconsin.

The Del-Bar geometric detail is even found in its light fixtures.

supper club consists of endless patterns of what appear to be small cups and saucers.

But Dresser was not a Wright knockoff. He used the low ceilings, liberal use of wood, and flagstone walls only as a starting point. He wasn't afraid to take chances: he designed the igloo-like Tommy Bartlett Robot World complex, which is walking distance from the Del-Bar.

Not unlike the Bridge, the Del-Bar began in the late 1930s as a roadside log cabin (now the wine room) that opened on weekends during the summer. Business dried up during the beginning of World War II when Jimmy Wimmer stepped in. He grew up on a farm in a rural section of the Dells known as Badger Valley. Jimmy's wife, Alice, told him he didn't know anything about running a supper club. Jimmy then reminded Alice she had a domestic science degree (University of Wisconsin, 1929).

The Wimmers were friends with the key players who developed the Dells nightlife and supper club culture. They knew Archibald "Nig" Kinney, who founded the popular Dells bar Swig at Nig's. Jeff said, "Nig started this supper club with Durlan Meyers from Baraboo. Durlan was the one who put together the first three letters of the Dells and the first three letters of Baraboo—the Del-Bar. They wanted it to be a steak house but they couldn't get beef because it was being rationed during the war. So they sold it to my father in the early '40s. And they split. Nig started Have a Swig at Nig's and Durlan went to Baraboo and named a resort Deva-Bera—for Devil's Lake and Baraboo."

Jeff paused and restated the theme for empahsis: "Deva-Bera."

Barbara and Wally Obois from the nearby Wally's House of Embers met at the Del-Bar. Barbara, who died in 2011, was from 57th and Halsted on the South Side of Chicago. She came to the Dells in 1958 and got a job at the Del-Bar. "Walter was a bartender there," she told me in a 2003 interview at Wally's. "He was supposed to be hip." Walter and Barbara were married six months after their first Del-Bar date.

Jane recalls, "When the Green Room [now the Copper Room on the north end of the supper club] was built in 1963, people got in their Cadillacs, got dressed up, and came here. It was positively dining out and spending the night. It was 'the Place.' There were droves of people."

All of the rooms and additions were made by Dresser. His favorite place to sit was the Garden Room, overlooking a garden and pond with Highway 12 in the background.

The Del-Bar is a supper club that still believes in linen napkins.

Johnny Depp dined at the Del-Bar when he was filming *Public Enemies.* He was placed at the Garden Room's Table 10, the most requested table at the supper club. The table is near a fireplace where a floor-to-ceiling window overlooks the pond.

The relationship between Wright architecture and rural supper club cuisine is strong and true. Wright's love of the earth was a large component of his philosophy of organic architecture. The Del-Bar flagstone was sourced in 1952 from a defunct blacksmith shop in nearby Rock Springs.

Dresser's daughter Stephanie Scheer is an acclaimed graphic artist in the Dells area. Several years ago she made the celebration of wine signs that greet customers near the hostess stand. In classic Wright block lettering one sign reads: WINE IS BOTTLED POETRY—ROBERT LOUIS STEVENSON.

John Rattenbury is one of the last direct links to Wright. He arrived at Taliesin West in Scottsdale, Arizona, in 1950. He still lives on the property, where he is a principal architect. Along with his late wife, Kay, he also worked on *At the Table with Frank Lloyd Wright: The Taliesin Cookbook.*

"We teach young people to cook for a couple of reasons," Rattenbury told me in a 2003 interview at Taliesin West. "One, we don't know how they can be allowed to design a house with a kitchen if they don't know how to cook, and also because

Barbara Fritz Dresser, longtime wife of Del-Bar architect James Dresser. He called her "Love Bug." James died in 2011 after sixty-four years of marriage.

cooking itself is multitasking. You have to do a whole bunch of different things at the same time. You have to be connected to the aesthetics of it and the taste of it. Everything has to be timed together, especially when you're doing this for a group of fifty, sixty people."

Emerging at the zenith of Wright's work, the Del-Bar arrived right on time.

James Dresser met his future wife, Barbara Fritz, at her twentieth birthday party near Spring Green. "James had come up from [Taliesin West] in Arizona," she said during a conversation in her Dells home and studio, which her husband designed. "He had stayed there longer to practice the violin. He and another young apprentice from Ireland rode to the party [from Taliesin] on horseback."

They became engaged after three weeks. And they got married three months after that.

"Mr. Wright walked me down the theater at Spring Green," she said with a soft smile.

The Dressers were married for sixty-four years. James always liked to call Barbara "Love Bug."

Barbara was born in 1927 in Oak Park, Illinois. Her father, Herbert Fritz, was one of Wright's first draftsmen. Her grandfather Ernest Fritz on her mother's side was one of Wright's first masons.

"My mother [Mary] was a farm girl who lived about ten miles from Taliesin," she said. "She would take my grandfather on her horse and wagon to Taliesin and he would spend the week there as a mason. Then she'd go pick him up and bring him back to the farm. My father was one of two who escaped in the fire. He broke his arm but he was quite an athlete and they think that's what saved him."

Taliesin burned down in an August 1914 arson fire incident in which Wright's mistress Martha Borthwick Cheney and several others were murdered. The living quarters of Taliesin II caught fire in 1925 due to electrical problems or lightning.

Wright deployed the same eye for detail into dining as he did into his architecture. He was so supper clubby he even *wore*

James Dresser's studio remains untouched in the Dresser home, outside of the Wisconsin Dells.

linen. Here's Wright talking about his breakfast attire in *Frank Lloyd Wright: An Autobiography*: "Me? I have on raw linen. Loose-sleeved jacket buttoned at the wrist, wide baggy trousers tied close around the ankles." Wright reflected how Taliesin's eggs were still warm, fresh from the Wisconsin farm, and the Guernsey milk came from the herd in a nearby green meadow.

"James also loved to cook," Dresser said. "And he was very good. He would slice a cucumber absolutely straight. Portions were exactly the same. He would arrange things on the plate so it was an artful presentation. Not for company, just for family. He cooked everything and he was always experimenting."

Dresser designed the circular house with a concrete dome where the couple lived in the mid-1950s on the west side of Madison, Wisconsin. The Round House was featured in a three-page spread in the March 10, 1953, issue of *Look* magazine. Bar-

The Wisconsin Dells—a sense of place.

bara is pictured in the center of a circular kitchen, which was the centrifugal force of the house. Plants were grown year-round in huge copper cones that hung from the ceiling above the kitchen's redwood cabinets.

"The Del-Bar was our favorite place," Barbara said in her current organically designed kitchen, lined with cherry wood. "For many many years. He was always thinking ahead, scrawling ideas down on napkins."

The oral histories of Dresser fill the Del-Bar, but there is also a "Dresser table" down the road at the latter-day Field's at the Wilderness supper club and steak house. He designed Field's in the late 1990s. "He started from scratch there," Barbara said. "The Del-Bar, he was remodeling a log cabin. He took a lot from Mr. Wright. Every morning without fail he would read for at least an hour on architecture or the environment."

Barbara stopped and added, "This place is so empty without him." A tear welled up in her eye.

Her Sheltie, named Ditto, sat by the kitchen table. The dog was named Ditto because it was the second Sheltie in a row for the Dressers.

Allan Brennan is the senior waiter at the Del-Bar. He started working at the Del-Bar in 1973. "Lots of people ask about Frank Lloyd Wright," he says while eating a salad before a weekday shift. "They come through here and it immediately gets their Wright senses going."

Brennan was born in 1955 on a dairy farm in Baraboo. "The first time I came here I was a junior in high school," he says. "I applied for a job. I was hired that summer as a busser. It was a summer destination when I started. Now it is year-round. When the Ho-Chunk [casino] came in it changed everything. The landscape? There's a lot more traffic and a lot more restaurants.

"The Del-Bar has evolved. In a lot of ways it has become a nicer restaurant. The menu has been built up and there's a lot of details in the ambiance. The lighting in this restaurant is beautiful. It's just a very easy place to come, even though it gets busy in here at times. It is a big restaurant. But it seems it has kept its identity how it started out."

A rave July 29, 1953, review from the *Chicago Sun-Times* is blown up and framed by the Del-Bar's main entrance. Correspondent Wade Franklin wrote that the Del-Bar was "unsurpassed in the country," and the soup is "tasty—and hot!" Franklin concluded, "Food can only be so good, no matter what you pay for it, but the Del-Bar's prices are moderate. That makes it unbeatable."

This biting commentary was long before the Food Network.

The Del-Bar menu has changed with the times. Seared sea scallops with wild mushrooms and vermouth are popular, but longtime regulars still know to ask for the dry-aged Angus steaks. "We serve a lot more fish nowadays," Brennan says. "We have a better variety of fresh fish. People definitely eat more vegetables and salads. The fish fry is still big on Friday night and we have prime rib on Saturdays. To me the steaks and the fish fry are the tops at the Del-Bar."

Along with the architecture, of course. One of Wright's organic commandments was that love is the virtue of the heart. And the heart still beats strong at the Del-Bar supper club.

The jumbo shrimp is a big deal at the Del-Bar.

12

Ding-A-Ling Supper Club

8215 West Race Street, Hanover, Wisconsin
(608) 879-9209 • www.ding-a-lingsupperclub.com

The name certainly rings a bell.

The Ding-A-Ling Supper Club has been in unincorporated Hanover since the 1940s. Hanover has a population of only 250 people. There is a church, a stop sign, and the supper club, which sits quietly along the abandoned Milwaukee Road railroad tracks about fifteen miles southwest of Janesville.

The Ding-A-Ling is owned by Jerrad and Kyla Wilke. They are a young cattle and crop farm family from tiny Orfordville, five miles down the road from Hanover. Jerrad and Kyla were born in 1980. Kyla grew up on a goat farm but wanted to try her hand at running a supper club. Jerrad wanted to stay on his 850-acre family farm.

Things were working out well during a Thursday night stop at the Ding-A-Ling in the spring of 2012. The supper club seats about 130 including the bar, and the place was half-full with locals in a kaleidoscope of loud red Wisconsin Badgers and forest green Green Bay Packers gear. The Ding-A-Ling is a casual supper club. T-shirts, neckties, and shorts are all welcome. Everything fits.

Kyla was dividing her time between hostessing, bartending, and answering the phone, "Ding-A-Ling . . ." all during a busy supper. It was funny to hear her

For generations a warm light has shined over the Ding-A-Ling
Supper Club in rural Hanover, Wisconsin.

Reservations not always necessary at the Ding-A-Ling.

A family-run supper club (clockwise): Jagger, Kyla, Jerrad, and Jemima Wilke.

answer the phone that way. "A lot of people think it's a strip club," she says.

Jerrad arrived around seven PM straight from the farm with their son, Jagger, and daughter, Jemma. Kyla was pregnant with their third child, due in the summer of 2012. Alan Jackson's "Don't Rock the Jukebox" played over a radio behind the bar.

There is no Hanover library to conduct research on all things Ding-A-Ling. Hanover was even overlooked in the WPA (Works Progress Administration) book from 1941, *Wisconsin: A Guide to the Badger State*, part of the American Guide Series.

"This is all from what I know," Kyla says. "It could be completely wrong. Originally this was called the Hanover Inn. The original owners lived in the back room but through time many additions were put on. There used to be a hotel near the railroad tracks. Hanover was very popular. There was a cheese-making plant near the supper club and I looked that up through the [Footville] historical society about a week ago. There was a big train station in Hanover." Then a tornado rolled through Hanover in 1911. "That tornado wiped out the whole town," she says.

Kyla is pretty certain of one thing. The Ding-A-Ling gets its name from a copper bell that has hung at the front door for as long as anyone can remember. When customers enter the supper club, a loud "ding-a-ling" announces their arrival. "That is the number one question people ask when they come here," Kyla says. "I remember that bell being there when I was a kid. And it's always been crooked."

Kyla's mom, Kristie Dooley, worked in the Saks Fifth Avenue distribution center, forty-five miles away in Rockford, Illinois. Her father, Mike, works at a manufacturing center in Beloit, Wisconsin. "I wasn't going to have anything to do with the goat farm," Kyla says. "Too hard. It wasn't fun."

For whom the bell tolls: Doug McLay, Ding-A-Ling customer since 1958.

Customers make artifacts to donate to the Ding-A-Ling Supper Club.

She graduated with a degree in social work from the University of Wisconsin (La Crosse). "I moved back home because I couldn't find a job," Kyla says. "I ended up getting back together with the same farmer I dated all through high school when [said] I never would have anything to do with farming again." She smiles. "We got married."

The couple was married in 2000 and Kyla started waitressing, bartending, and hostessing at the Ding-A-Ling in 2002. Kyla and Jerrad wound up buying the supper club in 2006 from previous owners Merrill and Marianne Perius and Julie and Ode Flister. "At the time I had a social work job in Beloit and was getting bored," she says. "I was going to go back to school to get my master's degree. But this place had been for sale forever. I threw it out to my husband and he said, 'Absolutely not.' I tried to convince him and he was not about it at all. Of course we were first married, we didn't have kids, and [the question] was, 'Do we want to put everything we own into buying a supper club?'"

She finally convinced him.

Kyla worked hand in hand with the previous owners to buy the Ding-A-Ling. "They were in their seventies and were getting tired of it," Kyla says. "They had it for twenty-seven years."

Of course, when you buy a supper club you buy the customers. Doug McLay has been coming to the Ding-A-Ling since 1958 when his father introduced him to the roadside establishment. He is a regular for the Tuesday night chicken and dumplings. "My dad was a refrigeration repairman," McLay says, with a nod to the past. "There was an ice cube maker right over there. He brought me in here and I sat down at the bar and watched him repair that ice cube maker." McLay was sixteen at the time.

"The building dimension has not changed since then," says McLay, who owns rental properties in the Janesville area. "The bar is the same. It's a total throwback and that's the uniqueness of the place. You don't find these in the southern part of the state. Up north you will find more supper clubs. I love these places. Guys will come in here and hash their stories about the farming day. These are people who truly care and they give 110 percent for their survival. And the people that own this place have done a wonderful job."

The Wilkes installed a new roof and new olive green vinyl siding. They reinsulated the warm supper club and installed new windows. They redid the bathrooms, and neighbors handcrafted new dining room tables. Other regulars donated handcrafted items like a Ding-A-Ling saw blade and a Ding-A-Ling wall clock.

The Ding-A-Ling does not have a jukebox. Before ordering fajitas, McLay says, "There used to be an old forty-five jukebox and one of the songs on there was [Chuck Berry's 1972 hit] 'My Ding-a-Ling.' Everyone always played it."

Kyla says, "I'm still learning what a supper club is. We didn't go to any supper clubs in Beloit or Madison. Most supper clubs have been in the family forty, fifty years. They've owned their supper clubs longer than we've been alive. We were twenty-six years old when we bought this place.

"People my age don't even think of a supper club. I grew up across the street so my parents brought my brother and me in here when we were kids. There was a bar. There would be a two-hour wait. It would be casual. People would sit at the bar and have a couple drinks, then eat. Typical Friday night fish fry [beer-battered cod]. Saturday night all-you-can-eat prime rib. Brandy old-fashioneds. After dinner ice

Jimmy Buffett never sang about a strawberry margarita at the Ding-A-Ling.

cream drinks. It was a very small-town setting. Everybody knows everybody. It was very comfortable."

The Wilkes only tweaked the menu. They learned their customers lean on supper club standards. Unique appetizers include the Hanover Haystack, a big mound of shredded onion rings. The Ding-A-Ling steak and lobster special is popular on Sunday and Wednesday nights. Chicken and dumplings are another staple.

New menus, old tradition.

Kyla also cooks, and she makes pretty stiff drinks. She says, "Game on!" to stop a conversation to make a strawberry margarita. She does inventory and ordering.

Jerrad has a minimal role at the Ding-A-Ling. "He doesn't expect me out to milk cows," Kyla says. "So I don't expect him here."

With his children at his side, Jerrad says, "We used to milk cows but about a year ago we sold them and mainly focus on grains, corns, beans, cash cropping. We do have some beef cows. It's me and my dad [James]. I'll be the third generation.

"I come down here [to the supper club] every day. . . . I wasn't keen on the supper club. I've been coming here since I was five years old, when they had carpet on the walls in the back. But she kept bugging me about it. Finally I said, 'Whatever, but don't expect me to be down here every day helping you.' Me and my buddies sided it, roofed it. We mainly fix everything."

Jerrad leans over to help Jagger, four, with his chicken wings and fries. "He wanted to try them because he saw other people eating them." Jagger screeches at his father, "Dad, you didn't even cut them!" Jerrad gently tells his son to just pick up the wings and eat them. He then adds, "At night, I'm in charge of the kids."

The Ding-A-Ling draws people from Janesville, Beloit, and Rockford. On a Saturday night with good weather, waits can go as long as three and a half hours. "And people wait," Kyla says. "They camp at the bar before they sit down for supper. It

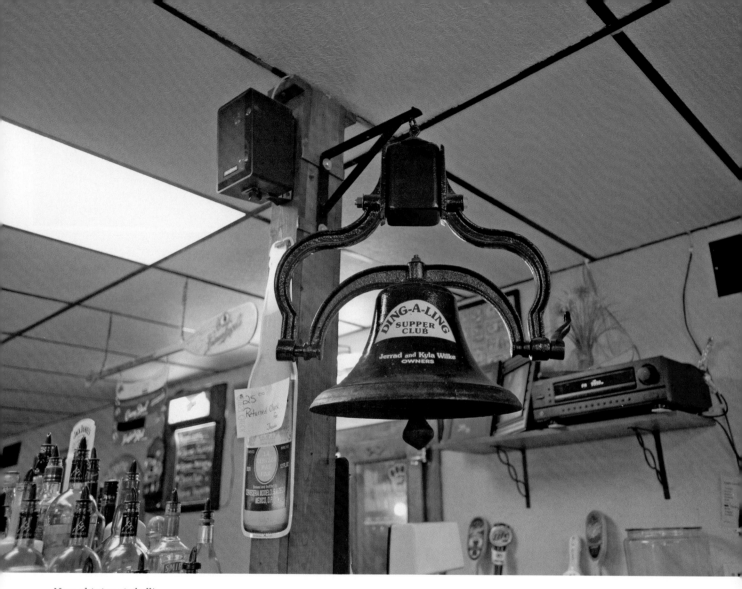

Now, this is a tip bell!

amazes me. But then there's nothing else in Hanover. I'd say the population is 250 on the high end. This is all there is in Hanover. There's not even a gas station. We do have a post office."

And everyone chimes in for a genuinely good time.

13

Moracco

1413 Rockdale Road, Dubuque, Iowa
(563) 582-2947 • www.moraccodbq.com

Jeanne Heiar is never far from her mother.

Her folks, Bert and Hazel Hillary, bought the Moracco Supper Club in 1966. This Moracco in south Dubuque is not spelled the same as the exotic Morocco in North Africa. And its vibe is all Midwest.

Jeanne was eleven years old when she learned to cook alongside her mother in the kitchen of the Moracco—which Jeanne now owns with her husband, Garry. The Moracco is in the hideaway Grandview Heights neighborhood, a mile south of the Mississippi River and downtown Dubuque.

"My mother worked the middle and did the grill side," Jeanne says during a Saturday afternoon conversation at the Moracco. "The tartar and lemon was on one side. The fryer cook was on the other side. You learned to work together because when she had her steaks done my sisters and I were ready to go at the same time."

The Moracco has a legacy menu with some parts from Hazel Hillary's recipe books.

"She died in 1985," Jeanne says. "But there's her handwriting in the book. Mom would never give out recipes, but now I feel we should give them out. You don't want them to get lost."

One of the most popular requests at the Moracco is the cheese spread, made from Hazel's recipe of sour cream and cheddar cheese mixed with a dash of cream cheese and whipped with a huge mixer. For forty-five minutes.

Some supper clubs have older customers.

No one knows why the Moracco Supper Club is not spelled the same as the Morocco in North Africa.

Moracco owners Jeanne and Garry Heiar with Jeanne's parents in the background.

Bert Hillary still finds time to find his way to the Moracco. He was sitting at the bar with his wife, Betty, during an Indian summer afternoon at the Moracco. In 1985 their spouses died six months apart. Bert and Betty were married in 1987.

"We will be married twenty-five years come February 21 [2012]," Betty says with a smile. "If we make it." Bert goes for younger women: he is ninety-five years old. He's drinking a Manhattan. She is eighty-seven. She's drinking a martini with an olive garnish.

"I was farming, and the owner here [Armin "Butch" Herbst, who had the supper club from 1958 to 1966] died," Bert recalls. "His wife [Genevive "Whitey" Herbst] was planning on selling it. I came here on my tractor and bid half of what they were asking for the damn thing. And I got it. Luckily I had five daughters. They took care of the kitchen."

Bert doesn't even know why the supper club was called the Moracco.

"We were going to change it to Hillary's Supper Club, but everyone knew it as the Moracco even then," he says. "I went into town to the bank and said, 'I'm going to buy Moracco, I should be able to get all the money I want."

Bert is a five-star wisecracker. A visitor tells Bert that he is from Chicago. Bert smiles and replies, "That's good country. I got in there once and couldn't find my way out."

Bert and Hazel grew up in nearby worldly named Cuba City before getting married and moving to the Dubuque area. He found his way out of Cuba City. Bert's farm was five miles south of Dubuque along Highway 52. Hazel was a waitress at the now-closed Leiser's Supper Club north of Dubuque.

Bert remembered an organ player who performed near the Moracco supper club bar during the early days of their ownership. Betty says, "He always played 'Somewhere My Love (Lara's Theme)' from *Dr. Zhivago*."

Betty was wearing a sweater freckled with small cats. She says, "We used to come here four or five nights a week. But now we're living in an assisted village so we get our meals in. We still come here once a week." She was ordering a seafood platter. Bert liked the cod.

Betty drives her husband to the Moracco in a 2008 white Cadillac. He says, "My driver's license has expired. With my age, they're going to check me pretty good."

A toast with previous Moracco owner Bert Hillary and his wife, Betty.

The supper club seats about two hundred in three distinct rooms including a large banquet/dining area. The main dining room still uses an illuminated 1960s number system where each member of the waitstaff has an assigned number. When the light turns on from the kitchen, the waitstaff knows the food is ready. You won't see this at Grant Achatz's Alinea on the north side of Chicago. The dimly lit bar area is framed by wood paneling painted in Moroccan colors.

The establishment opened in 1945 as the Moracco Truck Stop along old Route 151. The twenty-four-hour truckers' home served breakfast, lunch, and dinner until the early 1960s, according to Garry Heiar.

"Everyone wants to know about the name," Jeanne says. "The only thing we found in one of the books given to us by the previous owner was that one of the first owners served the army in Morocco."

Garry adds, "During Prohibition he had a Moraccan Room in the basement. When they got a call about the authorities, they would move all the booze to that room."

The original version of the Moracco burned down in the 1950s. The current one was rebuilt with native tan stone and scenic windows fronting the two-lane highway.

In a tradition that dates back to truckers on the highway, the Moracco makes ham salad on-site and a fine braunschweiger spread with crackers. "We eliminated relish trays about twenty years ago," Jeanne says. "With health inspectors everything has to be thrown out. It got to be such a hassle."

A stage awaits its actors.

Jeanne shifts in her chair and a look of pride comes across her face. "But we still have linen napkins," she declares. "It is expensive, but I'm a freak on paper napkins. I hate them. My son would like to eliminate the linen napkins right now because they're so expensive. But it adds an extra touch. It's more than a fast-food restaurant."

The Moracco goes through one thousand linen napkins a week. "We get them in every Tuesday. We fold them and have them ready to go," Jeanne says. "We try to get them all done by Tuesday night."

Such attention to detail earned the Heiars a "Restaurateurs of the Year" award in 2006 from the Iowa Restaurant Association. The award is given yearly to a business owner who exhibits originality, quality, and service to customers.

Garry grew up on a farm just south of Dubuque. The Moracco adds a family-farm spin to the supper club experience. Jeanne's brother Danny Hillary is still a family farmer south of Dubuque. Garry's brother Larry is a dairy, hog, and beef farmer in Lemont, Iowa, about twenty miles south of Dubuque.

"Our farm background is here in how you cut your steak, where the meat is coming from, the chicken, the eggs, the fresh garden products," Jeanne says. Garry adds, "Work ethic is a major part of that connection. Farmers work long hours. This can be long hours." Jeanne says, "You have to be there a certain time to milk the cows. You have to be here a certain time to open. People like to see you here, see you working in the business. When my parents started, Mom cooked. Dad bartended. He didn't know how to bartend and learned how. They weren't open during the day then. Where we were brought up dinner was called supper. Our kids say, 'Dinner is not at noon, Mom. Dinner is at night.' It should be called a dinner club, but we were raised with supper clubs. They weren't open all day."

The Moracco opens at 4:00 PM and service starts at 4:30. Like clockwork, the regulars walk in between 4:30 and 6:00. The Moracco can stay open until 2:00 AM.

Regulars include Jeffrey and Kay Slade of Dubuque, who have been holding court at the Moracco pretty much all their lives. "This really hasn't changed," Kay says at the bar while waiting for a table. She is an area accountant who was born in 1956. She did accounting at the legendary Dubuque Packing Company before it went belly up.

Kay's grandparents were regulars at the Moracco.

"Sure, there's been color changes and they redid some of the bar," she says. "You see younger kids come in and they're becoming professionals. We keep saying we've put two of their kids through college working the bar." Garry and Jeanne Heiar had four kids between the ages of twenty-one and thirty-six at that time. Hillary, twenty-two, is a waitress and hostess who began working in the kitchen at age thirteen. Nick, twenty-five, is a bartender who began as a busser at age sixteen. Greg, thirty-six, was a bartender and host starting at age sixteen. Today he is assistant basketball coach at Wichita State University. Tim Heiar, thirty-five, was working the bar flanked by a pair of televisions. Tim is now a business partner and general manager of the supper club.

Kay's husband, Jeffrey, is a third-generation optician from Dubuque. "I come here primarily for the prime rib," he says. "In fact I make sure they save me a piece of prime rib. Always." The Moracco prime rib is seasoned for two days before it hits the oven, where it is slow-roasted for hours. Prime rib is only served on Saturday nights. Always and forever.

"The beauty of a place like this is that it is consistent," Jeffrey says. "No matter what you order, time after time it will be the same. Because people put their heart and soul into it. It is their name and reputation. It's not like an Applebee's or whatever."

Born in 1957, Jeffrey came of age at the tail end of the old-fashioned explosion in supper clubs. "It's interesting because Dubuque is on the border [of Iowa and Wisconsin]," he says. "In Wisconsin, old-fashioned drinks are done with brandy. Here, it's bourbon. You can tell who is from Wisconsin and who is from Iowa based on them ordering a mixed drink." His wife adds, "An old-fashioned is like candy. I had to stop drinking them because I was gaining too much weight. Lots of sugar, but they're so good."

Garry says, "The old-fashioned is our most popular drink. It must naturally go with dinner." Jeanne adds, "I don't think a lot of people make them at home. They

Ed and Jeanne Carr in the foreground; Ed is a dead ringer for Johnny Carson.

don't have the syrup and everybody has their own technique. At home you will either have a beer or a highball. Something easy."

Highball. Now that's supper club talk.

Jeanne Carr, a retired Nordstrom's clerk from Dubuque, also comes for the prime rib and fish. She and her husband, Ed, have been coming to the Moracco for more than twenty years. Between sips of an amaretto stone sour she adds, "I'll tell ya, you eat a lot better here than some different parts of the world. We went traveling last year and we decided the best meat is right from here."

Garry had a handle on the Moracco's travelin' roots as a truck stop. He says, "All of these places are near where the old highways were. It's almost like a roadhouse situation. Lots of these supper clubs have great views."

Dubuque isn't Morocco, but then Morocco doesn't have anything quite as quaint as the Moracco Supper Club. Got it?

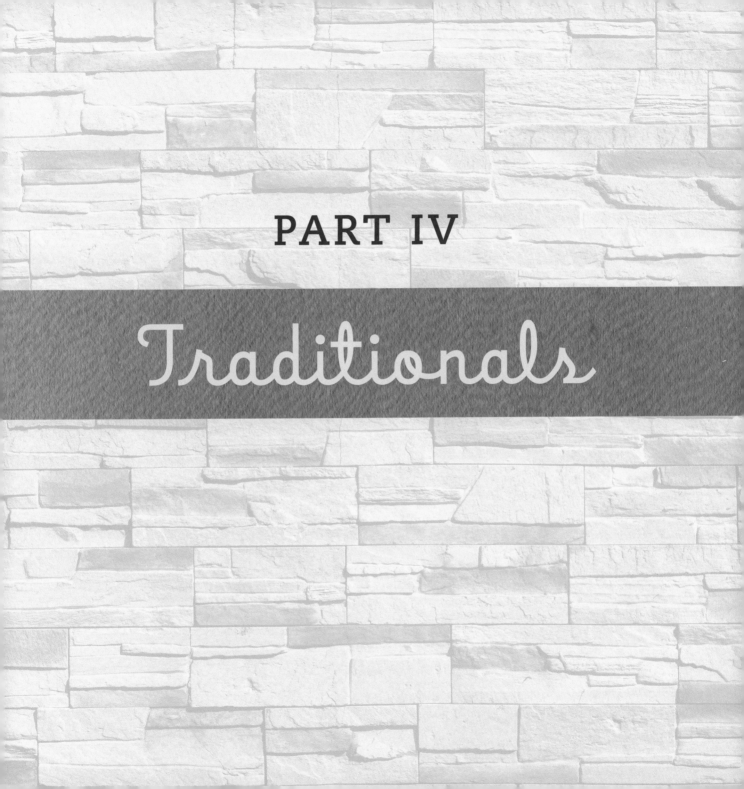

PART IV

Traditionals

14

Smoky's Club

3005 University Avenue, Madison, Wisconsin
(608) 233-2120 • www.smokysclub.com

Everything has its place. Oscar "Ozzie" Huber knows this. He has been a dishwasher at Smoky's Club in Madison, Wisconsin, since 1964. Oscar figures he has washed "a couple million" dishes in his lifetime. Dinner platters. Soup bowls. Wine glasses. Beer steins. Over and over and over again.

On a busy autumn Friday night Oscar reaches for a white dinner plate from a packed rack of stained dishware. He confidently picks up the plate with his left hand and brings it to a sink. He grabs a silver sprayer with his right hand and blasts the plate. He smiles from under the brim of a dirty white baseball cap. He is satisfied.

Oscar is blind.

Supper clubs are about a climate of vivid belonging. Oscar belongs here. "I'm the oldest thing in this kitchen," he says. "This is my second home."

Smoky's is a classic Wisconsin supper club by way of its hearty steak-inspired menu, family warmth, neon sign, and linear architecture accented by beige Lannon stone that was quarried just a couple blocks away. The torch classic "Smoke Gets in Your Eyes" often can be heard in the parking lot.

Oscar was born with glaucoma on August 6, 1946. He has endured twenty-seven eye operations. Over time the retinas blew out in each of his eyes; Oscar went completely blind in 1991. "All I see is light," he says. "No shadows. I don't

Smoky's Club. Classic neon is a sign of a good supper club. The Lannon stone was sourced just a couple blocks away from Smoky's.

Beloved dishwasher Oscar "Ozzie" Huber in the fall of 2011.

see pretty blonds. I used to see a lot of pretty blonds."

In the 1990s Oscar began working with a brown and gray guide dog named Fitch. Oscar brought Fitch to work, where the Smoky's staff installed a small bed for the golden lab. The bed was installed under the dish line where the dirty dishes were unloaded and stacked on trays. Fitch was well trained and never complained about the noise and excitement of a busy kitchen. When Oscar was off duty, he would remove Fitch from his harness and the dog would beg for carrots. Fitch loved carrots. Otherwise Fitch would loyally wait for Oscar to finish work.

Oscar is on disability and works two nights a week at Smoky's. He no longer has a guide dog, but a cane helps him negotiate his path. He does a 5:00 to 8:30 PM shift on the kitchen sprayer. Smoky's co-owner Tom Schmock will gently take Oscar by an elbow and lead the Midwest's best dishwasher to the kitchen.

"It's different now," Oscar says. "Two partners help me. They bring the dishes to me, I rack 'em, push them through, and spray them off. Another guy takes the clean ones. I'm at the sprayer. I don't carry no dishes. But I know the dishes." He stops and twirls around to the sink. "This is a hash brown dish. These are monkey dishes for tomato juice. [A monkey dish is a universal restaurant term for a small liner-type dish that also can serve side condiments such as salad dressings.] This is a bar glass. I feel them."

Oscar began his career in the original Smoky's, a two-story house with a horseshoe bar a block from the current location, on what was then the outskirts of town. Owner Leonard "Smoky" Schmock and his wife, Janet, lived upstairs with their children, Tom, Larry, and Barb. Frank Lloyd Wright visited this version of Smoky's, arriving with his dog through the rear entrance. He ate early because he was traveling to his home in Spring Green, Wisconsin.

Smoky's at 2925 University Avenue in 1963—down the road from the present location.

Madison, Wisconsin, began expanding in 1970 and construction tore up University Avenue in front of the present-day Smoky's. The tricked-out Shorewood House apartment building is in the background. That was built in 1966.

University Avenue expansion took out the first Smoky's, and in 1969 the supper club moved into what had been Justo's Club, owned by Jennie Bramhall, the wife of former Chicago Bear Art Bramhall. After retirement from the NFL Bramhall moved to Madison and became the radio voice for the University of Wisconsin football team. Smoky's came on the scene just as the Brahmalls retired from the supper club game.

Oscar heard about Smoky's when he lived in a rooming house in east Madison. A Smoky's employee told him about the job opening. "I came here on a Friday night and started that night," he recalls. "Washing dishes by myself. I didn't know what I was doing. I didn't have a job."

Oscar remains in the kitchen while Tom walks out into the dining room. "Oscar always has had the best work ethic," Tom says. "We were just kids when he started working in the business. He was half blind and couldn't drive. He would ride his bicycle to Smoky's every night. And work until we closed the kitchen at eleven, eleven thirty. Every night. I always wish I had ten more like him. Unfortunately his vision went and he can't do the work he used to. So we keep him on two nights a week . . . just to keep that link."

Like his brother Larry, Tom Schmock was a busboy at Smoky's, where the dimly lit dining room seats about 120. He remembers the white napkins with the white tablecloths. "We had to fold them every night," he says. "Of course Janet [his mother] was too pennywise, which was good at the time. It was too expensive to change tablecloths every time. So we would just lay another white napkin over the stain. We'd get two or three turns out of a table by just putting a napkin over a napkin."

Janet says, "Do you remember, boys, when we lived upstairs I washed all the tablecloths in our old washing machine? I hung them out on the line and the truck drivers would come [down University Avenue] and I'd start to cry. They'd get dirty and dusty."

In 1947 Janet was a waitress at the since-closed Hoffman House on the east side of Madison. Leonard Schmock was a Hoffman House bartender who had just returned home after serving in the US Navy in World War II. He tugged at her heart. She made him dance. There was no doubt. They were married three years later.

Janet is the product of a farm family in Black Earth, Wisconsin. Her parents, Erling and Ellen Punswick, came from Norway to Blue Mounds, Wisconsin, where Erling built a log cabin that still stands today.

Erling grew tobacco and raised dairy cattle. When Janet was a young girl her parents sold the large farm due to Erling's arthritis after years of operating a horse-drawn plow. Erling and Ellen bought a smaller, forty-acre farm and again grew tobacco and raised dairy cattle. Janet worked as a maid around Madison before meeting Smoky.

As an early Friday night crowd files in, Larry Schmock says, "Both of my parents were in the supper club atmosphere. As soon as he got out of the war she was making gunpowder up at the Badger Ammunition Plant in the Baraboo Hills. After the war they wanted to get their own place; they had been saving money. This was perfect for them, a good starter place."

Leonard was from Bloomer, about two hundred miles northwest of Madison. He came to Madison in 1937 to play football and study agriculture at the University of Wisconsin. After the war Leonard continued to fly and did crop dusting for regional farmers. He also worked as a bartender at the Cuba Club and as a salesman for Del Monte Foods before he knotted dreams with Janet.

"We had looked at quite a few restaurants the first year we were married," Janet recalls. "We even looked at country clubs." In 1952 Janet and Leonard finally bought Hogan's Club, a half block east of Smoky's. The supper club had been owned by Gus Hogan. Smoky and Janet changed the name, bought the entire building, and lived upstairs.

The club had twelve tables and twelve bar stools. On busy nights customers dined in the kitchen. "Smoky tended bar and for five years I cooked in the kitchen," Janet says. "We had no children then. We would work until three or four in the morning. I baked the pies."

When the University of Wisconsin Badgers were home on football Saturdays during the 1950s and '60s, Smoky's would serve between four hundred and five hundred dinners. And dinners have always included homemade soup and salad.

"We boiled meat bones to make the soup stock," Janet says. "We use whipping cream in our creamy soups. We could make up any soup. We never took recipes. The classic was the cabbage au gratin."

Tom adds, "I remember when I took over the soup duties. Tuesday was my soup-making day. We had six-gallon kettles. I would do seven or eight of those. Then on Friday I'd make the seafood chowder, which would be another three [kettles]. So you're talking at least sixty gallons a week."

Soon the children arrived. Larry was born in 1955, Tom in 1957, and Barb in 1961. They all went to school in Smoky's neighborhood. Janet made lunch for all of them when they came home from school. Tom recalls, "We didn't have a lunch room at our grade school but we had the luxury of walking home for lunch every day and having roast beef, mashed potatoes, and gravy. We never had peanut butter sandwiches."

Larry and Tom bought out their mother and father in 2000. Barb is a nurse in Madison and also bakes her famous chocolate chip cookies—Barbie's Batch Made from Scratch—at Smoky's.

Smoky's daughter Barb Schmock and dishwasher Oscar Huber in Smoky's kitchen, c. 1980.

Smoky Schmock setting up the bar, circa 1963.

Smoky's friends loved donating Smoky-related stuff to the supper club.

Even the smallest supper club is defined by big personalities. Leonard "Smoky" Schmock was one of the biggest. His nickname was derived from his last name. Janet says, "He comes from Bloomer, where up there they say *schmoke*. They're German. When he was here he was always called Smoky."

Even at the end of his life, Leonard would work from seven AM to five PM six days a week. He died at home after a long illness in March 2001. He was eighty-five.

Everything has its place. "He'd always sit at the [west] end of the bar," Tom Schmock recalls. "At four o'clock every day his crowd would come in to see him. They'd have a cocktail hour, then go about their way. Before that, during the day he'd come to the table in front of the window [facing University] and bring out the office—which was a cardboard box—with bills, checkbooks, charge slips, lay it all out on the table and go through it every day."

Smoky's friends would check in on a daily basis while he was doing his book-work. Some would bring him Smokey the Bears, which used to hang from the rafters of the supper club. A Smokey "prevent forest fires" poster remains affixed to a wall at the west end of the bar.

The walls and ceilings of Smoky's were once filled with blowfish, signage from defunct Madison restaurants, and garage sale stuff, most of which was bequeathed to Smoky from customers and salesmen. Inflatable Oscar Mayer wieners hung from the rafters. "We had golf clubs that women would bring in after their husbands died," Tom says. "They'd ask us to hang them above their table." Everything has its place.

The supper club looked like a target for *American Pickers*. The place was cleaned up in 2009, although a 1940s sousaphone from the University of Wisconsin marching band still hangs from a wall. And there's a stuffed muskie, a memory from when Smoky used to take his boys fishing in Hayward, Wisconsin.

"A lot of people didn't understand it," Tom says. "They'd walk in and turn around and walk out. They thought it was too much. Some people miss it; some people appreciate what we've done. The fire inspectors didn't like all the fishing nets hanging in the dining and bar areas. They collected dust and grease."

Tom remembers a story of one particular artifact. "A navy flyer, who is younger than my dad was, he lives in Illinois and he comes for the football games. We used to have this king crab mounted on a big red velvet board. I remember that, but it's been long gone. He was stationed in Hawaii and he would fly up to Alaska. He got the crab just for that purpose. He went back to Hawaii and had it sitting out in the sun for a month to dry out. He mounted it on the board and brought it in here just for my dad."

Wisconsin football legend Elroy "Crazy Legs" Hirsch was a regular at Smoky's. Green Bay Packer Fuzzy Thurston always impressed young Larry and Tom. Mickey Mantle and Indiana basketball coach Bobby Knight stopped in. So did television host Gene Rayburn, of *Match Game* fame.

"There were four or five supper clubs in town then," Tom Schmock says. "Now we're the only one left besides the Esquire."

Leonard and Janet came of age in the Madison supper club scene. They went to the Cuba Club and Minnick's Top Hat and danced at the Chatiliquer. Another regular stop was the fish fry at Crandall's (now the Tornado Room) near the state capitol.

The family is adamant that Smoky's is a traditional supper club. "What makes us a supper club is that we have the crocks to put on the table with all the fresh vegetables, the carrots, green onions, celery, and radishes," Tom declares. "That's not always done at a traditional restaurant. We also have cottage cheese and pickled beans and that's typical supper club fare. And when my folks started out, supper clubs were traditionally on the outskirts of town. This was on the outskirts of town. This was farmland.

"We still sell a lot of brandy old-fashioneds and brandy Manhattans. You come into a darkened room with a bar in the middle and you

Even a University of Wisconsin tuba has found its way into Smoky's. In 1992 a customer who played in the school band donated the tuba to the supper club.

Anyone who has been to Smoky's never forgets the damn house rules.

University of Wisconsin football legend Elroy "Crazy Legs" Hirsch was a fan of Smoky's.

almost feel like having an old-fashioned. I wouldn't want a beer or a rum and coke. The old-fashioned leads you into the whole supper club experience, for sure. We also have grasshoppers and a martini club with a couple thousand members. It's part of that old nostalgia."

Old Nostalgia—sounds like a good supper club name.

But Smoky's never had a Friday night fish fry. "And we didn't start prime rib until the late 1990s when we started cutting our own rib eyes," Tom says. "The Cuba Club was right down the street and they pretty much invented the fish fry in Madison. We were always known as the steak house. This is a supper club. Don't come here for fusion. It's always been basic.

"But on Friday we sold a ton of [Canadian] walleye pike. I remember when I was in high school and I had the night shift we'd batter the fish and deep-fry it, which means you have to get the fish nice and dry, otherwise the batter doesn't stick. I put out all the fish on layers of towels—five layers thick. It was like we had a fish fry, but we didn't. We didn't do cod or perch, which was popular at the time. But we did these big walleye dinners and sold as many as we could cook on a Friday."

Smoky's garnered a national profile in airline magazines in the late 1980s and early '90s through its mention as one of the country's "Top 10 steak houses" by the Knife & Fork Club of America. Although the ads no longer run, Smoky's still carries that memory.

"Jack Roach started that down in Texas," Tom explains. "He wanted to sample these independent steak houses using his own criteria. I don't know what the judging was like, but they'd come in and never say they were here. He created this top ten list. You could use that to advertise but we couldn't afford it at the time."

Smoky's appeared in the in-flight magazines for United, American, Northwest, and other airlines. "We got all this great advertising nationwide," Tom continues. "We got a big boost in business. It went away because one steak house owner wanted to be on the list but was disqualified for having a chain. That woman is Ruth Fertel."

That would be Ruth Chris. In 1994 Fertel, who owned forty-two steak houses nationwide, sued Roach and the Knife & Fork Club and won the suit. She contended the list was bought and paid for by her rival Dale Wamstad, owner of Del Frisco's Double Eagle Steak House in Dallas—a perennial favorite on the list.

Smoky's third-generation purveyor Steve Knoche of Knoche's Old Fashioned Butcher Shop, established 1938, in Madison, Wisconsin.

It turned out Jack Roach was really Houston publicist Thomas Horan, who assembled the list based on his own visits. He was not a food critic. Horan was paid $1,000 a month by Wamstad to assemble the list as Jack Roach, according to a November 9, 1994, Associated Press story.

The steak house list stopped.

Smoky's has used the same purveyor for decades. Tenderloins come from U.W. Provisions in Madison. Sirloins, New York strips, and T-bones come from Neesvig's

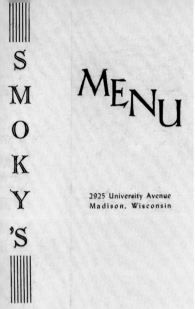

S M O K Y 'S

MENU

2925 University Avenue
Madison, Wisconsin

Before Dinner

Martini	.75
Manhattan	.75
Daiquiri	.75
Barcardi	.75
Old Fashioned	.75

After Dinner

Stinger	.85
Grasshopper	.85
Creme De Menthe Frappe	.75
Creme De Coco	.75
Peppermint Schnapps	.65
Brandy Alexander	.85
Gin Alexander	.85
B. & B.	.85
Brandy	.60
Cognac	.85
D.O.M. Benedictine	.85
Cherry Heering	.85

DINNER MENU

Shrimp Cocktail 75c	Home-made Soup of the Day or Tomato Juice	Marinated Herring 75c

All Steaks U.S. Gov't Choice

LARGE FILET MIGNON	4.75
LARGE SIRLOIN	4.75
LARGE T-BONE	4.75
SMALL FILET MIGNON	4.25
SMALL SIRLOIN	4.25
SMALL T-BONE	4.25

We cannot be responsible for the appearance or the tenderness of any steak ordered "well done"

> **CANADIAN WALLEYED PIKE**
> prepared with Chef's own recipe,
> lemon wedge, our own tartar sauce
> 2.75

GROUND SIRLOIN STEAK	2.75
BROILED AFRICAN LOBSTER TAILS	6.00
JUMBO SHRIMP (we bread our own)	2.75
CHICKEN (deep fried - tender)	2.75

Dinners Include
Home-made Hashed Brown or French Fried Potatoes
Relish Dish - Our Own Pickled Beets
Crisp Salad Bowl with Choice of Dressing
French, Thousand Island, Vinegar and Oil
(We make our own dressing)
Roquefort — 25c
Homemade French Fried Onion Rings — 50c
Mushrooms — 50c
BEVERAGE: Coffee — Tea — Milk

Sandwich Menu

OPEN FACED TENDERLOIN STEAK SANDWICH
Includes Toast, Potatoes, Relish, Beverage ... 2.25

CHICKEN BASKET
Includes Toast, French Fries, Relish ... 1.75

TENDERLOIN STEAK (on a bun)	1.00
GROUND SIRLOIN	.65
CHEESEBURGER	.75

Our Own Hashed Browns — 25c
French Fries — 25c
Onion Rings — 50c
Home-made Soup (cup) — 35c
Salad Ala Carte — 50c

BEVERAGES		DESSERTS	
Coffee	.15	Ice Cream	.25
Milk	.15	Sherbet	.25
Tea	.20	Chocolate Sundae	.25
Iced Tea	.25		

Basic graphics for a great menu.

Ground Sirloin Steak, $2.75 in the early 1960s.

in the Madison area. "But now that we started the prime rib we use Knoche's from a family that's been around Madison forever," Schmock says. "It's a family we know very well. They have a top-notch butcher shop and we've been buying ground beef from them because we also own a bar and grill down the street."

Knoche's is about a mile away from Smoky's. The butcher shop was started in 1938 by Nancy and George Knoche. The five-thousand-square-foot cement block shop sells wholesale to about forty-five bars and restaurants in Madison including the acclaimed Quivey's Grove.

"When we started there weren't the big stores around like Kohl's," third-generation owner Steve Knoche says. "Now there's so many of them. The ma-and-pa shops like us are pretty much gone. Supper clubs in Madison are pretty much gone, too: the Cuba Club, the Top Hat. Smoky's is a supper club with the old-time atmosphere and kind of a homey feel."

Knoche, who was born in 1953, maintains a homey feel with his customers. "People like the one-on-one with us," says Knoche. "We know people by name. On

Thanksgiving this guy comes in every year with a sheet. We cut his turkey piece by piece and tie up the leg, tie up the thigh, and bone the whole thing out. Nobody does that anymore. We have high-end product and that's how I keep the store going. I try to get locally raised Wisconsin beef. We get some out of Illinois and Minnesota. People are loyal to all this. Smoky's buys certain ribs from us because they are the best ribs around. We get them from Cargill in Chicago. We're the old-fashioned butcher shop. We cut the meat fresh every day." Tom Schmock adds, "When we started the prime rib they told us how they hand-picked all the primes that come in."

Destiny seemed to pick Tom and Larry Schmock. "This is all we ever knew," Tom admits. "We actually grew up living in a restaurant and lived upstairs until we were eight or ten years old, then my mom and dad could actually afford to buy a home. And then the home was only two blocks from the business. The business was the family and the family was the business."

He pauses, laughs, and says, "In that respect I guess you couldn't call it a normal family. It was always a good thing. We were always expected to be at work every Friday and Saturday. That was the work ethic instilled in us."

This is why staff becomes family at Smoky's. Hostess Helen Simonini began working as a waitress at the supper club in 1957. Helen and her husband, Reno, opened the first Tastee Freez in the state of Wisconsin in 1952, six years after they were married.

That was a long time ago. "The Tastee Freez was down the street," she says on a busy Friday night. "We only served ice cream so it was hard to get business in the wintertime. We closed up and I started to work this job in the winter. After we sold the Tastee Freez my husband worked for the post office and he bartends here part-time."

Tom obtained a two-year degree in visual communications from the Madison Area Technical College and worked in a Madison portrait studio for a couple years. "I thought about what I wanted to do the rest of my life," he says. "So I came back to the restaurant and started cleaning every morning. Oscar would join me. We'd watch *The Three Stooges* on television. Oscar would bring doughnuts. We would do

Girl's Night Out! c. 1956. Left to right: Helen Simonini, Charlene Richmond, Norma Volk, Pat Garske, and Janet Schmock, the beloved wife of Smoky.

the cleaning. My mom showed me how to make soup, how to order beef. I wrassled the bookkeeping away from my dad because he was a little reluctant to give it up. He'd go away on long weekends and while he was gone I computerized all the charts. He always called the computer the 'confuser.' I've been doing the books ever since.

My role here is mostly in the back of the house doing books, but on weekends I can help out, which means I can host, cashier, bus dishes, cook, and whatever else needs to be done. And now both of my sons and both of Larry's sons are working here."

Customers don't hang around all night at Smoky's. Change is always in the air, especially in a city as progressive as Madison. "The drunk driving laws and smoking laws have really impacted supper clubs," Tom says. "Men in supper clubs used to wear ties. Ladies would have a purse. High heels."

The growing popularity in Big Ten football—along with the on-field improvement of the University of Wisconsin Badgers—influenced the sartorial splendor of Smoky's. Men stopped wearing expensive suits on Saturday night because of the chance that someone in the post-game crowd would spill something on them.

Larry says, "Our family would always go to the football games and we would race back here in the station wagon. Within fifteen or twenty minutes after the game was over, the bar would be full. Coaches from different districts in the state would get together and ride the bus to Madison. They would reserve a big table at Smoky's after every game at Camp Randall. Then the crowd would file in. Sometimes we had three-hour waits. And it was no big deal. We never had a complaint. We moved our opening time from five o'clock to four o'clock. They'd be drinking in our parking lot and somebody would go out and call their names. It was big fun."

The increased popularity of tailgating has hurt Smoky's. Tom explains, "Everyone eats at the tailgate party. They're shitfaced by the time three o'clock rolls around, so why bother? They're not looking for supper. They may come to the bar around seven o'clock for sandwiches. And night games are awful for us. It is so different now than it was twenty years ago."

Some people see the changes. Others truly feel the deeper meaning of life's cycles.

15

Fisher's Club

428 Stratford Street, Avon, Minnesota
(320) 356-7372 • www.fishersclub.com

Like a long summer night's sunset or a lucky penny in the sand, Fisher's Club is waiting to be discovered along the shore of Middle Spunk Lake. The cool summer water is as smooth as a baby's bottom and is part of the Lake Wobegon Trail, a forty-six-mile hiking path among the goldenrod and wild roses of central Minnesota. The lake current gently rolls between now and then. Once seen, never forgotten—a first love for sure.

The light tan, pine green–trimmed lakeside roadhouse was opened in 1932 by the spunky George "Showboat" Fisher after he retired from major league baseball. Showboat got his nickname because he dressed better than anyone else on his minor league baseball team in Buffalo, New York, his son George "Junior" Fisher once told me.

An avid fisherman and hunter, Showboat dreamed of operating a club in the land of ten thousand lakes. He was raised on a farm in Saint Anna, about five miles north of Avon (population 1,144, about twelve miles northwest of Saint Cloud). Showboat died in the spring of 1994 at the age of ninety-five.

I have visited Fisher's Club twice: in the summer of 2008 and in the summer of 2011. Like baseball, it is a seasonal operation, opening the last weekend of April and generally running through the last weekend of October. Many things are finely turned double plays at Fisher's: sandwiches and baskets, the lake and

Fisher's Club was opened in 1932 by former major league baseball player George "Showboat" Fisher.

Historic bottle lockers at Fisher's, where regulars keep their bottles of hooch.

the summer moon, the eggs and potatoes in Sally & Hazel's Perfect Potato Salad.

And the bond of the locals who gave me their business cards after my 2011 visit. Their names were embossed together on each card: MARILYN & BOB OBERMILLER, for example. This was clearly a calling card from another era.

Old-timers debate whether Fisher's is a supper club or a bottle club. It met most of my criteria for a supper club because of its remote location, low ceilings, screen windows, and live entertainment on Saturdays. Handmade posters that hang above the bar warn DANCERS: DO NOT STOMP FLOOR and NO CRABBY PEOPLE ALLOWED. The lightly breaded walleye—a secret recipe—is as crisp as a late autumn walk.

Fisher's is also a bottle club because guests bring in their own bottles of liquor for setups and regulars have their own lockers, made out of fine Douglas fir. Only beer and wine are served at the bar. There are very few bottle clubs left in the United States.

"My dad put those lockers in fifty years ago," George "Junior" Fisher said in 2008, gazing at an empty dance floor where the past was present.

No bottles are on-site today. The lockers are historical artifacts.

Minnesota state law changed in 1986. So Junior backed his Suburban to the front door. Every bottle of vodka, bourbon, gin, and whiskey—all labeled with the owners' names—were hauled into the vehicle. A few hours later, after the inspector left, Junior drove back to Fisher's and reloaded the bottles back into the club. Junior then contacted the bottle owners to tell them to pick up their stash ASAP.

Manager/owner Karl Petters went for the supper club vote. "At a supper club, people tend to stay for a longer time than they would at another place," he said. "It's a social gathering." His wife, Karleen, agreed. "We're open only for supper," she said.

Fisher's motto is "A fairly good place for quite some time." If you catch a folksy drift, it's likely because the fine *Lake Wobegon Days* author and *A Prairie Home Companion* host Garrison Keillor became a partner in the rustic club in 2005. Junior never really wanted to call the operation a supper club because it diminished any luster of "Fisher's Club." He wasn't so fond of the club's new motto, which, as locals say, sounds like it was "Keillorized."

Well, these characters were right out of *Lake Wobegon Days.*

Karl and Karleen Petters, general managers of the Fisher's Club.

Pop rocker Bobby Vee lives near Avon. His 1960s hits include "The Night Has a Thousand Eyes" and "Come Back When You Grow Up." In 2005 he recorded the ballad "47 Wonderful Years" with Sally Fisher, who was then eighty. Sally was married to Junior, who was seventy-nine in 2005. They co-owned Fisher's for forty-seven years until they sold it in 2005. The song is a tribute to Fisher's Club and Avon as much as "New York, New York" honors Jilly's and Manhattan.

"The food is so great and Sally and Junior are such a unique couple," Vee said in 2008. [In May 2012 Vee announced on his website that he had been diagnosed with Alzheimer's disease.] "I was talking to Sally one day and she said, 'Junior and I took road trips and would go to New Orleans. I'd take out my ukulele and we'd sing songs.' So we brought her into my studio. I sang with her—just barely. She changed the words to that song 'My Buddy' [popularized by Al Jolson and Bobby Darin among others]."

So "47 Wonderful Years" has lyrics like:

We've been told growing old is the pits

We thought we'd be here forever and never quit . . .

I had to ask Vee if working with Sally was as much fun as the band he had in Fargo, North Dakota, that briefly included Bob Dylan. "It sure was," he answered. "I didn't have to help her out much. We pressed some songs up and gave them to her friends. It was so much fun for us to do that for her—it meant everything. After that she said how she had fifteen, sixteen songs she recorded on a little tape recorder so we dubbed them down to CD. She's a saucy singer."

Sunset over Middle Spunk Lake adjacent to Fisher's.

Sally Fisher died on October 16, 2008—just five weeks after I met her. Junior died shortly after on March 2, 2009. I told you about the meaning of couples around Fisher's Club. The dance hall area still sports the bright red patterned wallpaper of Sally and Junior's youth. Junior and Sally were married fifty years. They took over the club in 1959. They expanded the kitchen and installed the lively wallpaper. Junior and Sally ran Fisher's until 2005, when they sold to a group of fifteen investors that included Garrison Keillor and Jon Petters, Karl and Karleen's nephew (Karl and Karleen came aboard in 2007). Now many of the owners' children, nieces, and nephews have found summer work at Fisher's Club.

"Really, we bought it just to preserve the place," said Jon Petters, who remembered playing cribbage at Fisher's. "We used to come here when I was a little kid and have deep-fried jumbo frog legs from India."

In 2006 the new group added a rambling outside deck that overlooks the lake. "They had a jukebox in here at the same place it is at today," Sally said on that August night in 2008. Today's jukebox includes such songs as "Born to Boogie" by Hank Williams Jr. and "A Jukebox with a Country Song" by Doug Stone. Sally's favorite line at Fisher's was "The only thing that changes are the lightbulbs."

The dining room's walls are covered in knotty pine. "It was painted once in 1944—and since then it's never been touched," Junior said. An autographed photo of New York Yankee Johnny Blanchard hangs on a wall near a *Sporting News*–type cartoon outlining Showboat's baseball accomplishments. He had eight hits in his first nine major league at bats.

Showboat's stint in the majors was stranger than Lake Wobegon fiction. The left-handed hitter retired with a Hall of Fame–like .335 batting average in seasons with the Washington Senators (1923–'24), Saint Louis Cardinals (1930), and Saint Louis Browns (1932).

"He hit .374 with the Cardinals and made so much money they shipped him back to the minors," Junior said in 2008—and he still seemed bothered by that transaction.

During the years that Showboat ran his supper club he was around to give batting tips to young Minnesota Twins. He told the Cuban Twins legend Tony Oliva to always keep his bat down because "that's where the work is." Showboat couldn't stand hitters swinging at pitches up and away from the strike zone. "You drink the high balls and hit the low balls is what I always used to say," Fisher told Rob Held of the *St. Cloud Daily Times* in 1973.

Showboat was only thirty-three when he retired from major league baseball. He wasn't fond of year-round jobs and his flashy nickname dictated a minimal need of money. Here is a keen observation on George Aloysius Fisher from an April 19, 1930, issue of the *Sporting News*. The Saint Louis–based publication was jaked about the Cardinals rookie sensation:

The beloved Sally and Junior Fisher.

The writer found George Aloysius at the Forest Park Hotel last night reading a magazine in an obscure corner of the lobby and contentedly puffing away at his pipe. Attired in street clothes, Fisher looks more like a young banker than a baseball player. Quietly but well dressed, he is handsome enough to be a movie star. A finely molded face, bronzed by the sun, is set off by a pair of dark blue eyes and neatly combed black hair. And he has a spontaneous smile that reveals two rows of perfect white teeth.

A summertime supper club seemed like a perfect tonic for a magnetic sportsman. Period postcards promoted Middle Spunk Beach as "Undoubtedly One of Minnesota's Better Beaches." It's this type of Minnesota modesty that became Garrison Keillor's muse.

Showboat installed a dance floor in 1937, and the music combined with cold beer and slot machines made Fisher's a popular destination in central Minnesota.

George "Showboat" Fisher after a hunting trip.

Fisher's was so much the rage that Showboat often spent summer nights sleeping by the front door with his shotgun and his hunting dog to protect the day's gambling takes. Junior and his brothers Lewis and Dick would fish area lakes all around Avon for sunfish, northerns, and crappies. Showboat would host a complimentary Friday night fish fry at the rural outpost.

Junior remembered when baseball legend Ted Williams visited Fisher's Club in 1939. "He was fishing up here and had an hour and a half to get to Minneapolis eighty miles south," Junior said. "He had a date with some gal. And he made it."

Every Fisher's Club meal leads off with the classic hors d'oeuvre tray featuring meatballs in homemade barbecue sauce, garlic toast, liver pâté, pickled herring, crackers, carrots, and celery. "We served it that way for forty-seven years," Sally said. "Well, we used to have fresh tomatoes."

Up to four hundred dinners are served on a peak Friday night. About 60 percent of them are the tender and moist walleye, according to Karl Petters. The spicy coleslaw with a key poppy seed component is based on a recipe from the legendary 21 Club in New York City. "My mother [Flo] got it there when my dad played in New York," Junior said. Flo cooked in a tiny space behind the current bar wall. The kitchen was expanded to eight hundred feet in 1959 when Junior and Sally took over.

The Beeboparebop Rhubarb Pie that has been popularized in *A Prairie Home Companion* is baked here from scratch by Alice Thelen, who has lived in Avon since 1963.

Fisher's Club and Resort in Avon, Minnesota. Plenty of parking!

Plenty of parking!

Liz and Lew Fisher. Lew is the youngest son of George Fisher Sr., the club's patriarch.

The new group of owners unearthed Fisher's spirited bootlegging history (circa 1933). "We had the best moonshine in the United States," Jon Petters said. "Because we're in these hills, it was a place the feds had a hard time cracking. Al Capone came here. My dad had four fifteen-gallon kegs in the attic. Once a day my mom would go up there and shake them. We could not figure out what she was doing."

Sally was a former host at KASM-AM radio station in Albany, Minnesota. She smiled as she recalled getting the occasional ad from a place selling duck-feathered pillows. "I said to my boss, 'My, they must make a lot of duck-feathered pillows.' He said, 'No, that's when the whiskey's ready. That's how they spread the word.'"

As I was getting ready to leave after a Friday night dinner in 2008, another of Showboat's sons, Lewis, then eighty, dropped by with a clear bottle of "Minnesota 13" moonshine as a group of us sat on the lakeside deck. Lewis brought his French poodle, Buddy, along for the ride. I wound up drinking the sweet, tequila-type liquor under a full moon that glistened over the lake.

I will never forget that night.

"A guy named Warner Davis was cooking this stuff up until he died ten years ago," Lewis said as he looked at the bottle. "I'm gonna give that bottle to you." Lewis does not make moonshine these days, but he does make fifty to seventy-five gallons of wine a year. Lewis said Warner had a home on nearby Pelican Lake where they used to cook moonshine together.

Here's Lewis's recipe. "It's really pretty simple," he said. "You take four bushels of corn and one hundred pounds of sugar. You take ten pounds of baker's yeast. Mix the sugar, yeast, and water so it makes the mash where you slush it around. It ferments within a day. If you want it to go faster you add a little lukewarm water. You have to be careful. You'll kill the yeast if you get too much heat on it. You let it sit for a week. The still is what makes it from mash into alcohol.

"That was good sippin' stuff."

The gang at Fisher's Club got a charge out of seeing the guy from Chicago drink moonshine.

The history of Minnesota 13 goes back to 1932, near the end of Prohibition and the same year Showboat opened his club. The moonshine got its name from a local seed corn variety. Lewis recommended drinking it with a sweet companion like 7-Up. Or in my case, Mountain Dew.

"If you take a good whiff of it, it will burn your nose," he said with a playful smile. Lewis then poured a dash of the moonshine on the table. He pulled out a match and lit the moonshine on fire. A blue flame erupted into the cool summer night.

Buddy was nonchalant, as if he had seen it all before.

Showboat had game, and it would have played well in a place as big as Chicago, where constables can be encouraged to look the other way. Lewis said, "They raided these places continuously. If the feds were in town the sheriff had to be with them. So the sheriff knew the feds were in town so he'd call up Dad on a Wednesday night and say, 'George, you still serve those good fish on Wednesday night?' Dad would say, 'No, no, it's changed, it's Fridays now.' The sheriff would go, 'OK, I forgot.' He had plenty of liquor here, but the old sheriff always tipped him off."

Lewis said the hooch was cheap to make, recalling how sugar cost six cents a pound in the early 1930s. "You'd go to a grocery store in Avon—at that time a town of maybe 120 people—and wonder why people were buying nine pounds of sugar a month. That's how they caught a lot of 'em. The stills were made of copper in those days. The Minnesota 13 moonshine we were drinking was made in a fine stainless steel still."

Say that three times after three shots of moonshine.

Lewis even attributed the birth of the NASCAR racing industry to moonshine. These are the things you hear at supper clubs. He reported, "The guys who were running moonshine in the hills of Kentucky and Tennessee had to have a car that was faster than the feds' car. These moonshiners would get together on a Saturday afternoon to see who had the fastest car. Pretty soon they built a track out on the fields."

The gentle folks of central Minnesota are resourceful souls.

"Stearns County and Avon was equaling or exceeding most of the stuff that was being done in Wisconsin during the time when they had primarily dairy farms here," Bob Obermiller said. "There was a creamery in every little town every five-mile radius. They started to open in the late 1800s. My dad [Ed] ran the [Avon Farmer's] creamery here. That all ended in the mid- to late 1950s when all the Kraft people were buying milk directly from the farmer. But during that era there was more butter shipped out of Stearns County than any county in the United States. They would ship two hundred thousand pounds of butter right out of Avon. The quality of the land wasn't as good for corn as it is in southern Minnesota, Iowa, or Illinois. So they had a lot of pasture land and that's why the dairy farmers came in."

The humble and proud Bob Obermiller played pro baseball with Showboat's other son, Dick, who lives in Colorado. Obermiller is the unofficial sports historian at Fisher's Club. He has a big black notebook with handwritten notations of every at-bat Showboat had (340) in the major leagues. Obermiller is a year younger than Lewis.

Obermiller and Dick Fisher were teammates at Saint John's University and played minor league ball during the summer of 1951 in Duluth, a chilly long way north from Avon. "The old Northern League was Duluth, Superior, Saint Cloud, Fargo, Aberdeen, Sioux Falls, and Eau Claire," the old first baseman recalled. A supper club league.

"I lived two or three blocks from here," Obermiller said over a 2011 dinner at Fisher's. His wife, Marilyn, listened in as she had done for fifty-four years. "We'd swim here every day during the summer. I'd come here with my mother and father for the free Friday night fish fry. The place was closed for two years [1944–46] during the war." When Fisher's reopened, Showboat added the bottle club.

Lewis added, "We fished every day of the week, my brother Dick and my brother George. My dad fished. We fished all day. We caught bass, crappies, sunnies [bluegill], northern, a few walleye. We caught and cleaned the fish." The fish went straight from Middle Spunk Lake into the frying pan at Fisher's. The lake still holds bass, bluegills, and walleye and runs as deep as ninety feet in spots. But game fish cannot be sold in Minnesota; restaurants rely on distributors. Fisher's Club's popular walleye comes from Canadian lakes.

"My dad was a very good talker but not a very good worker," Lewis said. "My dad went through life without getting his hands dirty too often. My mother was the cook here a lot of years. As the business grew it got too much for her, but she still had the job of cleaning three cottages that were across the trail. But my dad was a good PR guy." In 1958 Showboat ran for the Minnesota senate. In 1974 he shot his age in golf—seventy-four.

A three-by-two-foot snack window with sliding screen was built off the kitchen in the early 1940s to serve hot dogs, ice cream, and soda to kids on the beach. A popcorn machine was installed in 1939; it worked until the summer of 2011. The present-day porch was added in 1954.

Obermiller continued, "From '46 on, we would sit on the little benches outside. George [Senior] was the bartender. Inside he would sit on his little stool and when there was no business we never talked about anything besides baseball. This was when Dick and I were in high school and early college. I'd say he was on the outside of the bar five to ten years before he died. He was there most of the time greeting everybody.

"George also had a big loudspeaker on top of the roof. Every time they played the Wurlitzer [jukebox] we'd listen to the music outside. George was the biggest Bing Crosby guy you ever saw, so about half the songs were Bing Crosby." Lewis added, "My dad thought he could sing. And the more he had to drink the better his voice became."

In keeping with community entertainment outreach, on July 4, 2009, Keillor broadcast a thirty-fifth anniversary of *A Prairie Home Companion* from Fisher's Club. More than ten thousand people descended on the small town. No one in town could remember the last time a satellite truck was in Avon. Later that summer Keillor did two private shows from the supper club. Karl Petters said, "He did a six and eight o'clock show. It was very casual. He walked around; it was a comedy-singing thing. The place was filled up. He requested that corn on the cob be served. We served it free between 3:30 and 5:30 and he was outside shucking it."

When Keillor and the new ownership took over in 2005 their main goal was to keep everything the same. How many times do you hear that when a new sheriff comes to town?

"The first thing they did was ask Junior who insured the building," Lewis said. "My brother said, 'I never carried insurance on it.' All these years, with all this wood in here, he never carried insurance other than liability insurance. No storm insurance. Nothing."

Only a couple of things have changed over the years at Fisher's.

"We get served a heck of a lot sooner than we used to," Obermiller said. "There was nothing about waiting for two hours. We always waited two hours and no one cared. Everybody knew they were going to wait that long and they sat and visited with everybody in the whole place."

Supper clubs are full of intense rituals such as having a favorite place to sit, but then so are corner bars on the South Side of Chicago. But things can become extreme at Fisher's. Karl Petters recalled, "I never realized it until we started here but people have ownership on a table. They've been sitting there for a number of years. Most of the time people reserve a table and if they don't call, then we should give it away. One night there was a couple that always had a table right next to the bar. They didn't come so we gave it to someone else. Well, they came a little bit later. They sat at the table next to it. And they sat there and just looked at the people like this . . . " And Petters went into a blank trance.

He continued, "It went on most of the night. They didn't even order anything. They just sat there and looked at them. It was absolutely amazing in that kind of thing can be that important in your life."

Several tables are known by name. The oak Weber table honors Mr. and Mrs. Weber from Albany, Minnesota, who had their first date at Fisher's in 1946. Francis and Betty Weber were Friday night regulars until Francis died in May 2010. The Monroe table honors Marilyn Monroe simply because Sally once picked up a cardboard figure of Norma Jean at a suppliers trade show. Even in Avon, some like it hot.

The Fisher family lived about four blocks from the supper club. George Fisher walked the straight path. "There was no leeway with my dad," Lewis declared. "He came home one night around eleven. We slept out on the open porch in the summer. He said to me, 'Hey, Sport . . .' He called all of us Sport. I don't think he remembered our names. He said, 'Hey, Sport, didn't I tell you guys to cut the grass?' We had a big yard. I said, 'We forgot, Dad, we'll do it right away in the morning.' He said, 'No, you're going to cut the grass tonight.' My mother said, 'For chrissakes, George, they can't see. And what are the neighbors going to think?'" George didn't care.

The "Sports" cut the yard by the light of a kerosene lamp. One of the boys walked with the lamp while the other pushed the lawnmower. "We cut that sucker until three in the morning," Lewis said with a smile. "Guess how often we forgot to cut the lawn again—never."

Sense of community and camaraderie are the marks of a good supper club. Memories of good times often overshadow the food itself. Showboat planted the seeds for that commitment. Obermiller explained, "George promoted trap shooting. He owned the property across the railroad tracks [the former Great Northern that is now the Wobegon Trail] and he would have a trap shoot about two or three times a year. We'd have to pick up the clay pigeon that didn't break in the swamp of the lake and bring them back. We'd walk out in the slew. In addition to that they had some of us help clean the beach periodically because George was responsible for helping to keep the beach clean for the town of Avon."

It just part of was Showboat's message in a bottle. Or supper. It doesn't really matter.

Fisher's Club endures.

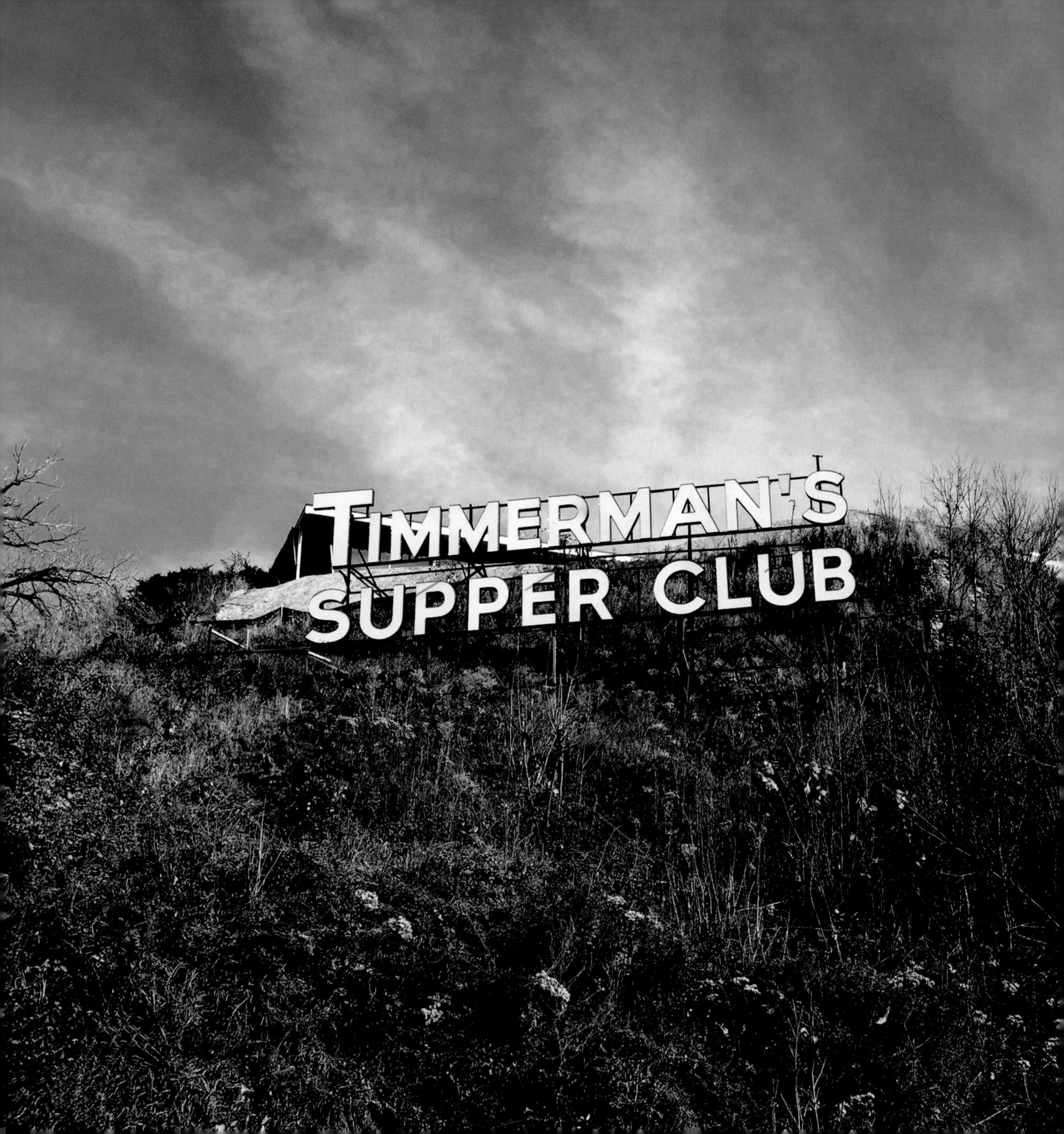
TIMMERMAN'S
SUPPER CLUB

16

Timmerman's Supper Club

7777 Timmerman Drive, East Dubuque, Illinois
(815) 747-3316 • www.timmermanssupperclub.com

It can be a bad idea to fire up the coals on nostalgia. Like meatpacking houses and buttoned-up blouses, the past will never come around again.

But sometimes the past is present. Such is the case with the elegant Timmerman's Supper Club in East Dubuque, Illinois—and the only true supper club in the Land of Lincoln. Helen and Bob Timmerman opened the club on August 27, 1961, on a bluff overlooking Highway 20 and Lake Lacoma, the backwaters of the Mississippi River. Helen's first choice for her supper club was on a site adjacent to the river, but the current location has worked out well.

The large white Timmerman's Supper Club signs on each side of the cliff have taken on iconic status over the years as the Hollywood signs of the hilly Galena (Illinois) territory. The Timmerman's sign on the east is neon, the western sign is LED.

The 175-seat dining room is accented with vinyl awnings and slanted picture windows that frame the panoramic view. The supper club has fifty-two windows on its main floor. That is a lotta sight for your bite.

Timmerman's offers the best view in Illinois apart from the skyscrapers of Chicago. This was not lost on the Timmermans when they opened the Sky-Line Room

Over the years the Timmerman's signage on Highway 20 west of Galena, Illinois, has become an icon for tourists.

The August 27, 1961, opening night at Timmerman's was not advertised on Yelp.

on the top floor of their supper club. The ceiling lights still have star-shaped filters. The menus of the early 1960s promoted "A Rocket View of Dubuqueland," even though the room faced Illinois. America was in a space race. Increasing mobility through bus and automobile created a new dimension of regional discovery. Even television viewers were getting their kicks on Route 66.

One of Timmerman's earliest menus promised entrees "From the corn belt of the Middle West" with items like "Double Thick Lamb Chops, Mint Jelly" ($5.75 with relish tray, tossed green salad, choice of dressing, rolls, butter, choice of baked, French fried, or hash brown potatoes, coffee, tea).

Atop the menu is the royal black and burgundy logo of the Dubuque Packing Company, which used the fleur-de-lis logo later adopted by the New Orleans Saints football team. The city of Dubuque was settled in 1788 by Quebec-born Julien Dubuque. It is the oldest city in Iowa. The regal logo denotes that their meat is the real deal.

And this is where the past is present.

Mark Hayes and Gary Neuses are just the fourth owners of Timmerman's. Their fathers were employed by the Dubuque Packing Company, founded in 1891 across the Mississippi River in Iowa. Mark's late father, Merilin Hayes, worked in the packing house for thirty years, winding up in the sausage department. Gary's father, Jerry Neuses, also worked in the packing house, where he was employed for a quarter-century until 1981, when the beef kill was shut down. He now counts money in the cage at the greyhound racetrack in Dubuque.

The packing company is gone. So are Helen and Bob Timmerman. But Jerry still helps his son cut the meat for the Sunday brunch at Timmerman's. "You either worked at John Deere or you worked at the packing house," Mark Hayes says. "Those were the two major employers of people around Dubuque."

Jerry recalls, "My neighbor Russ was a peddler for Dubuque Packing. That's what they called suppliers. I started in 1966 and peddlers

Timmerman's Supper Club overlooks Lake Lacoma, the backwaters of the Mississippi River.

were before my time. Russ started in 1949. He started on the hog kill and he went from there to selling meat. He'd go out four times a week on his route, selling meat off the truck to supper clubs and grocery stores."

Eastern Iowa was a mecca of meatpacking in the late 1950s and early '60s. In 1955 the first *Fortune* list of the largest companies in America was published. The Rath Packing Company in Waterloo, Iowa, was ranked 110—ahead of Coca-Cola (126), Anheuser-Busch (148), and Kellogg (186). At its peak in 1957, Rath employed

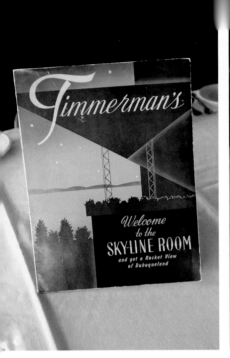

Timmerman's came of age during the space race of the early 1960s. The top floor of the supper club was called the Sky-Line Room, with "a rocket view of Dubqueland."

more than eighty-five hundred people. At one time it was the largest meatpacking plant under one roof in the world.

During the 1960s the Dubuque Packing Plant employed thirty-five hundred people under the watch of Robert Wahlert, the son of owner Harry Wahlert, who had purchased the plant in 1931 in the middle of the Great Depression. "Workers were paid well," Robert Timmerman says. "Harry found a guy on the floor loafing and reached in his pocket, threw down a bunch of money, and asked him to pick it up. There were a lot of stories like that about Harry."

In 1978 Dubuque Packing was the third largest beef slaughterhouse in America. People in the area called Dubuque Packing "the Pack" and the operation was located near the Mississippi River along Bob Dylan's Highway 61. Mary says, "My relatives in San Francisco bought Dubuque hams—in San Francisco."

The Dubuque Packers were a minor league baseball team who played in the Midwest League from 1956 to 1967 and 1974 to 1976. The 1961 Packers? They included future major leaguers Tommy Agee and Tommy John. Sixty-one is an important number around Timmerman's.

Rath went under in 1985, a victim of union busting through the Iowa Beef Packers (IBP), a company formed in 1960 in Denison, Iowa. IBP opened plants in rural areas that were cool to unions and hired immigrant workers who were less likely to unionize.

Meanwhile, in the late 1970s, Charles Stoltz became president of Dubuque Packing. In 1981 he fired fourteen hundred workers, earning the title of "the most unpopular man in Dubuque with the working man—maybe the most unpopular man in the history of Dubuque," according to the 1997 book *The Dubuque Packing Company & Charles E. Stoltz* by late Dubuque newspaper columnist Thomas Gifford.

"Harsh feelings," Jerry says. "We were out in wonderland. We didn't know what to do. I found odd jobs. I went out with a peddler. He paid me on the side with cash."

During the late 1940s and early '50s, Mary's parents, Jack and Mary Dempsey, ran the Moracco Supper Club in Dubuque, Iowa. Mary Timmerman declares, "Our neighbor worked at the Pack for twenty-nine years. You had to be there thirty years to get a pension. He didn't get a pension."

In 1982 Stoltz sold the plant and the fleur-de-lis trademark to a group led by his brother–in-law, Robert Wahlert. It reopened as FDL Foods, Inc., where Wahlert cut union wages before completely shutting down in 2001.

Today major purveyors like Reinhardt Food Service and *Sysco* are used to source the supper club's meat.

Timmerman's owners Mark Hayes (left) and Gary Neuses.

Mark Hayes was born in 1968 in East Dubuque. Gary Neuses was born in 1969 in Dubuque. People started families in Dubuque. The future was promising. "The Wahlert family owned the packing house and donated the money to build the school

I went to," Gary says. "To get Helen started they donated the [$9,000] bar and the coolers from the Dubuque packing house. In return, she bought their meat."

And she stuck the company logo on the Timmerman's menu.

Harry Wahlert established the Wahlert Foundation in 1948, which distributed millions of dollars to area institutions such as Loras College, Clarke College, and Wahlert High School, Iowa's largest parochial high school, whose notable alumni include actress Kate Mulgrew and former Chicago Bull Kevin Kunnert.

Gary Neuses came to Timmermans's for his senior prom. "We had a class of about three hundred, and thirty of us came here," he recalls. "This has always been known as a special occasion place. We still don't see much of a younger generation coming to supper clubs. They're going to chains. It seems like you have to be forty and up to go to a supper club, unless you're going to a family function, an anniversary."

Mary Timmerman adds, "You're going to have a drink or two. Helen used to say, 'If you want to eat out, go to McDonald's. If you want to dine out, come to Timmerman's.'"

Yes, this is the way Helen Timmerman wanted it.

A full-page ad in local newspapers promised, "You'll thrill to this completely new luxurious supper club, for an incomparable dining pleasure for an enchanting evening . . ."

Helen once threw out late country legend Waylon Jennings because he wouldn't remove his cowboy hat. Former bartender Louis Miller recalls, "Helen had dress codes. Waylon came in on a Thursday night with about twenty people, his band and crew. They sat by one of the front windows. Helen went over to Waylon and asked him to take off his hat. He said, 'I'm not removing my hat; do you know who I am?' Helen did not know who he was and she said, 'I don't care if you're Jesus Christ and the twelve apostles, you're not eating here.' So everybody left. She lost maybe $400, $500."

Helen died in October 2003 at the age of ninety-two. Her stylish pedigree can be traced back to 1942 when she and Bob opened their first establishment, a bar in Happy Corners, Wisconsin. Next they opened the 150-seat Chateau Supper Club, where Helen's half spring chicken sandwiches became the rage in the region. The chickens came from Helen's family farm. Bob died in 1970 but Helen kept on moving. In 1984, KDUB-TV called Helen Timmerman the Belle of the Tri-States, and after her death her son Robert said she was "liberated before liberation was in."

Born in Lamar, Missouri, Helen was the oldest girl in a family of thirteen children. She came of age on a farm in Kieler, Wisconsin, about ten miles from the supper club. Helen became an accomplished cook at an early age because she helped prepare meals for her siblings.

"My mom was not what you would call a 'normal' woman," Robert says in the winter of 2011. "First, she was a nun. She didn't take her permanent vows. She got Bell's palsy. She was sent home because her face was paralyzed." The palsy eventually went away and Helen met Bob.

"It wasn't fashionable for women to work in the 1950s and '60s," says Robert, who was born in 1937. "But my dad hurt his spine pouring steel in a foundry here. My mom had to go to work and her sisters frowned on that. I was a football player. I had a college scholarship. Although she was working, my mom tried to keep tabs on me. I had to be home at ten thirty. One night I came in at midnight. I assumed she wouldn't come home until one from the supper club. I slowly opened up the garage door. There was Mom. Notice I didn't say Dad. I'm coming up the steps real quiet . . ."

Robert gets up from a dining room table and tiptoes around an empty dance floor. Little kids watch him with wide eyes. They seem scared. Robert whispers, "I'm coming up the stairs real quiet," and then he raises his voice, *Whaack*! Remember, I was a two-hundred-pound football player. She hit me and I fell back. If I hadn't have caught the railing, I might have been seriously hurt. She slammed the door and did not say a polite good night. That is my mother."

Helen's first job was as a waitress in the early 1940s at the Julien Hotel in downtown Dubuque. That's where she debuted her feisty chicken sandwiches. She asked hotel management if she could make the sandwiches and keep the money for herself. Management agreed.

"It helped the hotel," Robert says. "People would eat a greasy chicken sandwich and down another gin and seven. We served chicken sandwiches after her funeral. It was a big deal for our family. It made the legacy of the restaurant business."

Helen liked to dance and wear big hats. "She liked sequined dresses," Mary says. "She didn't buy her dresses off the rack. She had her dresses made. A seamstress from Cedar Rapids would come here. Helen would pick out all her fabrics. The seamstress didn't even need a pattern, she was so good. The seamstress would have a free dinner here. She would go back to Cedar Rapids make the things up, fit it on Helen—and have another dinner."

It was common for Helen to work up a tizzy during a shift and, after the supper crowd peaked, she would retreat to her small penthouse above the supper club. Robert says, "She'd shower, dress up, and come back down and sit at the bar."

After Helen's husband, Bob, died, she acquired a German shepherd to watch over her during late hours at the supper club. "Sometimes pots and pans would be stacked crooked and you would hear a clang, clang," Mary recalls. "You didn't know if someone was in the kitchen. Helen had one dog, Happy, and that dog was really mean. She sent him out to get him trained, but he was so mean. Happy was running loose one day in the supper club before they opened. A salesman came by. The salesman was supposed to knock but he just walked in. The dog went after him. He ran to his car and tried to get his car door open and Happy chewed the back of his pants off."

Robert had a minimal role at the supper club. He planted the big locust trees that border the hills along Timmerman's to stop the erosion. In 1974 when Helen built the Timmerman's Motor Inn across the parking lot from the supper club, Robert bartended in the motor inn lounge. All five of Robert and Mary's children worked at the motor inn.

Robert became a full-time history teacher and head football and wrestling coach in the Dubuque public school system. "With my Ma, I'd peel potatoes," he says. "That was one thing I remember doing around here. As soon as I left you know what Ma got? An automatic potato peeler!"

The narrow, winding road up the hill to Timmerman's Supper Club was commissioned in 1959 by Helen.

She was the straw that stirred the drink.

"Ma had a whole lot of trouble building that road," Robert says. "It was called 'the Battle of the Hill.'" Mary adds, "The East Dubuque city council's interest were in the bars downtown [just three miles west of the supper club]." One city council member owned a bar in downtown East Dubuque, which between the 1950s and early 1980s was the neon-drenched Rush Street of northwest Illinois—or at least the Calumet City, Illinois.

East Dubuque's Sinsinawa Street ("Sin Street") featured girlie joints like the Coliseum and the Isabella Queen. There were hillbilly bars where John Prine's backup band the Famous Potatoes alternated sets with strippers, only to sadly learn they shared the same booking agent that landed all of them on Sin Street.

At its peak in the 1960s and '70s, there were more than thirty bars and clubs in downtown East Dubuque. You can still get a foot-long steamed chili hot dog at Mulgrew's Bar & Grill, now the oldest surviving bar on the strip. It served the first liquor in East Dubuque after Prohibition ended in 1933.

The "Sin Street" history goes as far back as to 1926, when the Dubuque *Telegraph Herald* called East Dubuque "Little Cicero" in reference to Al Capone's then-headquarters in Cicero, Illinois. During Prohibition people ran booze out of East Dubuque illegally. Speakeasies prospered along the scenic Mississippi River. Capone hid from the Chicago heat at the Hilltop in East Dubuque. The Hilltop was the template for the ballad "Hernando's Hideaway" from the musical *The Pajama Game*.

In its early years, Timmerman's, on the outskirts of town, was considered competition for downtown high life.

"When we were dating many years ago, East Dubuque was a beautiful place to go," Mary says. Robert says, "We used to dance at the Tick Tock. It boomed in the 1950s because you couldn't get a drink in Dubuque, or for the whole county for that matter. People came from all over. You could carry in booze at the Melody Mill, a big dance hall."

The Melody Mill was on Highway 3 about a mile north of Dubuque. Razed in the mid-1960s, it was the centerpiece of Union Park, billed as Iowa's largest park when the ballroom opened in June 1923. Guy Lombardo and Tommy and Jimmy Dorsey were among those who played at the Melody Mill on their cross-country tours. In later years the Melody Mill turned into a popular music venue, booking the Everly Brothers, Johnny Cash, Jerry Lee Lewis, and others. They all had to love the view from the fifty-five-acre site in the rolling Mississippi River valley.

Most Midwest supper clubs have iconic catfish on the walls. Timmerman's is not like most Midwest supper clubs.

Even in 2012, Timmerman's serves prime rib every night of the week. The supper club also has a popular Friday night fish fry with farm-raised catfish. As recently as the 1970s the catfish came directly from the nearby Mississippi River.

"We have white tablecloths and linen napkins, which you don't see in the chains," Gary Neuses says. "Another difference with a supper club is that we serve bottled beer. We don't serve tap beer. We serve Bud, Miller Light, Miller Genuine Draft, Heineken, Corona, Sam Adams. We don't serve local beers. Potosi is nearby. Galena Brewery. When tourists come by they all ask for local beer. But locals won't drink local beer. And the majority of our clientele comes from Dubuque and Galena, the Tri-State area."

Maybe that's why the Timmerman's Motor Inn across the parking lot has struggled over the years. The motor inn has been a separate entity from the supper club since 1994 and has tumbled in and out of bankruptcy. Helen operated the supper club and motor inn until 1985, when it was sold to David and Patti Thiltgen. Hayes and Neuses began working at Timmerman's under the Thiltgen ownership.

The Thiltgens renamed most of the rooms within the supper club. The Sky-Line Room became the 170-seat Palisades Room. The Pilot Room is the upstairs penthouse where Bob and Helen lived.

The Thiltgens sold to Juan Rodriguez in 1998. Rodriguez was born in Piedras Negras, Mexico, just across from El Paso, Texas. His parents, Indalecio and Diamantina, were migrant workers. Every spring they worked the Vass melon farms in central Wisconsin. When Rodriguez was two, his family settled in East Troy, Wisconsin. Rodriguez began his restaurant career at age fifteen by washing dishes at the Alpine Valley ski and rock 'n' roll resort. He moved to Galena in 1975, when he became a chef at the Chestnut Mountain Resort. In 1990 he bought half of the supper clubby Log Cabin restaurant in downtown Galena.

Rodriguez turned the business over to Hayes and Neuses in 2003. But he remained in the kitchen, cutting all the precious meat. "It was an opportunity for us," says Neuses, who majored in marketing at Loras College in Dubuque. "We had worked here, and this was always part of our side gigs. We made very minor changes. We just replaced what is here. We changed the color of the paint a little bit. We added new [dark brown floral] carpets."

The Thiltgen family brought in the burgundy dining room chairs, but the thirty-five burgundy stools around the bar date back to 1961.

Live entertainment used to be a big thing at Timmerman's. Helen liked to have a good time and she built a dance floor with a small stage adjacent to the main dining room. Mid-1960s cement blocks with a floral pattern separate the supper club's entryway from the small ballroom. Robert says, "My mother would cook until about nine thirty, go upstairs and shower and put on a real fashionable dress. After my dad died, hopefully somebody would ask her to dance after supper."

Dubuque piano player Geri Goodman held court with the Timmerman Trio from 1961 until 1985. "We were always told to play twenty minutes and off ten," Goodman said in a 2000 interview while touring the supper club. "The psychology behind that is that people would dance real hard and drink real hard. Helen Timmerman was quite a lady. It was like she was throwing a party every night of the week. That was her whole idea of the supper club scene. She loved being the center of attention. She loved to dance and that music meant so much to her. We played the foxtrot, the waltz; the cha-cha had already made its appearance. But after the Twist and the Frug it became impossible to please everyone."

Current ownership finds live music cost-prohibitive, but they do have DJs on weekends. Mood music is piped into the dining room through vintage ceiling speakers. "We played music from the '50s when I started here and people thought that was cool," Neuses says. "Well, now people go, 'That stuff is old.' I had to move decades so now we play music from the '70s. The dance floor was the key to a supper club in the day. I don't know if that's necessarily the key anymore. Bottled beer was and is. You'd go to the bar before and after dinner. You would make a night of it. Now there's nowhere near as many people doing that because of drinking laws. It changed the tradition of how things work.

"But we do want to turn tables. We figure an hour and a half for a table of two or four and two hours for a table of six or larger. We're a special occasion place with anniversaries and birthdays so a lot of times they're not going to leave. You know that ahead of time. We had a fiftieth birthday party where they got here at six thirty and were here until we closed at eleven thirty."

Helen would have loved the celebrity spin on today's cuisine. With ample cable food channels and magazines it seems that everyone is an expert on food. "It used to be if a steak came out medium, rare, or whatever, they ate it and didn't complain," Gary Neuses complains. "Now a lot of people are critics. If it is not done perfectly, they send it back and expect compensation of some sort. People are just more arrogant these days. That's how society is. It's a different time period. Where it used to be 'sir, ma'am,' now its 'Hey, you, buddy.' A hostess seating you is part of the supper club experience, as is the fact of customers becoming your friends. You know what they're doing and where they're going.

"Old-fashioneds are still one of the top five drinks we still make today. People in their forties are starting to drink old-fashioneds. Obviously the martini thing was a big hit ten years ago."

Between 1984 and 2001 the Chicago Bears trained in nearby Platteville, Wisconsin. Timmerman's would open early to accommodate the team. Neuses says, "I was working here. I remember William ['the Refrigerator']) Perry. They had a prime rib special so they could eat as much as they wanted or as little as they wanted. It was a boost for business, because we not only got the Bears but we got their fans. Mike Ditka was here. They'd eat and be gone before the public got here.

"Another time Nelson [the band comprising the twin sons of pop singer Ricky Nelson] were in town for a concert. It was a bad snowy night and no one was here. They went out and got their guitars and played in the middle of the dining room and played for about twenty-five minutes."

Every regular of a bar or restaurant generally has a favorite place to sit. But the majestic windows at Timmerman's offer lots of options. Neuses says, "But even if they want a window table they will sit with their back to the window so they can see everybody else. It is more of a social atmosphere. I have one lady who wants to sit right in front of the Gazebo [by the entrance] so everyone who walks in can see them. She comes in with her friends around six o'clock every Friday. People literally have to walk by them and stop by and say hi. The only time they call us is if they are not coming. They are getting older so it has been more often than not they call. Before it was virtually every Friday night."

History is an important part of the dramatic landscape at Timmerman's Supper Club.

Mark Hayes and Gary Neuses see it, they hear it, they feel it. They taste it. How do they keep the history alive while also charting their own path?

"For the most part the people keep the history alive," Gary Neuses answers after a thoughtful pause. "They constantly ask who started this. Where the name 'Timmerman' came from. I've learned the history of the restaurant. We kept the name because it was a nobrainer. It was well known. We'd talk to people who would fly in from Arizona for dinner because it brought back a memory of a certain night. Maybe they went to school here and their homecoming dance was up here. Or maybe they met their sweetheart up here."

Or maybe they see their memories in the windows of time.

A passport to adventure.

17

The Mill

4128 Highway 42-57, Sturgeon Bay, Wisconsin
(920) 743-5044 • www.millsupperclub.com

All of the old-time Wisconsin supper clubs have their moments. It took Don Petersilka Jr. a while to learn how to live in one. Don is third-generation co-owner of the Mill Supper Club, at the intersection of Highways 42 and 57 about three miles north of Sturgeon Bay.

Minor and Louise Dagneau opened the Mill in 1930, making it one of the oldest supper clubs in the state.

The Mill has been in the Petersilka family since 1963, when Milton and Marie Petersilka bought it from George and Olga Henkel, who had bought it from George and Sarah Paul in 1950. With those old-fashioned names you know the door has always been open to German settlers in this quaint county of twenty-seven thousand people. Don Senior and Janice Petersilka bought it from Milton and Marie in 1978. The Mill has been operated by Don Junior and his wife, Shelly, since 1991.

Don Junior has a mellow, zen quality. He generally works the bar in the dark brown knotty pine room where people wait for dining room tables. The drink orders come at Don in a furious manner, especially during the summer months when Door County is filled with tourists from Chicago and Milwaukee. Don smiles

The Mill Supper Club opened in 1930 in Sturgeon Bay.

Shelly, Allison, and Don Petersilka—a family affair.

A vintage photo of the Mill.

and pours his old-fashioneds at a measured pace. He has found balance between the old and young.

"My daughter Anna was probably eight years old," Don says a few days after Christmas 2011. "It was Christmastime. We were living upstairs from the supper club. She came downstairs and said, 'Dad, I know both of you probably can't make it, but it would be great if one of you could come to my Christmas program.'"

He pauses and says good night to neighbors walking out the door. A sticker on the door window is from the Door County Chamber of Commerce 1962: "Wisconsin's Air-Conditioned Peninsula Playground."

He continues, "What my daughter said makes you step back and reevaluate how many hours you put in and what your priorities are. That was fourteen years ago. I would have been forty-two. She was in Catholic grade school. It made me think I should spend more time with my kids and hire somebody to do some of my work."

All of Don and Shelly's kids have worked at the Mill: Allison, born in 1984; Don III; and Anna. The women have tended bar and Don III does the fish boil, a Door County staple. None of the children are interested in becoming fourth-generation owners. "I'd sell if the right price came along," Don Junior says. "I'm not that sentimental."

But he is. He has stopped to smell the roses.

Don was born in 1955 and was raised only four miles from the Mill. No one is sure how the Mill got its name, the common conclusion pointing to a four-winged windmill that was originally on the south side of the supper club in the peninsula prairie.

Don only left Sturgeon Bay for the four years he attended the University of Wisconsin at Stout, where he majored in graphics and minored in business. "I started washing dishes here when I was ten years old," he says. "I bussed tables and didn't have to be in the kitchen anymore. I started tending bar at fifteen. I know I couldn't drive yet. I liked the bar." Don's younger sister and brother also worked at the supper club, although they are not involved in the business.

The bar is Don's favorite domain because it is the original piece of the building. It is a link to the past. The bar features sixteen faded red bar stools, and behind the bar there are miniature handcrafted schooners celebrating Sturgeon Bay's shipbuilding history. The pine

James Cordier has handcrafted more than three hundred model boats in Sturgeon Bay. They are for sale at the Mill Supper Club.

and walnut ships were made by James Cordier, a retired Sturgeon Bay cop and Great Lakes sailor who has lived in town his entire life. Cordier was born in 1918.

He began making one ship a week after his 1955 retirement. The Mill sold Cordier's stained ships for up to $300 each. "I've done over three hundred ships," Cordier says in the winter of 2012. "I started with smaller ones and went up to six masts. The largest one is thirty-five inches with a twelve-foot bow." The ships are not replicas. The sails have detailed curves, and there are miniature windows in the hull. Cordier imagined all his ships. He stopped making ships in 2000 when he lost the vision in one eye.

James was married sixty-four years. His wife, Laura, died in 2010. The Cordiers had a fleet of six children. The only places in town where Cordier eats are the downtown Red Room for its burgers and at the Mill for its chicken dinners and coleslaw.

Watch out—Santa's looking for a reindeer at the Mill.

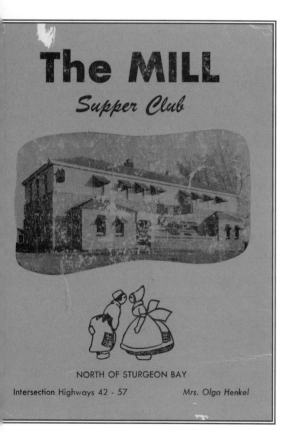

One of the Mill Supper Club's earliest menus.

When the spirit moves him he still visits the Mill with one of his children or his caregiver. He walks into the old bar and sees one of his ships with his good eye. The ship is set against thick cherry pine that is connected through hearty tongue-and-groove joints.

Don says, "In 1983 we refinished the outer walls in the bar. There was a guy who worked at [Palmer] Johnson yards [yacht shipbuilders]. He was a painter, a varnish person. We were gone deer hunting. He came in and rough sanded some of the stuff. He put on another coat of hard clear varnish and we helped him when we got back from deer hunting. That's the only time we did anything with the wood other than wipe it down with a cloth."

The original Mill was only fifty-four by sixty-nine feet with a lobby, a white maple dance floor with sixteen booths, and a "small soft drink parlor," which is today's bar. A menu circa 1940s says "Dance and Dine at the Mill—Where Friends Meet." And "Special Chicken Plate Lunch (at all times) 35 cents." A 1950 menu promotes "Before Dinner Cocktails"—Tom Collins, John Collins, rum collins, all seventy cents. And then "After Dinner Drinks"—pink squirrel and grasshopper, for example, eighty cents.

"I think the Mill was more hard drinks than soft drinks," Don says with a smile.

An empty original pine candy rack hangs behind the bar. Looking at the shelving with a watchful eye, Don says, "It must be built well. People keep knocking into it [in the narrow back bar] and it keeps standing."

Hanging around a supper club all night is a staple of any good supper club. "The maple dance floor is now our dining room," Don says. "The booths were gone when my grandparents came in, but as a kid I remember they had buttons on the wall. You would push a button and a number would drop out of a box. That would tell the staff they wanted service at the booth."

The large rear dining room seats 120 and was added in 1973. Don is unsure when the twenty-six-seat avocado-colored side room was added.

But Don was certain about Shelly Kiehnau. They attended the same church and had some of the same friends. Shelly was the daughter of Reuben Kiehnau, a dairy farmer who had a small plot of land about thirteen miles north of the supper club. Shelly's mother, Doris, tended to a big garden and did all her own cooking and canning. Doris had nine children, including Shelly, who was born and raised on the farm.

"I called to ask her out," Don says. "She thought I was calling to ask her to work here." That's how well Don's commitment to the Mill was known around Sturgeon Bay (population 9,000).

Shelly already had a job. She was a receptionist at the *Door County Advocate* newspaper. She had been to the Mill as a kid for family weddings. "Weddings were big here and at the Scandia Supper Club, which is where the intersection [42 and 57] is now," she says. "Actually we would walk back and forth across the road for weddings."

Don and Shelly were married in 1981.

"That's a long time when you're in this business," Don says in a separate interview.

Shelly makes all the desserts. During the summer she makes eight pies for a weekend: banana cream (one of the most popular), coconut cream, lemon meringue, rhubarb, and others. "A few more during the week," she says. "I make the torts."

Her cherry cheese and drumstick chocolate pudding torts are framed by a graham cracker crust. "I make them year-round, I make whatever I feel like making," she says. "I like to change it up so they're not getting the same dessert all the time. It's quite a few when it's busy."

Don's mother, Janice, mentored Shelly when she became co-owner in 1991. "She basically taught me the whole deal," Shelly says. "She didn't write a whole lot down. She lives in the area and would be here a lot with me. And she learned from her mother-in-law. A lot of it was verbal and repetitive experience."

Three generations of Mill Supper Club owners; left to right: Don Petersilka Jr., Don Petersilka Sr., and Milton Petersilka, who started the ball rolling in 1963.

Third-generation owners are tough in any business, but Don thinks it was harder for Shelly to work at the Mill than it was for Don to try to keep the tradition alive in the long shadows of two generations. "It was tougher for me," Shelly says. "I liked my job. I had been there almost fifteen years. Then I quit. It was a big adjustment in terms of hours. You're working days, back working at night. It's very hard to raise a family that way. You get used to that. But there were guilt trips."

Shelly says that she and Don divided responsibilities pretty much the way Don Senior and Janice did. Don handles the bar, the front of the room, and the business. Shelly is in charge of the kitchen, although she is not head chef. "We never changed the dynamic, although Don helps me out in the kitchen," she says.

While standing behind the bar Don concurs. "I think I help my wife in the kitchen more than my dad did with my mom," he says. "That was another generation. Guys wouldn't go in the kitchen and did the other stuff. We help each other. If I'm gone, she picks it up for me and if she's gone I do as much in the kitchen as I know how. I don't know how to make desserts but I can do a fair amount of other things."

The Mill has consistently been one of the most acclaimed supper clubs in Door County.

"We used to have a sign outside that said MILL SUPPER CLUB, but the food company told us we had to get a little more up to date," Don says. "Still, all our literature and menus say 'supper club.' We're always known as a supper club."

In a separate conversation Don's daughter, bartender Allison, adds, "A supper club has a full bar, which is separate from the dining area. Usually steak, seafood, chicken. Supper clubs are all older and have been in families for a while."

The Mill meets the supper club requirements of a Friday night fish fry, Saturday night prime rib, and the Door County legacy of a Sunday night chicken dinner.

"The Mill is famous for the chicken dinner [no white meat orders]," Allison says. "It's my great-grandmother's recipe. It pretty much falls off the bone."

Her mother adds, "It is roasted in the oven, not deep-fried or pressure-cooked. It's roasted like my mother would have done." Roasting a chicken brings out additional flavor. And if a couple of economically bought birds are roasted on a Sunday, the chicken can be used throughout the week. Shelly says, "It is served with homemade dressing, not boxed. Honest to God. Janice and Verna [De Meuse] made the dressing and Verna is eighty-nine. She only quit two years ago and still made the dressing."

The chicken is also served with potatoes, gravy, cranberries, and rolls.

Janice Petersilka was born in 1930, the same year the Mill opened. She says the Mill launched the chicken dinner tradition in Door County. "The previous owners started the chicken dinner in 1950," says Janice, who was born and raised in a farm family about a mile from the Mill. "The recipe has never changed. One night I was hostessing for Shelly. A fellow paid his bill and said, 'My God, this chicken and dressing tastes just like it did thirty-five years ago.' I said, 'Well, it really is the same.'

All the dressing is [made of is] salt, pepper, sage, dry day-old bread. We use chicken fat. Now don't go telling this to anybody.

"When we were there the chicken came from the Bay Food Butcher Shop right in Sturgeon Bay. My husband's dad and mother wanted to add another night so they thought Sunday night chicken dinners would be a good idea. And it really took off. But it was a lot of work. We made all the dressing and roasted the chicken. On a good night we sold more than 250 dinners. Then we started it on a Wednesday night and that took off real good too."

The traditional Door County fish boil is held at six PM Tuesday and Thursday from mid-June through mid-October at the Mill. Locally sourced whitefish is served with red potatoes, carrots, onions, homemade coleslaw, rye bread, and Shelly's classic cherry pie.

The whitefish almost always arrives the morning of supper from the Weborg Brothers Fishery in Gills Rock, Wisconsin, at the tip of the peninsula. Caught in Lake Michigan, the whitefish is served broiled, which creates a mild taste, or deep-fried.

"One time I drove up there and the fish weren't ready," Don recalls. "I was talking to Jeff, one of the brothers. A guy came down the hill by their fish house. He's driving a 1949 Chevy pickup. He's beeping the horn. I thought, 'What are you beeping the horn for? Are they supposed to jump out and wait on you?' So Jeff goes in the fish house and fills up three plastic bags with whitefish filets. He came out and handed it to the guy. The guy never got out of his truck. And down the road he went."

Don asked Jeff who the hell this guy was.

"Jeff says, 'It was Pastor Anderson. He delivers fish once a week to shut-ins and people who can't get around.' I thought to myself, 'That's a small-town story.'"

The Mill offers seven fish options. "The perch is fresh, we get that from Sysco Foods," Don says. "They used to fish them in the bay, but the population fluctuates. They took away so much of the quota hardly anyone fishes perch anymore. We have baked cod. Walleye (lightly breaded), pan-fried and deep-fried. All-you-can-eat redfish. Plus the regular menu."

Of course, the fried Wisconsin white cheddar cheese curds are the most popular appetizer, followed by the house-made spinach and artichoke dip served with warm pita chips. "We always have a fresh vegetable," Shelly says. "Whatever is in season. Squash in the winter. Things people normally don't have. I like to be a little different, I guess."

Shelly's brother Kevin took over the Kiehnau family farm and stepped out into organic farming. "It was a great idea," she says. "He eventually sold off his cattle and is working for Organic Valley [in La Farge, Wisconsin, west of Madison]. He helps farmers get started and helps people who want to convert into organic farming. But small farms in this area have had a hard time making a go of it."

Shelly does not buy organics for the Mill. "It's very pricey," she says. "I don't want to pass it on to our customer. I want it to be affordable for people to come here to eat. I use organics at home. I believe in it."

She also believes in getting rid of the china that predates her arrival on the scene. "I'm sure Don's grandparents had that china," Shelly says. No one knows how far back the china goes, and staff debates on how to explain the pattern on the china. "Everybody loves that pattern," she says. "Apple or cherry blossoms? We never came up with an answer. It needs to be updated. I gotta make the move."

Don says, "I think it's either apple blossoms or dogwood." Janice says, "I think it's dogwood. It was there when we bought the place and the Henkels had it. You can't buy it anymore. When we left the supper club [in 1991] it was eleven dollars for one gravy boat, eleven dollars for a platter. You didn't want to see those get broken. It may go back to the 1950s."

The Mill has a "locavore" legacy, even though Sysco is now the supper club's major supplier. A 1940s-era menu offers a steak and chicken dinner meal for a dollar, washed down with a bottle of Rahr All-Star beer for fifteen cents. The menu promotes the Sheboygan Liquor Co. for wines and liquors, "finest qualities meats" at Hopp's Meat Market, and bakery products made by the Sturgeon Bay Bakery.

During the mid-twentieth-century shipbuilding heyday of Sturgeon Bay, local farmers supplemented their income by working winter months in the shipbuilding yards. "Imagine working that hard," Shelly says. "This is an area of hard workers."

Don was one of them. His great-great-grandparents were first generation in Door County. Don's grandfather came from a legacy of farming and cherry orchards

One of the best supper club rules ever.

before buying the Mill. With a laugh his mother, Janice, says, "We came right off the farm into the supper club. A lot of supper clubs were started by farm families. I was the youngest of nine children."

Don says, "When I was a kid everybody had an orchard. We picked cherries to make money to buy school clothes. My grandparents told me I was German and Bohemian. My mother was English."

In 1945 German prisoners of war picked 508,020 pails of cherries in Door County, according to the Door County Historical Museum. They lived on assorted orchards and the county fairgrounds. Don's father hauled cherries with the POWs but they never made it to the supper club as they were constantly under guard.

Minor Dagneau owned the National Hotel in downtown Sturgeon Bay near the present-day Bank of Sturgeon Bay drive-through. The hotel had been built around 1900 by John Leathem to house sawmill workers, according to Ginny Haen, assistant curator of the Door County Historical Museum. Leathem was an early Sturgeon Bay settler who came to town in the mid-1870s as a lumber manufacturer and general merchandise dealer.

"People are still shopping for that good deal," Don maintains. "Our costs have been going up. We have to price our menu accordingly. They can eat that family-style chicken meal here for eleven fifty. That's not a bad deal. Yeah, there was lots of tourism this summer, but they were still looking for a value. That also means you don't make the money you probably should for the hours that you put in."

The Mill offers a genuine and well-paced dining experience.

"You try to care more," he says. "That's a supper club thing. My dad always said, 'It cost nothing to say hi, good-bye, thank you, please.' And it will get you a lot. Sometimes people are genuinely surprised if you come and talk to them when they're sitting at the bar. Being nice will go a long way."

18

Kavanaugh's Esquire Club

1025 North Sherman Avenue, Madison, Wisconsin
(608) 249-0193 • www.esquireclubmadison.com

The greatest characteristic of Kavanaugh's Esquire Club is its complete lack of pretension. Madison's oldest supper club opened in 1947. It sits on the city's north side next to the upscale village of Maple Bluff like a fork to a silver spoon.

The governor's mansion is in Maple Bluff (population 1,500) and the community is the site of the Oscar Mayer Jr. estate as well as the birthplace of flashy Go-Go's guitarist Jane Wiedlin.

The Esquire Club has a plain white shoebox-like exterior facing a gravel parking lot. There are no neon beer signs in the windows or retro red shutters. The supper club could easily be missed driving along Sherman Avenue if it weren't for the sign of a steer-mermaid figurine hoisting a martini.

That's wild in a Jules Verne-on-mushrooms way. And that's classic Wisconsin supper club stuff: fish fry on Friday, prime rib on Saturday.

Some supper clubs have struggled to stay afloat in the early twenty-first century. Second-generation owner John Kavanaugh, born in 1949, is poised to hand off the operation to his son John Junior (born in 1972), and daughter Jackie (born in 1970). He has two other children who are not in the business.

(inset) Arguably the most unique supper club sign in America.
The Esquire exterior—original box retailer.

"This is all I know," Kavanaugh says in the supper club's dark pine Back Room before a Friday night fish fry. "They've brought back the 'supper club' term in the last couple years, but it has changed so much. We've kept the tradition of supper club menu items like hand-breaded shrimp, walleyed pike, steaks, homemade salad dressings, homemade soups. We do all that.

"I don't know how to make fat-free salad dressing very well. But we make our bleu cheese, our French dressing, our Thousand Island on-site. We make our own cheese dip, which was a traditional thing you got in a supper club with a lazy Susan. We do the salad bar on Saturday night that has the relishes. We hand make our own onion rings. All our dinners include the choice of baked potato, hash browns, American fries."

Kavanaugh is not looking at a menu; he knows this place by heart. It is all he has known. His father, John "Jack" Kavanaugh, and his mother, Jane, bought the club in 1947. The fifty-by-fifty-foot Esquire Club was four years old. John Junior was two years old. "This was out in the country then," he says. "The supper club thing evolved. The guy who originally built this place sold it and went over on East Washington Avenue and built another place called Ace of Clubs. It burned down. The Oscar Mayer meat plant [now Kraft] is right across our field. Our first dining room sat about thirty people."

Oscar Mayer became a kindred spirit to the Esquire Club. In 1919 Oscar Mayer expanded from Chicago to Madison. The plant opened its home office in Madison and remained under Oscar Mayer hands until 1988 when it was bought out by Kraft Foods. A portion of the Oscar Mayer Weinermobile fleet is still based in Madison. Jim Kinney, the husband of an Esquire Club waitress, used to be in charge of the Oscar Mayer transportation department. US representative and 2012 Republican vice-presidential nominee Paul Ryan drove the Weinermobile once during a summer job.

Beef and hog kills were done at the plant. During its heyday the Oscar Mayer plant employed between forty-five hundred and five thousand office and plant people. At four o'clock every Friday many of them would walk across the field to the Esquire Club.

"When Oscar Mayer was going strong, at four o'clock Friday, boom, the bar was two deep," Kavanaugh recalls. "And it was two deep until six o'clock. Maybe their wives would come in with the family and they would have the fish fry. And now the younger worker doesn't do that as much."

The younger worker does have fancier tastes in beer. "Craft beers are more popular now," Kavanaugh says. "When I was growing up you had the beer you drank and you drank it all the time. You might drink a Potosi at home but they would drink Budweiser, Miller, or Schlitz, or whatever was popular at the time when they went out because they didn't want to look like a hick. Now young people come in and say they feel like a Supper Club [beer] or a Guinness. There's not a lot of loyalty to their brand. A keg of craft beer is $160. It wasn't that long ago you were paying $50 for a keg of Miller.

"But young people are willing to pay the price for a craft beer or even a craft vodka. Back in the old days there were Oscar Mayer people who boycotted the bar at the bowling alley when the guy raised his price a nickel. They were captured in there for thirty-two weeks of bowling and of course the drinks were served in a thimble, and he raised it from twenty-five cents to thirty cents. They were upset."

Supper club patriarch John "Jack" Kavanaugh, back in the day and night.

The Esquire Club's interior is still dimly lit at four in the afternoon, and about half the dining room chairs remain from the 1960s. A black and white picture from the 1950s depicts Kavanaugh's father making a whiskey and water.

A new dining room features new furniture. The Wisconsin supper club tradition of the old-fashioned cocktail is still in vogue at the Esquire Club, although not as many drinks are sold as in years past.

"When I was pretty young we used to buy sweet and dry vermouth in fifteen-case lots," Kavanaugh recalls. "Now we buy it in a single-case lot. Martinis, Manhattans, and old-fashioneds were the drinks of the day. Now wine by the glass is

Looking out is better than looking in at the Esquire.

so much more popular. It is the drink of choice now, where it wasn't before."

Like every good supper club, the personality of the owner is reflected in the daily operation. The staff is friendly and businesslike. There is respect for tradition. Kavanaugh was director of the National Restaurant Association (NRA) between 2002 and 2011, and in 1987 he was president of the Wisconsin Restaurant Association (WRA). As he hands the supper club off to his children he is aware of the historic challenges of third-generation ownership.

"The old story is that 50 percent of the second go out," Kavanaugh says as he peers out a cloudy window. "And 80 percent of the third go out. There's a family succession group at the university [of Wisconsin], and they have a group that meets here and they talk about family planning. I asked them about this and they said unless your kids are working to get your ass out of there, they're not ready for it. It shouldn't be how I give it to them. It should be how they take it. I thought that was good advice. That is a huge deal. If you're a farmer or a restaurant guy, unless you have it in your blood, you really truly cannot do it. Because it is not a part-time job."

Kavanaugh knows full-time style as well as he knows Wisconsin supper clubs. "We use linen napkins and linen tablecloths at almost every lunch and dinner," Kavanaugh says, with a color portrait of his parents hanging over his shoulder in the supper club's Back Room. "We don't use them on our fish fry. With the state of the economy a lot of places are getting away from linen napkins."

Kavanaugh did make one dramatic change with the signage. He was almost too humble to add the family name to the long-standing Esquire Club. He reasons, "When people are traveling and they see Esquire Club, it could be an Elks Club, a Moose Club, or a gentleman's club or a private club. We wanted to show it was a family-owned place."

Change has come slowly around the Esquire Club. The present-day square bar that seats thirty-six was reconfigured in 1966. An upstairs and downstairs dining room was added in 1972. Another front dining room was built on in 1990 to attain the current capacity of three hundred supper clubbers. A new three-thousand-square-foot kitchen was installed in 2009.

Anybody is everybody at the Esquire Club—and that's what locals still call it.

"Our clientele is all over the board," Kavanaugh says. "Young families, high-end customers. The Little League meets here. Fergie Jenkins has been here for lunch, but I've never been a Cubs fan. Fishing groups. Sometimes I have the Republican caucus and the Democratic caucus meeting at the same time." The Yelp critics have suggested the Esquire is a favorite meeting place for Tea Partiers. Wisconsin is the birthplace of the Republican Party.

There is great debate around Madison as to how a supper club is truly defined. Kavanaugh does not think the popular Old Fashioned in downtown Madison is a supper club. It does not have a scenic view, unless you love looking at the state capitol building, and it does not have linen napkins. Smoky's Club has been around forever, but the majority of Mad City regulars call it a steak house as opposed to a supper club.

"Here, people look at supper clubs as more of a northern Wisconsin thing than a city thing," Kavanaugh explains. "And again, what's a steak house? We use certified Angus beef, which is top 80 percent of quality, and we have some steaks on our menu that are of the top 1 percent of that. A steak house will have a porterhouse and a rib eye. Sirloins are traditional supper club steaks but they're losing their popularity. A sirloin is a nice tasty steak, but they've been bastardized by a lot of the corporate stores. They tenderize it, needle it, and do this and that and people don't know what to expect from a sirloin like they used to.

"The other part is the price of the sirloin got expensive. In mid-2009 sirloin sold for twelve dollars a pound wholesale. It was no longer a value steak. In mid-2011 for high-end steaks we're paying close to thirty dollars a pound. I wanted them available so nobody in the city has a better steak than we have if somebody wants to order it. Back in the '70s we'd sell a couple hundred sirloins on a Saturday night. That business is gone."

Doug Griffin is an exhibit and graphic designer for the Wisconsin Historical Museum. Born in 1975, Griffin grew up in the supper club circuit of his native Green Bay, Wisconsin. "When my parents come to visit or my friends' parents come to visit, the Esquire is a great one to take them to," Griffin says over lunch at the Old Fashioned. "Because you're talking about folks in their seventies from the Green Bay area. You can take them to a sushi place in Madison. Or an African restaurant. Or you can play it safe and take them to the Esquire and they will be really happy. It does have a Republican following. It is a bit different than a lot of places."

For example, the Esquire is known for its battered chicken. Kavanaugh says, "We cooked the chicken from scratch. As I grew up, the batter was better to eat than the chicken. We had a six-ounce tenderloin that came with a choice of French fries or a salad. It was a smaller meal and over the years, apart from the fish fry, probably one of the most popular meals on our menu."

The Esquire fish fry is a rarity around Madison in that the supper club features ocean perch. "Up in the valley of Appleton and Green Bay they always use lake perch," Kavanaugh explains, adding that the Green Bay area sources from area lakes. "They did family style. A [Friday] night like tonight, we might sell four hundred to five hundred pounds of ocean perch and fifty pounds of lake perch. In Madison there's not many places selling ocean perch but that's been our traditional family style. The lake perch is from the pike family, so it's a little sweeter. Ocean perch can be a little more fishy. They do a much better job with ocean perch than they did years ago."

During the 1960s the Esquire Club meat was cut by local butcher Don O'Dair. "He would call us at nine in the morning and deliver by eleven," Kavanaugh says. "Then he would call us at one o'clock and deliver in the late afternoon. Monday through Friday. Now you're paying cash charges, they want you to order once a week. Being in Madison you get spoiled. If you're in the Dells or in a small community you probably have never experienced that personal treat. You get spoiled."

The volume of fast-food restaurants in the 1970s and '80s also influenced older supper clubs like Kavanaugh's. "I'm finishing up nine years of service as a director on the National Restaurant Board," Kavanaugh says. "One of the committees I served on years ago was where people would say what was happening in their neighborhood. And on this board is everybody from independents to McDonald's. With the economy the way it is, people have downsized themselves. An Applebee's guy was concerned about losing his customer to a Culver's. And a Culver's guy might go to McDonald's—where we would consider someone not coming here is at lunch, if they don't have the time and want instant gratification. Today, with the economy, lunch is probably the part of business that's down the most.

"We have customers we see every Friday but we don't see them on Saturday or Monday. In a supper club, you know your customers, you really do."

Kavanaugh likes to call the Esquire a neighborhood place, and he likes to tell this story: "The weather was terrible on one New Year's Eve," he says. "Somebody asked someone else what they were doing for New Year's. They said, 'Naw, we're not going to do anything. We're just going down to the Esquire and eat.' They didn't necessarily consider that going out, you know what I mean?"

Of course.

The Esquire is a true Wisconsin supper club, 365 days a year.

19

The Lighthouse Inn Supper Club

6905 Mount Vernon Road SE, Cedar Rapids, Iowa

(319) 362-3467 • www.crlighthouseinn.com

A lighthouse in the middle of Iowa—it would be like corn growing in the Great Lakes.

But there is a twenty-eight-foot tall lighthouse with white vinyl siding and a lighted lantern room along sleepy Mount Vernon Road, about seven miles east of downtown Cedar Rapids. It is the signal for the Lighthouse Inn, a still-rural supper club that dates back to 1912.

Mount Vernon Road is part of the old Highway 30 (Lincoln Highway). Tourist cabins that were popular along the highway were built adjacent to the Lighthouse Inn. The cabin scenes from the 1934 Clark Gable and Claudette Colbert comedy *It Happened One Night* were filmed at the Lighthouse. Colbert played an heiress who met an out-of-work newspaper reporter on a bus ride through the heartland.

Some things never change.

Al Capone crashed at the Lighthouse to stay out of the shadows of big-city Chicago. John Dillinger hung around the Lighthouse because he had family in Cedar Rapids. Local history buffs ask for a seat to the left of the Seabreeze Lounge entrance at the Lighthouse Inn. That's where Dillinger laid his gun on the table.

Al Capone found refuge in the shadows of the Lighthouse Supper Club.

The Lighthouse Supper Club dates back to 1912.

The gun went off and left a hole in the wall. The hole was patched up in a 1988 remodeling project.

Stories like this fly around the supper club, but no one knows why in the world the place was ever named the Lighthouse.

There are hints. On any given Friday night the Dick Watson Combo ("Music for All Occasions") could be serving up Bobby Darin's lounge classic "Beyond the Sea" in the Seabreeze Lounge. The bar was added to the supper club in 1943 and is filled with nautical knickknacks and paintings imported from south Florida.

The lounge was built with native oak. The wood was not cured since the addition was made during the war. "It kept up nice, but we've put a lot of work into it," Lighthouse co-owner Theron Manson says. "It would have been easier to bulldoze it and remodel it, which I wanted to do in 1986. But there was public uproar. One old guy grabbed me by the arm and shook me and said, 'Who do you think you are to tear down the Lighthouse?'"

Live music used to be a staple of Midwest supper clubs. Not so much anymore. Live music is costly no matter the venue, and it is even more expensive out in the country. The Lighthouse Inn does not make money from having the Dick Watson Combo in the lounge, but the band is there because the customers like it. And the customers always come back.

"We have people come from as far away as Daven-port for dinner and dancing," Manson says. "We're off the beaten path so I have to do something to get people out here. We don't charge a cover. Northeast Iowa is blessed with a lot of good musicians. We have a history of jazz musicians coming to the Lighthouse. Ray Blue [from the Cotton Club in New York] has a son who goes to Iowa and when he is in town to visit his son he'll sit in."

The historic back bar in the Seabreeze Lounge of the Lighthouse.

The Watson songbook recalls the merry and moody twinkle of Jackie Gleason LPs that have crash-landed in Goodwill stores across America. *Music Martinis and Memories* (1954), *Music for the Love Hours* (1957), *Champagne, Candlelight and Kisses* (1963). Gleason actually recorded forty-one of these lush, themed records between 1953 and 1971.

"We do the standards here and people connect with that," Watson says during a break. He was born in 1940 in Indianola, Iowa, near Des Moines. "There's not many groups around doing standards. Somebody has to do it, so here we are. It goes with the supper club. When I think of a supper club I think of a place that has linen on the table and good service and nice folks taking care of you. That's what we have here."

The Dick Watson Combo will tell you it don't mean a thing if it ain't got that swing at the Lighthouse.

The Dick Watson Combo takes requests. On a busy autumn night in 2011 they were playing Roger Miller's "King of the Road" for the first time. Watson was stumbling through the words from behind his piano. Israel Newman was on bass. He lived in nearby Iowa City, working on a PhD in music and computer science at the University of Iowa. Sax player Larry Fountain was sitting in. And loyal drummer Craig Woods has been with Watson for forty years. "That's unusual for a drummer," Watson quips.

The Dick Watson Combo takes many requests, because, after all, they play "music for all occasions." Manson remembers his favorite request: "A lady was here dancing with a gentleman. They left and she called back and said, 'By the way, I left my dress in the restroom. Would you send it home with Dick?' Dick, do you remember that?"

Watson smiles softly and says, "I think it was shoes."

Manson continues, "It was wintertime, I think she had a coat."

But Dick Watson is happily married. He has been gigging at the Lighthouse since 1996. "We also play with a good trumpet player from the Quad Cities [about an hour east of Cedar Rapids]," he says. "That's a rich musical area. I go over there and play with them and they come here. Different areas accent different styles. If you go back and forth between places you can pick up extra things you might not pick up otherwise." Legendary jazz cornetist Bix Beiderbecke was from Davenport, Iowa, one of the Quad Cities. He played with a pure jazz ballad style that predated supper clubs. One of his best-known numbers was "In a Mist," which crooner Bing Crosby acknowledged as an influence.

Atop Watson's black piano there are free cassettes of Dick Watson music. Compact discs are $10. Like Jackie Gleason, the road goes on forever: *Live at the Lighthouse*, *Live at the Lighthouse 2*, and *Live at the Lighthouse 3*.

"The first one there's some single solos and the rest are trios," says Watson, who lives in Iowa City. "The second one the drummer likes the best because they miked him up better and his son sings on it. And there's a trombone player. The third one, I might like it the best because my daughter sings on about five tracks. We do trio on the rest."

Eve Adamson is the singer on *Live at the Lighthouse 3*. By day, she is a *New York Times* bestselling author who cowrote *The Real Housewives of New York City*, star Bethenny Frankel's *Naturally Thin* and *The Skinnygirl Dish*, and other titles. Adamson's resume also includes *Beer: Domestic, Imported and Home Brewed*, *The Complete Idiot's Guide to Being a Sex Goddess*, and *The Complete Idiot's Guide to Zen Living*.

"She could live anywhere, but she lives in Iowa City," Watson says. "She has a novel in her head but she can't afford to do that. She makes her living with these books and she supports her family this way."

Certainly there is a book in the novel idea of a Seabreeze Lounge in the Lighthouse Inn in the middle of Iowa. Even famed *Peanuts* cartoonist Charles Schulz doodled and signed a cartoon of Charlie Brown exclaiming "Good Grief!" on a bar napkin, but no one knows when Schulz visited the tiny tropical-themed bar.

Like a distant sandbar at sunset, Barbara Ross was sitting alone in a corner of the lounge in the fall of 2011. She was easy to see because of the way her eyes connected with the music. She has heard the supper club music just about every Friday night since 1989.

Music and supper club fan Barbara Ross.

Ross was born in 1930 in Sabula, Iowa, on the Mississippi River. "It is the only island city in the state," she says as the Dick Watson Combo plays the 1902 hit "(Won't You Come Home) Bill Bailey." Ross's mother, Bernita Durham, was a schoolteacher and her father, Maynard Durham, worked on the Milwaukee railroad.

"This is very rare to have a supper club with music, a dance floor, and ambience," Ross points out. "I've known about this all my life, but I'll tell you, when I was college age, the Lighthouse was a roadhouse. Nice girls didn't come here."

Manson once met John Dillinger's niece at a Cedar Rapids grocery store. "She said, 'My mother always told me that if anybody asked, we were not related.' I said, 'Do you ever come to the Lighthouse?' She said, 'No, nice girls don't go to the Lighthouse.' That's always been the standing joke."

Ross has experienced stand-up class. At age nineteen, during the mid-1950s, she was a restaurant cashier at the Drake Hotel along Michigan Avenue in Chicago. Ross is a refined, diminutive woman. The idea of her peddling cigars is as colorfully incongruous as a lighthouse in a cornfield. "I had a ball," she says. "I was going to college and needed a job. I also worked for Hickey Brothers Cigar Company [founded in 1901 in Davenport, Iowa]."

She bows her head and whispers, "They had stands in hotels where they sold cigarettes, cigars, and newspapers. One stand was in the Drake Hotel and I worked one summer doing that."

Ross spent most of her life as a schoolteacher in Maquoketa, Iowa. Her husband, Donald, was a mechanical engineer who found work in Cedar Rapids. "About 1989 we decided to make a night out of it," she says. "We decided young people go out on Saturday night. We can come out on Friday night. We would eat here and then come to the lounge. The Lighthouse is known for their ribs, which smell so good, but I love their baby cod."

Barbara and Donald Ross danced to the Dick Watson Combo. They were married thirty-nine years. He died in 2006. "Even after my husband died, I hear a little voice that says, 'Friday night, let's go to the Lighthouse.'"

In the big world of Dick Watson Combo requests, which song does Ross ask for? She pauses for a very long time. Her eyes become watery. She answers, "I'll Be Seeing You."

When Theron Manson was six years old his father, Morris, died in a tractor accident on the family farm in northeast Iowa. Manson was raised by his stepfather, Darrell Dake, a well-known stock car driver in the Midwest. Dake raced in 1960 and 1961 at the Daytona 500. He died of cancer in August 2007.

"He raced mainly dirt tracks and then some hard surface," Manson says. "He usually drove Fords; in the 1950s he drove Chevys." Dake was racing while Manson has stayed put around Cedar Rapids his entire life except for a stint in the service.

Manson was born in 1948 and worked at the Lighthouse as a teenager. He was dutifully employed by the colorful Harold "Woody" Woodford. "I bussed tables in the 1960s," he says. "I did the relish tray; four of the pickled herring, four of the stuffed celery. The relish tray stopped in '78 or '79. Younger people weren't interested in it.

"The living quarters were where part of the kitchen is now. There was a stone fireplace back there and it had a little living room with one bath."

Woody and his wife, Vi, lived at the Lighthouse.

"About eight o clock or so one night, Woody had too many," Manson says. "A lady complained her steak wasn't rare enough so Woody went out and picked the steak up off the table. He had a chef's knife in his hand. He cut it . . ." and Manson goes into dramatic samurai action and continues, "Woody squeezed blood all over the plate, then said, 'I don't know how rare you can get it.' My wife was in here eating when that happened. They just got up and left. He drank Pinch scotch. He was a nice guy but had a hot temper."

While Woody and Vi lived in the supper club, Woody's mother, Rose, lived in one of the old cabins. "She would sit it in the corner booth and come out and fold napkins and polish silverware," Manson says. "Toward her later years we would run food down to her cabin. We still have the linen napkins. It's expensive, but I insist on it. We used to have linen tablecloths. We used to have placemats. But I still have the linen napkins. It's tradition. If you're going to have a good meal, you have to have good coffee and good linen."

The Lighthouse is so upscale that the six dark brown curved Naugahyde booths were rescued from the Broiler Club atop the Sears Tower in Chicago. Manson bought them at a 1994 auction. The supper club's other booths are original, although they have been covered several times. The tables date back to the early 1950s. "If you look underneath they are grey Formica," he says. "I flipped them and put wood-grain Formica on top just to update it."

Woody and Vi were the supper club owners from 1953 until Josie and her first husband, Daryl, bought it in 1978. Daryl died in 1984, and Manson became co-owner with his wife in 1986. She operates the Chateau Salon, a beauty shop behind the supper club, where the cabins used to stand. Manson tore the last cabin down in 1980.

A pair of club chairs is always reserved for Theron and Josie in the Seabreeze Lounge. The bartender places a glass of ice water with a straw for each of the owners and the chairs point "gunfighter style," in Theron's words, to a door into the supper club.

"If you start at the beginning here you start at the Civil War," Manson says. "That's when the land was deeded out to John J. Daniels, a veteran of the Civil War. Andrew Johnson was the president at the time. Charles E. Wood and his wife, Daisy, had the restaurant in 1937, that would have been when Dillinger and Capone were here.

"Cedar Rapids police would follow the rules and not come out here. It was outside of city limits. Capone knew he would be perfectly safe. They could stay in the

Theron Manson co-owns the Lighthouse with his wife, Josie. She runs a beauty shop behind the supper club.

cabins for a week at a time. The supper club was a bootleg operation so whatever they needed they got—food, booze. One time Capone was here and left in a hurry. We don't know what the circumstances were, but he left a car here. Eventually the Cedar Rapids police department came out and towed it away. In the trunk was a Thompson submachine gun. The Cedar Rapids police department still has it."

Iowa City, about twenty miles south of the Lighthouse, was the state capital when Iowa was admitted to the Union. Manson says, "If you wanted to go from Cedar Rapids to Iowa City, this was the only way to go. It was a dirt road. It was mud. So this was the stop, a place to eat. They had the cabins out back. Travelers would travel until it got dark. Cars weren't so good with headlights. They'd drive until dark, have dinner, rent a cabin overnight, get up early the next morning, and hit the road again. That's how supper clubs started. They would avoid the city hotel tax and they would get a head start on traffic."

The Lighthouse has a long history with the Lincoln Highway. The highway was conceived in 1912, the same year as the Lighthouse, and mapped out a year later. It connected Times Square in New York City with the Pacific Ocean at San Francisco's Lincoln Park.

It was America's first coast-to-coast highway and most of it was dirt road.

"My wife had a customer who remembered the highway's premise of a paved road," Manson says. "When they got to Iowa the law was such that the farmer had to pay for any highway improvements that adjoined his land. The farmer could care less if they had pavement or not. So to get it done, they did what they called the Heritage Mile, which is between here and Mount Vernon [ten miles] down the road. It is a mile of paved road. Dirt road, a mile of paved road, dirt road again.

"Her dad had a Model T with the high wheels. They got stuck in the mud right in front of the Lighthouse, around 1916, 1918. The neighboring farmer got his horses out and pulled him out. She remembered that as a little girl. She's gone now but she related that story to us."

In the summer of 2012, Manson purchased an original copper Lincoln Highway road marker that had sat untouched for fifty years in an Iowa barn. He installed it in the supper club. He didn't want to put it in front of the Lighthouse—in the likely event it would be stolen.

After the stock market crash, the husband and wife team of Edwin and Wilton McCoy received the Lighthouse from the bank. Viola "Vi" and Virgil Rhodes bought it in 1940 and ran it until 1953, when Virgil was killed with other Cedar Rapids businessmen on a private airplane crash returning from a fishing trip in Minnesota. Vi then married the colorful "Woody" Woodford.

Ron Ameche, the son of Academy Award–winning actor Don Ameche (*Cocoon*, *Trading Places*) was next in line. A native of Kenosha, Wisconsin, Don Ameche and his wife, Honore, preferred their children to be raised in the Midwest as opposed to California. The Ameches also had a home in Dubuque, Iowa.

"After Vi died, Woody married one of the waitresses and moved to a cabin by the Mississippi River," Manson says. "He wanted to sell this. Ron Ameche leased it for a year in 1967–68 with an option to buy. Ron came in, tore the kitchen apart, microwaved it, did the fancy stuff with tapas—you can imagine how well that went over here. He was only here a year and that was when my wife and her first husband bought it." The late Ron Ameche also owned and operated Ameche's Pumpernickel in Coralville, Iowa.

Although Manson worked at the Lighthouse as a teenager, he never thought he would return to work at the supper club as an adult. "I didn't even think I'd be in the restaurant business," he says. "I sold wine. We semiretired in 1988 and tried to sell this place. We built a house in Fort Lauderdale, Florida."

He worked for a Florida auto dealership. He sold a beautifully restored black and white 1955 Chevy Del Ray to drag racing legend Don "Big Daddy" Garlits. The car is now in the Don Garlits Museum of Drag Racing in Ocala, Florida, with a plaque honoring Manson.

But Theron and Josie have now settled in to keep the supper club tradition alive. "We used to serve old-fashioneds every day," Manson says. "Then they went out. Now they're back. Almost everything old is new again. Martinis, the same way. We had a young lady come in and order a martini. She sent it back. I check the tables every night I am here, which is most of the time. When we have a complaint at the table we instruct the server to remove the offending item, whatever it is, and come get me. I want to know right away. We want to make them happy while they are still here. So I asked the young lady about the problem."

Manson leans over and whispers, in her voice, "It's way too strong." He then reassumes his deep supper club voice and says, "I proceeded to explain to her a martini is all booze, a little bit of vermouth. I had no way of weakening it outside of watering it down. She obviously didn't know what a martini was, so we ended up cutting her a sweeter, softer drink."

The Lighthouse has served prime rib on Friday and Saturday, and fish every night as far back as day one (1912). "Business is great," Manson says. "Our older clientele is dying off, as are supper club operators. But when you have the few instances, somebody is going to carry on and insist on certain things, the younger generation is nostalgic for that. We have lots of people who come because their grandma brought them here when they were little kids. And they all like it. And they like the food and the service. But now, people don't eat as late as they used to. We're open until eleven and I'm thinking of shortening my hours 'til ten."

The Lighthouse uses legacy recipes from the past, but they were not handed down. Manson protects them like a guard at a bank. "We had to pay for them," Manson says. "We have a specialty that is unique to the Lighthouse, which is garlic cabbage or garlic slaw. You have to like garlic or you're not going to like it. Because it is a cooked sauce, we cool it, shred the cabbage in it, and serve it with croutons." Guests can order garlic basil bread to go with the slaw.

Barbecued ribs are another Lighthouse special. "We make our own secret sauce, which is sweet and tangy," Manson says. "We cook the ribs for two days and the sauce is added as you order. The dressing recipes are a combination of hand-me-down from the original business with my wife's fresh homemade [without preservatives] French dressing recipe."

There is a tempered ambience at the Lighthouse. It is no place for people in a hurry. The cadence is more like a sea breeze. Like the best supper clubs, entrees are not cooked ahead of time. They are cooked to order.

"We're not Burger King," Manson says. "You passed that on the way out here. Broasted chicken takes twenty, twenty-five minutes depending on the size of the chicken breast. We make our own dressings. We bake our own bread. We try to source from people around here. There's a hobby farm on the new Highway 30 toward Mount Vernon and they have a wild selection of lettuce. We do a lot of business in summertime with specialty salads, topping them with grilled chicken or shrimp.

"People also think they're more of an expert on food and wine than they used to. You can go months and not have a single complaint but then it will be one person who is totally impossible to make happy and it becomes the old joke, 'We'll have the manager shot and your meal's free, and we'll close the place down. Will that make you happy?' We had a party of fourteen come in on a Saturday night. We were busy. The room was full. We got them in and they were as rude as can be.

"Our kitchen is very small. This supper club is so old the kitchen is in the middle of the building so we cannot expand. It's not air-conditioned. The chef loses five pounds on a busy night. And this lady was being ridiculous. We brought the food out, we serve on carts. The manager helped. I was helping. This lady sat the food in front of a child, said, 'Is that his order?'" The large group caused confusion in placement of orders.

Manson continued, "Then she used a four-letter word. Our manager said, 'One more word like that and you're out of here.'" She used it again. They were just a bad group. So he said, 'That's it, get out!' They didn't believe it. What they wanted, probably, was a free meal. But we put all the food back on the cart and pushed it all back in the kitchen. When they finally left, most everyone in the room got up and clapped."

Even with a century in one location, the Lighthouse still dictates a standing ovation.

PART V

The Future

20

The Peak Supper Club

43517 County Highway 38, Clitherall, Minnesota
(866) 403-1291 • www.thepeaksupperclub.com

Dwayne Codner was lost at the base of Inspiration Peak in midwestern Minnesota. The night was so dark he could not see down the road.

The native of Kingston, Jamaica, had fallen in love with a beautiful blond woman from what Sinclair Lewis called the Gopher Prairie. They were married in July 2006. Dwayne was twenty-six and Lori Stich, the daughter of the owner of a Minnesota bait and tackle store, was thirty.

Just three months after their marriage the young couple purchased the Peak Supper Club, on a three-acre dream site at the base of the 1,750-foot mountain that had inspired Lewis.

The Nobel Prize–winning novelist was from Sauk Centre, about ten miles east of the Peak. His modest boyhood home remains as a tourist site. On any given day in the fall of 2011 an elderly woman behind a desk in the front of the home will tell lost tourists she does not know the way to the remote Inspiration Peak, the second-highest point in Minnesota. She is missing one foot and cannot walk the quarter-mile to the top.

But you do what you can, and that is what Codner was thinking about a year into his new life in Clitherall. He had lived in Jamaica, Newark, Brooklyn, and Fort

The Peak Supper Club is different, including the wine and grill.
Minnesota blue skies are always a pick-me-up.

Lauderdale, which is where he met his bride. She was a nurse. He was a chef at the five-star J. Alexander's and at Shells Seafood in Florida.

Clitherall will never be confused with Jamaica, New Jersey, New York, or Florida.

"This was in the middle of nowhere," Dwayne says during a conversation in the supper club's Hunting Room. "First I thought I was in a witness protection program. You had to acclimate between the weather and people and everything."

On this lonely summer night after closing the Peak, Dwayne and Lori have a bonfire in the backyard of the supper club. Codner looks up at the stars. He had not seen stars burn this brightly since he was a boy in Jamaica. He was home.

"You have to give something up to gain something," he says. "And that's what we did. We gave up a different life. And it's good. Cities program you in a way that if you snooze, you lose. I had to learn how to relax. I couldn't believe the [slow] pace the first time I went to the Walmart in Fergus [Falls]. But during my first bonfire someone told me, 'Look up in the stars and tell me what you think.' It was phenomenal. It brought me back as a child. In Jamaica I would go to Ocho Rios with my aunt. There were no lights and I remember looking up at the stars and it was beautiful. All beautiful."

Florida's hurricane seasons had turned the Codners inside out. Lori explains, "We went through four hurricanes in five years. I called my family in Battle Lake and said we were moving home."

Dwayne holds a computer animation degree from the Art Institute of Fort Lauderdale, but the couple elected to follow his muse as a chef. "We put a few offers in on other restaurants in the area," Lori says. "My dad's cousins have owned this supper club since the late 1970s."

Cousin Irv Post added on the lower-level, one-hundred-seat Hunting Room. An upstairs room with a fishing motif seats another hundred people with sunset views streaming to South Dakota. "My dad's other cousin, Beverly, [and her husband] Tom Lorine had it the nineteen years before us. It was run down. Gray on the outside. We thought we'd make it more in line with hunting and fishing."

At the foot of Sinclair Lewis's point of retreat, the Inspiration Peak park has bear, deer, and fox. A mountain lion was spotted in the summer of 2010. From the prairie-covered crest of the hill, Lewis wrote, "there's to be seen a glorious twenty-mile circle of some fifty lakes scattered among fields and pastures, like sequins fallen on an old paisley shawl."

The first year was difficult for Lori and Dwayne within the supper club and out in the community. Lori explains, "We changed things at the restaurant but people had to adapt to us too, being kind of a different couple. People were open armed."

Dwayne laughs, "But everybody in town looked at me and said, 'Don't mess with me.' Actually I was proud of being the only black person here. Now a few [black] guys come in and I go, 'I gotta move.' At first I was fighting this. I couldn't stand this place. Our stuff

A meditation point for novelist Sinclair Lewis is the inspiration for the Peak Supper Club.

was still in storage boxes. We weren't sure we were going to stay. It's a 360-degree difference from what we were used to. Many people have been here their whole life. I put myself in their shoes and they were right. It wasn't their fault."

The young couple toughened up. They created a piercing reddish brown log motif and spruced up the North Woods interior at the supper club. They brightened up the upper level with new lighting. "Dark lighting had been the thing," Lori says. Dwayne adds, "We would like to see your face." The downstairs game room remains cozier and a bit darker in supper club tradition. They removed the orange 1976 disco dance carpet and tiles from back in the day when the Peak had live bands.

The Peak's two nonworking stone fireplaces were handmade by one of Lori's cousins. Every rock in each fireplace was bequeathed to the restaurant from the

Lori and Dwayne Codner with their son, William Benjamin.

fields of nearby farmers. Dwayne and Lori removed the mounts of animals and added new ones from Lori's father, Ben, and brother Craig, who is a taxidermist in Battle Lake.

The timeless eyes of antelope, elk, a mule deer from Montana, and what once was an eight-foot-tall moose look over the diners in the Hunting Room.

Dwayne has never held a gun in his life.

"We now pull people from 150 miles away," Lori says. "It's amazing. People love to come because it is a beautiful drive. The sunsets are gorgeous. We're huge in the summertime. The town I grew up in [Battle Lake] is about eight hundred people. In the summer it turns into ten thousand with tourists. There are a thousand lakes just in Otter Tail County."

Lori and Dwayne did not take a vacation between 2006 and 2011. In 2009 they had a baby boy they named William Benjamin.

Spiffy new Peak menus were designed by Dave Leesocker, who owns Menu Masters in Pelican Rapids, Minnesota. On the bottom right side of the back of the menu there is a small ad for the Dave & Andy Christian comedy ventriloquist act.

Holy moly! That's Dave Leesocker, too. "I have never seen him do this," Lori says. "They perform at churches and banquets. Dave gets the [menu] advertising for us so we don't have to do that. We just revamped the back page and he put his ad on there. I said, 'Dave, I didn't know you did that ventriloquism.'" He's a great guy."

The Peak Supper Club is open year-round, downsizing to three days a week during the winter. A snowmobile trail goes across the supper club's parking lot; it is popular with snowmobilers, who can number up to three hundred for lunch. "But it's a supper club," she says. "It's a huge draw at nighttime."

Lori's aunt Connie Lee (Stich) Cunningham is a country singer at the Tennessee Roadhouse in Alexandria, the biggest city (population 11,200) around Clitherall. "She's been singing since she was two," Lori says. "She went to Nashville and almost got a record deal but she didn't want to change her small-town country ways. They wanted to make her like Shania Twain. She has an amazing voice and plays every single instrument. She married the guy who owns the [Tennessee Roadhouse] restaurant and now she sings at the restaurant with my aunts. She used to perform at all the casinos around here."

Yes, the stars twinkle a bit brighter around the Peak.

Bob Pischke opened the future Peak supper club in 1957 as the Parkway Inn, a roadside stop selling cigarettes with a couple of gas pumps.

The inn was built from the shell of an 1871 schoolhouse, which remains as the back of the present-day supper club. "It was more of a bar with pinball machines and some food," Lori says.

The Peak has now been tweaked to the Peak Supper Club Wine & Grill. "If we changed the name it wouldn't be what it is," Lori reasons. "We go to Alexandria or Fergus Falls and people go, 'Oh, you own the Peak.' I talk to everybody. I talk to every table."

The supper club image was as foreign to Dwayne as a Minnesota Viking. "When I heard 'supper club,' number one I didn't know what 'supper' was," he says. "Why do they call it a Lion's Club or a Shriners club? Maybe you had to be accepted in?"

Lori says people do gather at the Peak. "They'll meet people from the other side and come from this side," she explains. "It becomes like a coffee shop. They spend a couple hours here and I tease them how I will start charging rent. Most of the times it is OK, but on busy nights we need to flip tables and get people in and out. The atmosphere has a lot to do with it, too. It's very clean and laid back. We get so many calls, 'What do we wear to your club?' They think it's an exclusive deal. I grew up here and I still don't know why they are called clubs."

Dwayne smiles and adds, "Supper around here starts at five o'clock. Supper is like eight in my family in Jamaica."

Dwayne left Kingston when he was ten. His father, Donovan, was a paratrooper in the Jamaican army. He died in an air and sea show when Dwayne was nine years old. Dwayne's mother, Thelma, attended catering school in Jamaica and made cakes for family and friends. "We're not the first interracial couple in the family," he says. "I found out a couple years ago Grandmother was also a nurse whose father had married a white Englishwoman."

Dwayne had never had walleye until he met his in-laws. "I'm a snapper guy," he says. "Walleye? I never ate it at her mom and dad's because they gave me an option, walleye or chicken." Lori says, "My mom will try pan-fried sunfish. He thinks that's pretty cool."

The Peak serves big portions of flavorful walleye that is broiled with paprika and deep-fried in homemade beer batter. Locals are also coming around to the supper club's seasonal Jamaican jerk pasta.

"Now there's no way being German or Norwegian you can handle the Jamaican herb spice," Dwayne says. "So I doctored it up a little bit, added a little cream sauce with onions. It has a smokier taste to it. It explodes in your mouth."

Dwayne slowly introduced an experimental touch to the traditional supper club menu. He brings back Jamaican spices from Golden Krust Caribbean Bakery when he visits family in Brooklyn. "My mom figured out a way to send me Jamaican beef patties," he says. "It's kind of like a crusted meat pot pie. Really good."

During the 1980s restaurants in the Alexandria-Clitherall corridor were known for broasted chicken. The birds were hand-battered and set in a natural pressure cooker, resulting in a crispy outside. "Before we started here we were known as the chicken 'n' rib shack," Dwayne says. "We didn't want to be known for that. We were going through thirteen cases of thirty-pound chicken a week. Do the math. Then we went up to twenty cases."

The young couple backed off. They brought in steak, pasta, frog legs, broiled shrimp stuffed with crabmeat, and tilapia and it all was a hit. "Now we go through twenty cases of chicken, maybe in a month," he says.

The pastas registered with younger diners. "Mahimahi," Dwayne says. "People said, 'What is mahi?' We called it 'the steak fish.' Then people would go, 'We're eating Flipper?' and we'd tell them, no, that is dolphin."

The Peak began to hold its own against what is regarded as fancy-pants clientele from Alexandria. Lori reflects, "People knew our place but it was never regarded as 'classy.' Then we started remodeling and changing the menu." Dwayne says, "It had been a biker bar, the place was full of smokers. The smoke in here was thick. We made it more upscale and family oriented."

The Peak holds on to certain supper club traditions. The supper club rolls out an occasional relish tray for Christmas parties. The Peak has a salad bar with home-made bleu cheese and ranch dressing, homemade macaroni salad, and homemade coleslaw with mandarin oranges.

The Peak offers prime rib on Friday and Saturday and has a Friday fish fry during Lent. "We're competing with the churches now," he says. "The fish fries are huge around here. There are bazaars, pancake feeds, stuff like that."

Lori says the Peak's customers are still mostly elderly. "Supper clubs are [elderly based] and they have been since I was a kid. Since we started the pastas and steaks it has kind of turned around. Older people are bringing their kids now. Then their kids' kids. That's exciting. My high school friends frequent here as well. I have friends from Iowa who come up to Clitherall Lake and come here. I grew up coming to these. My dad grew up coming here. He'd sit at the bar with his grandfather. But supper clubs are a dying breed."

Like a hunter with a bow, the Peak aimed to make its mark in regional cuisine.

In the spring of 2011 Dwayne and Lori participated in "Dining Around Douglas [County]," an Alexandria Area YMCA fund-raiser for needy families. The Peak was featured with twelve other central Minnesota restaurants that served food to 230 people at the Holiday Inn banquet center in Alexandria.

"This was the first time we did it," Lori says. "You bring your signature item. Alexandria is pretty profound but we thought we'd give it a whirl. We did our barbecue pork ribs, his homemade pasta, and sautéed fresh green beans in garlic and olive oil. We won two of three awards and didn't even compete in the dessert category. Here we are out in the middle of nowhere and Alexandria has all these million-dollar restaurants. We're obviously not. It was pretty exciting."

The YMCA found the remote Peak. "Some of it is word of mouth. We also ask our members what restaurants they would like to see," says Cahil Collins, contest coordinator and aquatic director of the Alexandria Area YMCA. "They won for the entree [pork ribs] and they won 'the People's Choice,' which is the overall award. Everybody in attendance votes for the best restaurant. The Peak won."

The Peak didn't compete in 2012 because Dwayne was busy with a large event at the supper club. Collins explains, "The Peak has one cook [Dwayne]. That's the operation. If they have a big group in, they can't release him. The good side of that is that you know you're going to get the same thing every time."

Collins, born in 1960, is from the Alexandria area. He knows about Minnesota supper clubs and he scouts out every restaurant before they are admitted to the competition. "The Peak absolutely has great food," he says. "It's a casual place so when you first go in sometimes it's a surprise just how good the food is. It is very special."

Tickets to attend Dining Around Douglas benefit the Y's Strong Kids Campaign. "We give out financial assistance to those who cannot afford a membership," Collins says. "We have 5,400 members and 17 percent of those are on some sort of financial assistance."

Lori grew up with Legg-Calve-Perthes disease, a deterioration of each of her hip joints. In February 2012 she endured her second hip replacement. The Shriners Hospital for Children in Minneapolis helped her out when she was young. "I said someday when I had a family and would be able to give back we would," she says.

And she did.

George "Mick" McMillin lives a mile away from the supper club on "the big hill out the door," in his words, and he finds the meaning of family in the rustic environment. A retired central Ohio roofer, the confirmed bachelor comes to the Peak every night, at least in the summer. His favorite spot is at the end of the bar, near the stuffed walleye.

Mick settled in rural Clitherall in 1994 after twenty years of traveling from Columbus, Ohio, to go hunting near Manitoba, Canada.

"I needed a place to go," says McMilllin, who was born in 1941. "I wanted to get closer to the Canadian border and I liked the lakes, hunting, and fishing here.

I wanted the isolation of the area. I went through Fergus Falls and said I was coming back in February looking for land. And I did. I knew nothing about this area. I spent nine days looking for something and I found it."

Dwayne apparently does not stand alone. Mick says Dwayne has made big changes at the Peak. "He is a spectacular chef," Mick says while Dwayne is in the kitchen, far out of hearing distance. "He has done things the others would never have done. That guy has worked in places that taught him to be a real chef. My mother ran restaurants all her life around Columbus. I grew up with this whole deal. That's why I'm a bit of a critic. I wouldn't venture in here tonight if this was a piece of crap. You can bet your butt on that."

Mick likes the Peak's prime rib, citing immaculate preparation (marinated and slow cooked with homemade au jus sauce). Lori considers that as a tribute to her husband's work in Florida. "Somebody asks for a medium rare steak and it is cooked to perfection," she says. "He knows how to cook

Regular customer George "Mick" McMillin.

them. Before we took over, nobody ordered a steak because nobody knew how to cook them."

The twelve-ounce Provolone Steak with sautéed mushrooms and onions and provolone cheese on the side is a big hit at the Peak. The steak is baked to a golden crust.

Food is sourced from distributors like Sysco and Reinhart FoodService. "We've tried local places," Lori says. "But it's easier to get it from one source." Her voice drops and she continues, "And cheaper, too, with the capacity we use. In the summertime we can serve two hundred to three hundred people in three hours."

The Peak experience opened up Dwayne's eyes to the ways of rambling Midwest living. "There are people who have big events here," he says. "They've stayed friends with people from way back. They congregate here. They call them up when they're here by the lake or the cabin, 'Hey, we're going to the Peak,' then it's, 'OK, I'll dress up and I'll come meet you there.' And it's not just two or three people. It's like fifteen to twenty people showing up, all knowing each other from back in the day. Wow! People really do that. I had never seen anything like this until I moved here."

Like other supper clubs in rural Minnesota, the Peak once had setups where customers brought in their own booze, especially for Manhattans and old-fashioneds. Insurance companies pulled back on coverage for setup establishments.

"Setups are going away," Lori says. "That was a big draw for a lot of people. Now we pour the alcohol into their drink."

Of course, Dwayne and Lori don't have to worry about driving home. The family lives in an apartment connected to the Peak, like old-school supper clubs when the owners had space atop the restaurant. "The pros are that we're next door," Dwayne says. "The cons are that we're here all the time. People knock on our door instead of making a phone call. One customer wanted to use the printer in our house." Lori says, "She was at the lake and her printer wasn't working. She said, 'I know you have a printer,' and I said, 'Well, yeah, but it is in my house.' We separate that. You have to do that or you will go insane."

Another time supper club customers invited themselves into the family's backyard bonfire beneath the Minnesota stars. "We didn't know them," she says. "But that's how people are here. Which is good and bad."

Dwayne had never even held a tool before he came to Minnesota. Now he has learned quite a few tradesman skills. "See where those pine boards are?" he asks, and nods toward a beautifully restored floor. "That was all carpet. My buddy and I did it ourselves. It was like one of those hidden talents you didn't know you had. Instead of watching Food Network, I'm watching DIY [network]. I'm looking on

YouTube on how to fix things. I had never held a screwdriver. I never used a cuttin' saw. I never mowed a lawn. So I've learned a lot."

Are Dwayne and Lori in the Peak for the long haul?

"We had a ten-year plan going in," Lori answers. "This is year five. Who knows? There's a big burnout from these. Lots of hours, lots of people time, being on all the time." Dwayne adds, "The previous owner burned out after nineteen years and he was at the point where you had to replace stuff. For five years we were replacing a lot of things."

Lori recalls, "When we took over a lot of people couldn't handle it. It was nineteen years of the same owner, of the same thing. All of a sudden we proved ourselves. We started getting our own following. Then the older people came trickling back because they heard how good the food was. It evolved into something a little bit bigger and better. Around here, if you're not here, you don't care. If they see you, they come in and support you. They say, 'They're here, doing their time.' People like seeing that—young people who have a mission. They want to see it work. If you're not at your place, they're not going to support you."

A devout soccer fan, Dwayne has gone as far as learning more about baseball and football, although he is a Green Bay Packers fan in Minnesota Vikings territory.

"My wife introduced me to a lot of different sports and cultures," he says. "Which is good. If you grow up in a box that is all you see and know. You have to get outside sometimes so you can learn more. That is why I am here. I want to be open to everything. So when I get older I can tell my son, 'I lived in the city, I lived in the country, I did this.'"

And he did.

21

Red Stag Supper Club

509 1st Avenue NE, Minneapolis, Minnesota
(612) 767-7766 • www.redstagsupperclub.com

With relaxed ambience and soft lighting, supper clubs have always set the mood for an exchange of ideas, secrets, and dreams.

Kim Bartmann grew up around the supper clubs of northern Wisconsin. The rambling hush of a small town can turn into big things. In November 2007 Bartmann opened the Red Stag Supper Club in a former warehouse in the trendy NorEast neighborhood of downtown Minneapolis.

There is no sign identifying the Red Stag Supper Club. The venue's bold nature is defined by a life-size red aluminum stag that stands above the front door. The sculpture was imported from an Illinois foundry. The sign is a signal shared by rural souls.

The Red Stag Supper Club is apart from the herd as the first LEED-CI (Leadership in Energy & Environmental Design for Commercial Interiors) registered restaurant in Minnesota, and one of the first in the United States.

"A supper club is typically a rural place where it houses all sorts of activities," Bartmann says on a Saturday afternoon at the Red Stag during late summer 2011. "You might go there for a drink after a softball game but you're also going to bring

The salvaged red stag is the only signage for the Minneapolis supper club.

your grandparents there for their fiftieth wedding anniversary. There's a certain kind of conviviality that is intrinsic to a supper club that we try to re-create here."

The Twin Cities are a nesting ground for plainspoken country tones, ranging from *A Prairie Home Companion* in neighboring Saint Paul to the detailed country-folk songs of Minneapolis chef and songwriter Ben Weaver.

"Rural things are very fashionable now," Bartmann says. "And they've become more so for a while. It has to do with the food movement, but it also has to do with fashion in Williamsburg [Brooklyn, New York] and Los Angeles. A couple months ago I stayed at a bed-and-breakfast in Lake Pepin [Wisconsin]. There was a couple at the breakfast table. He was clearly a very successful businessman. We told them we had gone to a rhubarb festival in a small town. I love small-town festivals."

The successful businessman with sharp black glasses responded to Bartmann and her friend by riffing on the tractor pulls of the small town that was his hometown. "It struck me that five years ago that person would not be highlighting his rural roots," Bartmann says. "Maybe he would be talking about his downtown condo or house in the suburbs."

Bartmann was born in 1963 in Appleton, Wisconsin. She lived in a small one-story farmhouse where her grandmother was born. Bartmann went to grade school in North Hollywood, California. Her father traveled to Japan a lot for the Giddings & Lewis Machine Tools company in Fond du Lac, Wisconsin, and moving to Los Angeles made sense for the commute. The family returned to Appleton when Bartmann was in the second grade, and she went to high school in Eagle River, north of Appleton.

Bartmann studied liberal arts at the University of Minnesota. After working in kitchens through college, in 1991 she opened her first restaurant in the Uptown neighborhood of Minneapolis. Bartmann began making regular summer pilgrimages back to northern Wisconsin in the early 2000s.

Bartmann's father, Richard, also owned a Suzuki dealership in Appleton. "When I was ten he bought an island that had been abandoned by the Wilke family," Bartmann says. "They were one of the twelve founders of the Aid Association for Lutherans [now Thrivent Financial], which was the first insurance company in the United States. The island was a very cool place. Everything was very old, built in the early

1900s. They just walked away at some point. So I grew up in this environment of everything being from the 1920s—the dishes, the linens, the books, the games. I still love that aesthetic."

Bartmann used the White Stag Inn supper club in Rhinelander, Wisconsin, as an inspiration for the Red Stag. The White Stag is down the road from Eagle River and Sugar Camp, where Bartmann spent her summers. "The White Stag is stunning," she says. "I didn't pattern this after that in any way but the White Stag definitely informed my concept of what a supper club is, although I've been to a million of them. The White Stag was probably the first one I ever went to."

Even the Red Stag's vintage chandeliers were sourced from a salvage yard in North Minneapolis.

The Red Stag Supper Club is on the ground floor of an open four-thousand-square-foot loftlike space that formerly was a mechanical warehouse. Bartmann looks between the posts and beams and proudly says, "It was the first mechanical contractor in the country to receive rolled sheet metal steel as opposed to small sheets. Who knew that was so interesting? The old guys told me all this stuff about this charming space. It was a total gut.

"A typical supper club is pretty ornate and over the top. It's fairly simple in here, but little touches of ornateness develop that [supper club] feeling." She looks up at the gaudy 1970s brass and swirl whorehouse chandeliers and said, "Like those ridiculous chandeliers [obtained from a salvage yard in North Minneapolis]. They work in the space. There's a lot of amazing interior design in supper clubs that doesn't exist anymore. People don't put the time into spaces that they once did. Chicago sets the bar pretty high for that, but not everywhere."

The warehouse ceiling was constructed with heavy Douglas fir, shaping the North Woods supper club feel. The dense Douglas fir paneling matches the ceiling. Bartmann says, "I misunderstood part of my LEED project and thought I was

The Red Stag Supper Club opened in 2007 in a former warehouse in the artsy NorEast neighborhood of downtown Minneapolis.

required to buy FSC (Forestry Stewardship Council) lumber, which is certified wood. I looked and looked. Finding FSC certified is not easy. But the biggest FSC distribution point in the country is about a half hour from here; a guy who went to the University of Minnesota founded it. He made Douglas fir paneling for Harvard University and had just enough left from that job to finish off this room. I found it at the last minute. And I didn't finish it until the last minute. I'm sort of a hobby furniture maker and I had never used water-based stains and varnishes. It is very difficult to work with because this wood is very soft. It sucks stuff up. There was no more of it in existence—anywhere. I just had to go at it, but it worked out."

Before assuming the regentrified NorEast name, the Northeast side of Minneapolis was known as Old Saint Anthony's. The neighborhood is three blocks from the Mississippi River and is considered the original part of Minneapolis.

The supper club's neighbors include a flower shop, a clothing store, and a boutique called I Like You, quite appropriately filled with handmade cards, clothes, and jewelry.

Minnesota senators Al Franken and Amy Klobuchar come to the Red Stag when they are in town. So does Sean Daley (aka Slug) from the hip-hop band Atmosphere.

More than a quarter of the materials used to build the Red Stag were hand salvaged, including the marble bar top and smoke-gray dining booths. Excess doors were transitioned into tabletops. The fabric used to reupholster the booths is made from recycled cassette tapes. No word if any are from the Morris Day and the Time catalogue.

The decade-old supper club chairs are from the Buckstaff Company, incorporated in 1899 in Oshkosh, Wisconsin, as a chair—and casket—maker. "Supper clubs usually have nice chairs," Bartmann says. "Because people sit around a lot. You make a night of it at supper clubs with music and a multipurpose aspect."

The contemporary supper club menu celebrates organic and sustainably farmed local ingredients. Organic chicken and eggs come from the Larry Schultz family farm in Owatonna, Minnesota. The supper club has received regional recognitions including best French fries and best Bloody Mary. "But you better have a good old-fashioned," Bartmann says. "It's a Wisconsin thing, but it's absolutely a supper club thing. Prior to this restaurant I had transitioned my other places to selling local foods, family farm foods, and engaging in other environmental concerns. I was interested in doing the buildout as a LEED-certified project. I had a bit of an ax to grind, although I don't want to use that phrase. A lot of LEED-certified spaces are very modern, very much like an ice cube. There's not a lot of life to them. They have a lot of light and that's very good. They are healthy spaces. I really believe in LEED certification. I've just finished my second one, which would be LEED Platinum. But

I was very interested in doing a LEED project with the aesthetic of a supper club: antiques, organic surfaces like marble, wood, the patterns in the carpets."

Rachelle Schoessler Lynn was the Red Stag interior designer. A native of Denison, Iowa, Lynn helped create Minnesota's current sustainable building design guidelines: Buildings, Benchmarks and Beyond.

Bartmann searched out Lynn at Meyer, Scherer & Rockcastle in Minneapolis, where she is a senior associate. "There had never been a restaurant in this space," Lynn says in a separate interview. "That gives you a lot of opportunity to do whatever you want. We had to think about the best location for the bar, the kitchen being in the back but semi-open, a little bit open but not wide open. The space isn't that big so we decided not to break it up into areas. It is all wide open. And one of the best things about the space is that it had all those windows."

The Red Stag uses natural light from six small original warehouse windows. The Red Stag also installed three new windows in large warehouse window spaces that had been boarded up. "It is very different to be there during the day for lunch," Lynn says. "And then being there at night."

The supper club was also the first facility in the country lit entirely by LED lights, which use 90 percent less electricity than incandescent bulbs. Bartmann says, "It's not dimly lit like a traditional supper club during the day, but it does the trick at night. We have linen napkins. In fact, we use the last independent supply company [Spruce Linens] in Minneapolis." The Red Stag also participates in a commercial composting pilot program.

"It is a very chef-driven restaurant, but very accessible. It still offers a lot of the same supper club fare. Beef stroganoff, a relish tray with pickled vegetables—but they're organic and sustainable vegetables. They're not from a jar, off a Sysco truck, whatever. That's been fun—and well received."

Lynn was born in 1968 in Denison and attended Iowa State University. She had a handle on the supper club motif, as Denison is the birthplace of wholesome mid-century actress Donna Reed. Everyone in Denison goes to the supper club–tinged

Cronk's Cafe and Restaurant, and during the summer Lynn's parents, Paul and Rose Marie, took the family to supper clubs around Lake Okoboji in northwest Iowa.

Bartmann said she wanted a retro supper club feel to the Red Stag, but what does "retro" mean to a designer? "We've talked about that a lot," Lynn answers. She also worked with Bartmann to create Pat's Tap, a popular Minneapolis gastro-pub skee-club with four skee-ball machines. "Is it 1950s? 1960s? Which part? We go through conversations and look at images together. Are you talking this kind of vintage, or that kind of vintage?" Bartmann wanted a supper club but she wanted a twist to it that mostly comes in the food. "The supper club came together nicely because the pieces were there. The back bar came from the guy [antique dealer] next door. We used the goldish-colored bar top from a Marriott hotel in downtown Minneapolis that was twenty-five years old. There was nothing wrong with it; they just wanted to update it. We found red

The Red Stag's ceiling is constructed of hearty Douglas fir.

carpet and just tried to create an older look. We had the wood ceiling and wood floor we could work with."

Resourcing vintage stuff is a trend being deployed by designers across America. Discarded wood from the historic Coney Island boardwalk in Brooklyn is now found in a Philadelphia mill works company and a furniture manufacturer that uses boardwalk wood for a $7,500 lounger.

Twin Cities advertising executives are inspired by the designs of the Red Stag vintage beer can collection.

The Red Stag Supper Club seats 120. The restaurant is packed on weekend nights with young, old, and neighborhood people.

The back bar is defined by a beer can collection that numbers into the hundreds and includes the omnipresent Billy [Carter] Beer. Bartmann looks at the collection and says, "My favorite is on the lower left. It is the quintessential rural thing. There is a Grain Belt Premium can that is branded specifically for Bean & Bacon Days in a small town [Augusta] in Wisconsin. It doesn't get any better than that. The design community in Minneapolis is very strong and they love these beer cans."

The bar serves about sixteen microbrews and a couple dozen bottled beers. The local Surly, Summit, and Fulton beers are the best sellers in the urban supper club.

Bartmann says, "Our first chef was from Texas so he understood it through the lens of a roadhouse, which is what a rural place in Texas is. We had lots of conversations about 'What is a supper club?' because he didn't know. That was kind of good, in a way, that he didn't know. He actually drove and looked at supper clubs to get an idea of what he was starting with and what he was contemporizing in his food. So we ended up with beef stroganoff made with elk. Handmade pasta that's really fresh. But we also have things people would expect in a supper club, the steaks and walleye. We'll have prime rib on Saturday. Sometimes it's pot roast. We do a Slow Food Sunday. A lot of supper clubs in northern Wisconsin will have pot roast, mashed potatoes, and green beans on Sunday for nine or ten bucks. Or roast chicken in north central Wisconsin on Sundays. That's why we do Slow Food Sundays." Slow Food is the nonprofit founded in 1989 to counteract fast food and the disappearance of local food traditions. Slow Food can now be found in more than 150 countries.

"I'm pretty committed to the arts community in Minneapolis," Bartmann says. "Music and late-night music is part of the whole of what a supper club is. Often there's a separate area for music in a supper club, but here we have one big room." The Red Stag often pulls a curtain across a side of the room where local jazz is featured under soft theater lighting.

In keeping with the community nature of traditional supper clubs, the Red Stag hosts a monthly "Green Ideas & Ham" series hosted by Environment Minnesota. Speakers include experts in transportation, renewable energy, clean water, and other issues.

"We're not open in the mornings, and I was trying to get some business meetings and other things happening when we're not open," Bartmann says. "We've done breakfast fund-raisers for other organizations. We just came up with this idea to do this regular series like a business breakfast. The best one was Arjun Makhijani [formerly in President Jimmy Carter's administration], who wrote *Carbon-Free*. The book was five years old but in the book he can prove that with existing technology America can be completely carbon free by 2030. No petroleum at all. It was amazing. It is good for our business to be making community connections like that."

The supper club's walls are speckled vintage art. There's a mint condition post-Prohibition menu from the now-defunct Wooden Nickel in Appleton, Wisconsin, offering a bottle of beer for fifteen cents. There are 1960s pictures of the Green Bay Packers taken by team photographer Vernon Biever. "I would be willing to bet you there are pictures he took of the Packers in some other supper clubs in Wisconsin and Minnesota," she says. *Life* magazine took a portrait of the late 1960s Green Bay Packers sitting on stacks of hay. "There's something sort of creepy about it," Bartmann continues as she walks through the front of the supper club. "They're all sitting on hay bales. The lighting is really weird. And it's all white guys, you know? They're all trying to look like porn stars or something."

The Red Stag looks forward while keeping one foot planted in the past. "I really wanted a good old-fashioned fish fry in Minneapolis," Bartmann says. "There are a few fish fries, but they could be improved upon. This all was kind of an exercise in nostalgia."

22

Cliff Bell's

2030 Park Avenue, Detroit, Michigan
(313) 961-2543 • www.cliffbells.com

Cliff Bell's supper club opened in 1935 in downtown Detroit. It was perfect timing. The expanding automobile industry brought adventure and wealth into the Detroit area. Even folks from then-rural Dearborn could take a spin into Detroit for a big-city meal at Cliff Bell's.

And the supper club remains a silver-toned metaphor for foodways as much as it is for the life, death, and slow comeback of the American automobile industry.

John Clifford Bell was a gregarious saloon keeper who operated speakeasies in the Motor City throughout Prohibition, just as his counterparts were doing in rural Wisconsin and Minnesota. He had his own private-label bourbon.

Cliff Bell's supper club was no small thing. The room was defined by fine mahogany and brass. It had air-conditioning and refrigeration, which was such a big deal the *Detroit Free Press* ran a photo essay on the newfangled devices. The supper club holds 319 people today.

Bell retired in 1958 but still hung around the supper club with his wife, Maude, as it operated under other names like A.J.'s on the Park and the Winery. Bell died in December 1977. He was ninety-one years old.

Between the 1930s and the 1950s, Cliff Bell's and the Town Pump Tavern were the bookends of Detroit's swaggering nightclub strip. Automobile industrialists had money to burn. Steaks were sizzling. Park Avenue had hole-in-the-wall gin joints, nice taverns, and burlesque houses.

Cliff Bell's supper club, circa 1950s in downtown Detroit.

m e n u

Cliff Bell's

2030 Park Avenue
EST. 1935

Cliff Bell's supper club declined with the rest of downtown Detroit. Henry Ford's dream enabled a straight, no-chaser flight out of urban blight. Cliff Bell's became La Cave, a Creole-inspired disco and strip club, before closing for good in 1985. The space sat empty for twenty years.

Cliff Bell's supper club reopened in January 2005 as Detroit was back in the spotlight hosting the Super Bowl. Of course it snowed like hell on Super Bowl weekend.

Detroit natives Paul Howard, his sister Carolyn, and her husband, Scott Lowell, brought back Bell's. They are the visionaries sociologist Richard Florida writes about in his Creative Class books. They are young people investing in a decaying downtown. By 2011 *Playboy* magazine listed Cliff Bell's as one of the best bars in America.

During a January 2012 weekday happy-hour visit to the restaurant, a high-strung street person hassled me as I walked near the front door of Cliff Bell's. The abandoned Hotel Charlevoix across the street looked like it could fall down at any minute. The hotel's empty windows were deep tear ducts.

But the scene inside Cliff Bell's was reinvigorating. It was like walking back through a misty jazz song into a Detroit of the 1940s. The original herringbone-patterned wood dance floor had been restored. Snappy Art Deco decor gave the supper club an enticing feel. The walls had pictures and portraits of Cliff Bell, just as a rural Iowa supper club will have pictures and portraits of its owner.

"This was built as a supper club," managing partner Paul Howard says. "It became a complicated question for us because it went through a lot of different incarnations in the 1960s through the '80s. Like La Cave. There was a lot of stucco and Styrofoam soffits with a dungeon theme.

"We opened in 2005 as Cliff Bell's with just a bar with a stage. When the kitchen came there was a lot of discussion about our identity and what is Cliff Bell's? Would

The romantic interior of Cliff Bell's, circa 1960.

we serve late-night dinner? Lunch? But the term 'supper club' came up again and again. It defines our core identity. We have that meandering nature of a supper club. People spend a long time here, which can cause problems because unlike a normal restaurant that can book a table every hour and a half, we never know. We have limited seating and it's hard to keep the place going without turning the tables. So we've tried to put some policies into place like having live music between six PM and one thirty AM so people can feel like they had a night and still be out by nine PM People spend a lot of time here."

A tip of the hat to Mr. Cliff Bell.

Howard is a Detroit native. His father, James, was an engineer at Chrysler, and Howard's mother, Sally, raised seven children. James Howard grew up on a farm in Grand Rapids, Michigan.

Howard says Cliff Bell's is in the city's "entertainment district." "I find Detroit pretty entertaining," he quips. Cliff Bell's is a couple blocks away from the new Ford Field, the home of the NFL's Detroit Lions, but the supper club does not attract much of a sports crowd since it does not have televisions.

Howard was born in 1974 as Lions All-Pro cornerback Lem Barney was winding down his career a few miles away at Tiger Stadium.

"Downtown really has gotten better," Howard says. "For one, the city is just so cleared out. The neighborhood north of here used to be the Cass Corridor. During parts of the 1980s it was the worst neighborhood in the country in terms of all sorts of crimes. Well, the buildings burned. They were torn down. They were rehabbed. Freeways went in, divided neighborhoods and isolated neighborhoods. Now that isolation can be good. People are acquiring buildings downtown."

But the Hotel Charlevoix across the street from Cliff Bell's is in a holding pattern. The once-resplendent Victorian hotel was built in 1905. It has been empty since the mid-1980s. "There are two big empty buildings across the street and they are owned by the same guy," Howard says. "He's owned both buildings since they were occupied so that will give you an idea of what he's been through."

What's going to happen?

"What's going to happen?" Howard repeats. His voice rattled around the room. "Somebody is going to get hurt. Until then nothing is going to happen. The city doesn't have the wherewithal to enforce the law in Detroit. If somebody has no money, no resources, they own two huge buildings, they don't want to sell them, and nobody wants to buy them anyway and, the city doesn't have any money . . ." He shrugs his shoulders.

Cliff Bell didn't have these problems.

A new mural was installed in Christmas 2011 honoring supper club doorman Roosevelt "Rosie" Callen Jr. The effervescent doorman has been known to feed and sometimes rescue the cats that have taken over the Charlevoix. "They surprised me with that mural over the holidays," Rosie says in a separate conversation. "I've always been a pet lover. I drove my parents crazy bringing something home as a kid, whether it was crickets in a jar, a stray cat, or a butterfly. I take care of the cats in the building across the street. I rehabilitate them and get them housing. I've seen up to ten at a time, but there are always babies. I work to get them adopted."

A tribute to Cliff Bell's doorman Rosie Callen Jr., who rescues cats from the abandoned Hotel Charlevoix building across the street from the supper club.

Rosie, born in 1979, is a Detroit native who now lives in Ferndale, just outside the city. He continues, "People were giving me money at the door to buy food for the cats. It took on a life of its own."

Rosie started at Cliff's in 2007. He works the door between 7:30 PM and 1:30 AM up to five nights a week. "One of the joys of working at Cliff Bell's is I get to hobnob with everybody that's anybody," Rosie says. "George Clooney. The director Abel Ferrara (*Bad Lieutenant*, *King of New York*). They filmed a lot of movies at Cliff Bell's because it's such a period place. Sometimes they use the employees as extras. Parts of [Clooney's] *The Ides of March* were shot at Cliff Bell's. Whitney Houston did some of her last film [*Sparkle*] at Cliff Bell's. I didn't know much of the history of the club until I sat down and became amazed with all the Art Deco. It makes you want to know more. I wasn't familiar with a supper club. I may have heard the term once in a Humphrey Bogart movie." Between 1940 and 1953 Bogie, Howard Hughes, and Orson Welles hung out at the real-life Players supper club on Sunset Boulevard in Hollywood.

And the sun is rising again over Park Avenue in Detroit.

"I'll tell you this, before Cliff Bell's reopened, the streetlights here weren't even turned on," says Rosie, who previously worked at the now-defunct Music Venue

Cliff Bell's today—modeled after the Green Mill in Chicago.

blues club in downtown Detroit. "My friends called this little strip the Forbidden Zone. No one would go down Park Avenue. It was a complete holocaust. Everything was burned out."

Howard says, "Nothing drastic has happened to us. Usually it's an operator. There will be a string of holdups, then they will get the guy. Then there will be a string of car break-ins. Then they get that guy and he disappears."

Cliff Bell's has American food and live jazz and blues. "When you hear 'supper club,' that's what this room conjures up," Howard says. "A dining room with a stage. A big bar. Cocktail waitresses. Dim lights." Iconic Detroit rocker Mitch Ryder even headlined a book release party at the supper club. The house Steinway piano was the Cobo Hall house piano during the 1960s, the downtown Detroit arena where rock acts like Bob Seger and Kiss broke through in the 1970s. Howard found the piano sitting on its side in a downtown warehouse.

"For the food we took a lot of cues from old menus we found. Nothing too contemporary. We've done great with lake perch, but it's hard to get it fresh in the winter. We've had prime rib on

Friday and Saturday nights. Shrimp and grits and steak and eggs are standards. We stick with classic recipes well prepared in-house."

Howard's design template was the historic Green Mill nightclub (without food) in Chicago's Uptown neighborhood. "The Green Mill is what made me want to do this," he says. "I've been in the bar business and have another place [the Bronx] in Detroit. It's a corner bar from the 1930s. I went to Chicago to see Cheap Trick [at the Riviera, a block from the Green Mill]. We went to the Green Mill and I always had that place in the back of my mind. A couple years later I came across this, which actually could be comparable to the Green Mill."

Cliff Bell was born February 3, 1886, in Cincinnati, Ohio, and came to Detroit as a teenager with his parents. His father was a socialist labor agitator and saloon keeper. His father gave Cliff his first job at the age of sixteen as a porter at his Detroit pub.

Prohibition hit in 1919. Cliff wasn't happy. He was thirty-three years old and found himself out of work. He called Prohibition "an unwarranted infringement on the personal privileges of red-blooded Americans."

Howard says, "He basically didn't put up with it. He operated speakeasies around town. While most speakeasies were basement bars in houses, Cliff was connected enough to be out in the open, to give speakeasy clubs names, for example. They had entertainment. They were an establishment, they weren't a secret."

In 1922, for example, Cliff ran a joint in the reclaimed space of the Grand Circus Chop House behind the Detroit Athletic Club. Known by regulars as the DAC Annex, members could sneak out of the dry club for a shot of hooch. Word got out and Cliff went to a lower-profile neighborhood operation called the Parisian Club in Detroit.

In 1930 Cliff opened the now-razed Erskine Bridge Club. The club was known for importing quality liquors from Quebec. A 1954 *Hotel and Restaurant Journal* article wrote of the club's history, "Few people it seems, recognize or remember the history of some innovation years after it appeared. So it is that hardly anybody remembers that it was Cliff Bell who introduced bar stools to the tavern or vice-versa. The Erskine Bridge Club, as near as anyone has been able to determine, was the first saloon to have stools by the bar."

So this was Detroit's legacy: car seats and bar stools.

Cliff's coming-out party for the end of Prohibition was the Commodore Club, which he opened in 1933 and brought in acts from Hollywood and New York. But the Commodore Club was not a supper club. Cliff Bell struck it rich with the supper club concept.

The original Cliff Bell's building was built in 1925 at its current location. Albert Kahn designed the building. He also designed the twenty-eight-story Art Deco Fisher Building in Detroit and the Ford Motor Company's Highland Park plant, which opened in 1909 and where Ford put the assembly line into play. The Cliff Bell building was intended to be ten stories tall, but after the Depression the project stopped at two stories.

"Cliff operated a speakeasy in the basement here too," Howard says. "Some of the remnants of that are still there." Howard found an egg-shaped speakeasy-era tile mosaic with "Cliff Bell" embedded in the tile. The four-foot-high, seven-foot-long mosaic now hangs on the south wall of the supper club.

Cliff Bell wanted the best supper club in Detroit. He hired architect Charles Agree to design the club itself. Agree also designed the Wittier Hotel on the Detroit River. "The supper club was state of the art when Cliff opened," Howard says. "Air-conditioning was new then. They had compressor-run coolers instead of ice boxes. There was a lot of Art Deco at the time, machine age. Chrome plate. He [Bell] considered modernism to be very jarring. He wanted Art Deco elements, but no neon. No chrome. Not a lot of polished metal." Agree went on to design sleek 1960s shopping plazas like the Oakland Mall in Madison Heights.

Agree brought out detailed supper club flourishes that have been embraced by a new generation. "I'm not tooting my own horn because I had nothing to do with it," Howard says. "But there are a lot of subtleties in the architecture here that come together, and there's something here that has an effect on how people feel."

The original Cliff Bell's ceiling was always uplit and the current ceiling lighting has the same subtleties. There's not a lot of direct light. A nephew of Cliff Bell's has brought photographs and newspaper clippings to the new generation of owners.

Howard says, "We looked at photos of these beautiful brass lamps that hung like a big brass bowl to light the ceilings. During our initial construction we found a golf club in Mount Clement that was going out of business. They had an English pub," and Howard gazes at the dramatic chandeliers. "Actually those were lenses from the pub and they were very close to the ceiling with white lenses. I actually spray-painted those silver, added long chains, and spray-painted the chains gold. There were nine of them; I got them for fifty dollars apiece. We were very lucky."

The supper club features twenty-five reclaimed cream-colored bar stools around the big bar. "The bar didn't used to come all the way around," he says. "We wrapped it around to get more bar space. The stripper stage was in the middle. It was shaped like a telephone. The other stage [for live shows] was already there. The dining room chairs came from the golf course and we redid them with upholstery. We built the booths ourselves."

Howard did not disclose renovation costs, but he did say the group did not receive financing. "We just did it on an initial shoestring and ran the place real lean for a couple of years," he says. "It was in real bad shape when we came in. The entire building had been abandoned for many years. There weren't many entries to get into this space so it was not vandalized. Restaurants didn't used to be ventilated well and there was bad ventilation. It was grimy. We did a lot of work on the exterior. It was originally a mahogany front that had been painted over. We put in mostly new wood and restored what was old. We had a three-year soft opening. We opened for the Super Bowl and the place was really rough even then. There were layers and years of bad renovations. It was hard to see through that La Cave theme. There were huge cast-iron chandeliers with candles and they were covered in cobwebs. There were no utilities, no working drains. It was very gothic. There was water damage. We were lucky to open. The city wanted places open and they let us."

Audrey McCrimmon Kolyer, "Miss Windsor 1944," still a Cliff Bell's regular.

Audrey McCrimmon Kolyer is thankful for these golden chains of events.

Kolyer—"Miss Windsor 1944"—was drinking chardonnay at Cliff Bell's bar during happy hour. She wore a jacket with leopard-print trim and a matching skirt. "I always dress up," she says. "During that era if you didn't dress up you didn't come in. I'm eighty-five. I came here on a date when I was eighteen. We sat down in the main dining room and had dinner. No cocktails because I wasn't old enough. But I never stopped coming here. It was so elegant. It really doesn't look that different now. This is a classic supper club. I'm from a small town outside of Windsor and when I came over here, it was *really* classic to me. And I'm a classy person. And I looked then like I do today. Can I say that?"

Kolyer has a home in Grosse Pointe, Michigan. Her husband, Harry, was a successful sports advertising executive who died in 1982. In 1964 they bought the brick two-story home from Joseph Mario Barolo, the founder of the Mario Olive Company, who started his company at the historic Eastern Market in downtown Detroit. "I never got to see the house," Kolyer says. "My husband loved the bar downstairs. It was all red leather. It sat six people and there were totem poles on each side of the bar. It had running hot and cold water behind the bar. That's why we bought the house."

When Harry and Audrey had supper at Cliff Bell's, her favorite order was the veal parmesan. She also had a friend from Toronto who sang at the supper club. "She was a French chanteuse," Kolyer said. "That's another reason I came here so often. I knew the bartender, who was her boyfriend at the time. Cliff Bell was the perfect owner. He made sure everybody was taken care of and he was always here. He talked to every table. He was very outgoing. Music was going all the time. This place was a gold mine."

In a separate conversation Howard says, "The acts that played here were local. Cliff was a showman and had his own house band. We don't believe a lot of traveling acts came here. I heard Etta James played here, but we can't confirm that. There is very little documentation."

Kolyer's posse includes Katie Stock, who owned the former Golden Galleon restaurant across from the Joe Louis Arena, and a former Detroit public relations man, Jim McDonough, who is Kolyer's nephew. McDonough looks around the happy hour crowd at Cliff Bell's and says, "You know what saved the place? Whoever owned it the last time lowered the ceilings two or three feet. They had all that plaster and nobody knew what was under it. When Paul's brother-in-law and sister looked at the place and started knocking out all the plaster they found this beautiful stucco."

"This once was the classiest town in the world," Stock says. "Detroit had so many grand restaurants and lovely supper clubs. Little Harry's, the Boulevard. Lots of supper clubs were along Jefferson. A lot of the auto industrialists lived in Grosse Pointe and Indian Village. These were their local spots. Little Harry's was a great, great place. Anita Baker bought it." The pop-soul singer tore it down.

Kolyer was half listening. Checking out the hipster waitstaff, she says, "When I came here the waitresses were all older. They didn't hire anybody young like they do today."

Howard looks around the busy Cliff Bell's. He thinks about the renewed energy of downtown Detroit. He takes time in choosing his words with the tempered cadence of ordering off an old menu. "Maybe a good analogy would be the people who held out in the Dust Bowl," he says. "They had the same sense of pride and would be happy to tell you about their lives. I guess I'm one of them."

23

The Butterfly Club

5246 East County Road X, Beloit, Wisconsin
(608) 362-8577 • www.butterflyclub.us

The ravines of Turtle Township near Beloit have always been fertile ground for the milkweed plant. This is not an across-the-Wisconsin-border dairy attraction but a destination for the monarch butterflies that lay their eggs on milkweeds where their larvae (caterpillars) feed.

That's how the Butterfly Club got its name in 1924. It is the most impressive supper club in southern Wisconsin.

"My kids are big into butterflies," says Mike Sala, who owns the Turtle Township supper club with his brother Hektor. "They show me the eggs on the milkweed plants. It is unbelievable."

The Butterfly Club is an unbelievable place. Start with the bar. That's what the regulars do. It is not uncommon for diners to spend an hour or more at the fifty-seat bar before adjourning to supper. The sleek, linear bar with fifty swiveled green chairs sits under a dropped ceiling. The bar is the centerpiece of a 110-seat cocktail lounge adorned with exposed brick, silver tile, and greenish opal paneling that matches a summer landscape. The south end of the bar features a view of the valley in which the milkweed plant grows among tall pine and blue spruce trees.

The Sala brothers purchased the club in 1999. They have since planted more than four hundred trees on their eleven-acre property. "Overall we have twenty-two big windows in the dining rooms and bar," Mike Sala says. "People always

The Butterfly Club is on East County Road X in rural Beloit, Wisconsin.

It looks like an airport lounge, but it is the swank jet-set bar at the Butterfly Club.

request a window seat." The dining room windows face south and bring in lots of sun in the winter months. The lounge hosts live blues and rock on Friday and Saturday nights.

The retro architecture came into play after a December 1972 fire destroyed the original Butterfly Club. It took nearly a year to rebuild the restaurant.

The supper club first opened in the summer of 1924 on five acres of land in the town that was then called Turtle. Hal and Mae Sherburne were the original owners and named their roadside diner to honor the many yellow and white butterflies that fluttered through the adjacent field. The Butterfly Tea Room was on old Wisconsin Highway 15, which rolled through Beloit to Milwaukee. Very slowly.

The tea room incorporated a kitchen and dining room on the main level and a bar and two more dining rooms in the basement, where intense card games went down among rows of gambling machines. In 1938 the complex was renamed the Butterfly Club.

During the late 1960s a big illuminated iron butterfly (no rock 'n' roll joke) was installed on the restaurant's roof. The place looked like a set from an Ed Wood sci-fi movie.

Mike Sala, born in 1965, and Hektor, born in 1967, have a unique take on the American supper club experience. They come from Korçë, Albania (population 80,000). Their father, James, worked in the coal mines of Korçë, but the brothers fled for the United States in 1990 when the country was at the dawn of communist rule. They obtained political asylum in Greece. Their father and grandfather were against the communist regime. The Republic of Albania was founded in 1991 and the former communist party was routed in the 1992 elections amid grave economic collapse and social unrest.

A large American flag on a tall stand is perched near the hostess table as guests enter the supper club. "We lost our freedom," he says. "Put yourself in the middle of the ocean and you see a light. That is your very lucky light. That is what the United States means to us."

The brothers first settled in Freeport, Illinois, because an uncle lived there. They understand family. Mike looks around the open space and explains, "A supper club is different than a family diner. The way we serve at a supper club is

Butterfly Club co-owner Mike Sala is proud to be an American.

A stamp of approval as you enter the Butterfly Club.

Joy King began waitressing at the Butterfly in 1960.

more slow and easygoing. People take their time. Then there's desserts or after-dinner drinks. Our ice cream drinks are popular. If you are in a hurry, don't go to a supper club. Beloit used to have five or six supper clubs. Now there's us and the Gun Club." [The Gun Club burned down in the summer of 2010 and may be rebuilt.]

The Sala brothers purchased the club from Rick Camboni, who had owned it since 1977. Camboni decided to sell the club in September 1999 in conjunction with the club's seventy-fifth anniversary. "We wanted to buy a supper club," Mike says. "We didn't want a bar. Or a pub. A supper club is a place you go with your family or your close friends. You have a meaningful time. Now, you see so many people eating in their car."

Welcome to America.

You rarely see Hektor on the floor at the Butterfly. "He's in the back cooking," Mike says.

Beloit is just five miles from the Illinois border. Why are there supper clubs in Beloit but none in northern Illinois? Or most of Illinois, for that matter? Many suggest that answer lies with Wisconsin's affinity for the brandy old-fashioned. Longtime Butterfly Club waitress Joy King explains, "They just don't serve the brandy old-fashioned in other states. The majority of our old-fashioneds and Manhattans are brandy. Very few whiskies." King started working at the Butterfly Club in 1960 and returned after the 1972 fire.

The dual Butterfly Club dining rooms seat 180 people and overlook a large outdoor deck. The dining room chairs are original. They were repainted and restored after the 1972 fire. "During the evening we dim the light in the dining room," Sala says. "We had supper clubs in Europe with linen tablecloths. The lights are down and there's easygoing music. But they're not as big as they are here. There's not as much space in Europe."

When the Sala brothers purchased the business, they inherited recipes that dated back to the beginning of the club. The recipes are handwritten in a notebook. Hektor says, "The garlic-pepper seasoning is a family recipe and I don't know how far back it goes. The [salt, black pepper, thyme, oregano] seasoning for the steaks are my recipes. The batter sauce and breading in the fish is an old recipe. You have to follow the recipe to be perfect."

A 2006 book on Wisconsin Friday night fish fries rated the Butterfly Club second only to the Serb Hall in Milwaukee. "We use old-style tartar sauce and a lightly breaded Icelandic cod," Hektor says. The year-round fish fry runs from 4:30 to 10:00 PM Fridays—and, due to popular demand, on Wednesdays.

"And prime rib [eight-ounce prime rib and three large white Honduran shrimp] is very popular every night, not just Saturday," Hektor says. "We try to do different things like combine seafood and poultry." The Butterfly Club is the only restaurant in the Beloit area that serves cinnamon rolls instead of bread before dinner.

The historic club has been used as a meeting place for the Beloit Snappers minor league baseball team and union meetings for the former General Motors plant in nearby Janesville, and when Miss Wisconsin visited in 2006 she caused quite a commotion. The Butterfly Club is the Sala brothers' second restaurant venture in the Beloit area, but their first supper club.

"You use your brain more here at a supper club," Mike says. "You want to create something special every day of the week. That was our challenge." And the Sala brothers are used to meeting all challenges. They are young Americans.

24

The Old Fashioned

23 N. Pickney Street, Madison, Wisconsin
(608) 310-4545 • www.theoldfashioned.com

Artists and writers draw from all the senses, but food memory is one of the old reliables. Snapshots of suppers past have fueled the success of the Old Fashioned, across the street from the state capitol building in Madison.

Chef Tami Lax, general manager Jennifer DeBolt, and their three partners have deployed childhood memories that include a hearty menu of prime rib and Scandinavian-style chicken dinners, colorful Schlitz beer signs, and the floor and portions of the bar made with reclaimed oak from a Buster Brown shoe factory in Ohio.

The Old Fashioned opened in 2005 in a brick three-story building built in 1873. It doesn't have the lean look of a traditional supper club and it is not out in the country like a traditional supper club. But DeBolt insists, "We consider this a traditional Wisconsin supper club. We offer a lot of the same foods you find in a traditional supper club. Our atmosphere resembles an older supper club."

On Friday nights there's often a two-and-a-half-hour wait for the traditional fish fry with lake perch, beer-battered cod, and walleye. "Honestly, this brings back people's childhoods," De Bolt says. "I've seen lake perch on a menu since I was a kid. Or you see a lazy Susan here, and it's oh-my-god."

But where the Old Fashioned breaks from tradition is its loyalty to local purveyors. DeBolt, who orders beer and cheese for the restaurant, says 80 percent of

Portions of the Old Fashioned bar are made with reclaimed oak from a Buster Brown shoe factory in Ohio.

the menu is sourced locally. Lax founded the Madison chapter of Slow Food and serves on the Slow Food U.S.A. APC Committee. Old-school supper clubs are into a slow evening, but not Slow Food.

DeBolt explains, "For us in Madison, people are really after the local aspect of things. They want independently owned businesses. We've been successful because we fit that niche. We meet a lot of demographics. Last week there was an eighty-two-year-old couple sitting next to college kids."

Even sexpot singer Tom Jones discovered the Old Fashioned. "It was a busy Friday night and he walked up to the host stand," DeBolt says. "They asked for his name for a table. The hostess had her head down. He said, 'I'm Tom Jones.' She said, 'OK, Mr. Jones, it will be two hours for your table.' He said, 'No, I'm *Tom* Jones.' She was like twenty years old so she had to ask somebody who Tom Jones was. In the meantime all these women are fawning and walking around him."

Jones still had to wait those two hours. "Johnny Depp and his group came in late and made room in a corner," DeBolt says. "Christian Slater was not very happy when we made him wait." That's the hearty Wisconsin way.

Customers can "Help Yourself" (Jones's 1968 smash hit) to four different Wisconsin cheese plates deploying nineteen local cheese purveyors. Hamburgers are made from organic local beef. The mellow bratwurst comes from Miesfeld Market in Sheboygan. And they insisted the brats

Jennifer DeBolt, general manager of the Old Fashioned in Madison.

be served on hard rolls, a Sheboygan tradition. So the rolls are driven into Madison four times a week from Highway Bakery in Sheboygan.

The bar menu offers one-dollar spicy pickled eggs and three-dollar landjaegers, a cured sausage from nearby New Glarus. On Saturdays DeBolt makes about four trips back and forth pulling a huge red wagon between the restaurant and the farmers market across the street.

The acclaimed farmers market is held around the Wisconsin state capitol building. The Old Fashioned, across the street, was ground zero in the 2011 protests to recall Governor Scott Walker—who prefers the Esquire supper club in Madison. "In the long haul the protests hurt the businesses around here," DeBolt says. "The streets were packed and I was the one at the door saying we weren't letting people in. One person in, one person out. All demonstrators."

The Old Fashioned did not serve free coffee or appetizers to the protesters. "One of the things they taught me in business school was to always stay neutral no matter how you feel," DeBolt said. "We did set aside one table upstairs in the private dining room for Jesse Jackson and his security. There were some actors from a couple of soaps. Then when the demonstrations ended around five o'clock we'd be dead because no one wanted to come downtown. That went on for a few months. Two businesses on the square closed because of all that. People were drinking iced tea and Miller Lite. And that's all they were doing."

The Old Fashioned carries more than 160 Wisconsin beers, including the Supper Club, created in June 2010 by Capital Brewing just outside of Madison. The supper club has thirty tap lines and also offers five different vodkas and three different gins from Wisconsin.

Of course, this brings up the restaurant's namesake. The old-fashioned is a staple of the Wisconsin supper club, but it's not just any old old-fashioned. The first use of the name "old-fashioned" went down in a bourbon whiskey cocktail in the 1880s at the Pendennis Club in Louisville, Kentucky. But Wisconsin is known for substituting brandy for whiskey. Winters are colder in Wisconsin than in Kentucky.

"That's what all of our parents drank when we went out as kids," DeBolt says. "The state is known for old-fashioneds, but they're not exclusive to Wisconsin."

On a typical Friday night the Old Fashioned sells about three hundred old-fashioneds. But don't expect the supper club relish tray. "We do about one thousand people a day," DeBolt says. "We'd have to hire one person just to slice lettuce and prepare it for us." The Old Fashioned employs 130 people.

Doug Griffin is a designer at the Wisconsin Historical Museum, across the state capitol square from the Old Fashioned. He is a "darn near daily" lunch customer at the supper club. Griffin loves the beer-battered walleye sandwich with shredded cabbage and house-made lemon caper sauce as well as the Friday-only clam chowder.

In 2010 the museum hosted a supper club installment of its Taste Traditions of Wisconsin series. "It was one of our most popular ones," Griffin says over lunch. "It's totally nostalgia. People react strongly to fond memory. It's not the food itself necessarily, but it's about the experience and where they were during the experience. I was talking to a friend about Door County fish boils and it is much the same thing. It's not that the fish boil itself tasted great. It's the fact you are in Door County. It's summer. With your family. And you're a kid and you're having a great time."

The Old Fashioned partners understand how to tie in the supper club's sense of place with food.

In his book *Standing by Words*, Kentucky regionalist Wendell Berry argues, "To know where you are (and whether or not that is where you should be) is at least as important as to know what you are doing, because in the moral (the ecological) sense, you cannot know what you have learned where. Not knowing where you are, you can lose your soul or your soil, your life or your way home."

So DeBolt and Lax visited about fifty Upper Midwest supper clubs taking notes incognito. "Jotting down, 'We can't forget Saturday prime rib,'" DeBolt says. "Things like that. We both grew up in supper clubs." DeBolt was raised in Watertown, halfway between Milwaukee and Madison. Her father, Roger, was a tool and die engineer.

Doug Griffin understands the Old Fashioned is not a supper club in the old-fashioned sense. "This is not an according-to-Hoyle supper club," he says. "They would

You still can't go wrong with vintage Schlitz beer ads at the Old Fashioned.

Pickled egg for a buck? No yolk!

Say cheese!

Say it loud and say it proud with old-fashioned Old Fashioned bumper stickers.

describe themselves as a tribute to supper clubs. And they very much are. The food would definitely not be out of place at a supper club, even though a lot of it is more upscale. You'll get a better burger here than you will at most supper clubs. It has the feel of a supper club with the decor and warm design. Lots of novelty items on the walls, old brandy bottles, Paul Bunyan, that kind of stuff."

The Old Fashioned seats about 190 including twenty-two bar stools. In early 2012 a second fifty-seat bar with thirty tap lines was added next door to the restaurant. Every brewery in the state of Wisconsin is now represented at the Old Fashioned.

In true supper club style, suppers are served with cloth napkins, and supper starts being served at four PM. But the ownership group never considered opening the supper club out in the country. DeBolt lives three blocks away from the Old Fashioned and Lax owns the popular Harvest, next door to the supper club.

And as some older supper clubs in the country fall by the wayside, the Old Fashioned continues to thrive in the city. "The small towns think we're crazy for charging $12.95 for a perch fry," DeBolt explains. "They're trying to do it at $8.95 but they're still falling away, unfortunately. Or the product suffers, the food suffers, one thing leads to another and they're done."

Postscript

Tribute to Supper Clubs Gone By

The door is never closed on a good supper club.

Some businesses go under, others are refitted into upscale office space. Others, like the futuristic Gobbler Supper Club in Johnson Creek, Wisconsin, sit empty waiting for a better day.

Preservation, after all, is just history in measured motion.

The supper club experience is at the core of family. Birthdays, holidays, weddings, and reunions are celebrated at a supper club in a leisurely fashion. The compressed, warm nature of the setting forces one to live in the moment. And the memories play on long after the physical supper club is gone.

Frank Bond's Supper Club, at 3243 S. Harlem in Berwyn, Illinois, was one of those places. Berwyn (Route 66), Cicero (Al Capone), and Oak Park (Frank Lloyd Wright, Ernest Hemingway) are the first ring of suburbs west of Chicago. With the city in such close proximity, a Berwyn supper club could not afford to be too humble. It would get lost in the culinary shuffle.

So at Frank Bond's a mammoth 1961 Vegas-inspired neon sign promoted "The Supper Club" (with an illuminated cocktails sidebar), almost dwarfing the name of Bond, who was head chef and owner. A bar featured live organ music from Charlie Stanek.

The late great *Chicago Daily News* writer M. W. Newman reviewed Bond's in June 1962 with this report: "Its opening salvo consists of a relish tray laden with herring, beets, liver pate, radishes, peppers and scallions. Plus breadstuffs. . . . This suburban supper club has white tablecloths, smart black-and-gold chairs, subdued lighting and pleasant decor."

There was ample parking for big cars at Frank Bond's Supper Club in the summer of 1962. Note how the huge neon sign covers all bases, with "Dinners" in small letters at the bottom.

Frank Bond's Supper Club was a popular Chicagoland destination for suppers, weddings, banquets, and, by the mid-1960s, rock 'n' roll shows.

By the mid-1960s Frank Bond's built an adjacent banquet room that served up to eight hundred people. Bond also added the Mardi Gras cocktail lounge for before-supper libation.

"Frank Bond's Supper Club was an old standby," said Berwyn-born songwriter Jim Peterik, who co-wrote the monster hit "Eye of the Tiger" for Survivor and 1970's "Vehicle" for the Berwyn-based Ides of March. "I think it was on its way out when the Ides started playing teen dances there in 1966, '67. At this point it was functioning more as a hall."

Research at the Berwyn Public Library revealed the last mention of Frank Bond's in the March 6, 1970, issue of the *Berwyn Life* when the Norman King Trio appeared with dinner being served in the Maria Regina Room, which had been "completely redecorated," according to the paper.

Peterik said, "The other supper club was Magnum's Chateau [on Ogden Avenue, aka Route 66, in southwest suburban Lyons]. I had my wedding there. It was the place to be. I saw some great acts there like the Four Seasons and Blood, Sweat and Tears—with dinner, or supper, of course. This was the height of fancy in the 1950s and early '60s." Local television personality Two Ton Baker—a major influence on late Memphis blues-rock producer Jim Dickinson—played piano at Magnum's.

The Chateau also had a huge neon sign that featured a fat green lobster. Customers could pick their own lobster for dinner from a giant tank in the front lobby.

Original Ides guitarist/vocalist Larry Millas grew up in Berwyn, a half mile from Frank Bond's. The Ides had formed in 1964 as the Shon-Dels. "Frank Bond's was a mainstay for us," Millas says before heading out to play with the Ides at a July 2012 Cicerofest gig. "When the Ides played there I was eighteen, nineteen. We played in the banquet room. There was a whole series of places like [teen club] Dex Card's Wild Goose [in north suburban Waukegan]. Events would be in these clubs in regular rotation."

Millas called Magnum's a Vegas kind of supper club. "You sat down at tables with big burgundy booths," he recalls. "A photographer would walk around with a camera and take pictures and you would get the prints mailed to you in a frame. The service was great. You'd have a prime rib dinner and see a show. The best prime rib on the planet and the best garlic bread ever. Of course there was butter and garlic and Parmesan cheese but it was like a cake. It was an event. There was a featured singer and a chorus line. I spent a lot of time there between the ages of seven and twelve. My dad [John] was a physician for the Magnum family so he was great friends with the family. Frank Bond's didn't have the 'scene' that Mangum's had."

Why was the Berwyn-Lyons corridor so popular with supper clubs when so few existed in Illinois? "Not to tread on this too lightly, but there was a mob thing in the Berwyn-Cicero scene, and Riverside was on the outskirts of the suburbs, so these were just enough away for someplace to go," Millas answers. "They were destinations."

Capone pallies "Screwey" Claude Maddox and Frank Nitti resided in Riverside while the wonderfully supper club–named Tony "Big Tuna" Accardo and Paul "the Waiter" Ricca were next door in River Forest. Millas says, "And a lot of people in the Berwyn-Cicero area were connected in other ways. There were a lot of doctors, lawyers, and stuff. That's what you did when you had money around here—you went to a supper club. I have so many fond memories of that time. They still seem larger than life."

No list of late great Midwest supper clubs would ever be complete, but here are several more memorable ones who did not get their just desserts:

- Marty's Showboat Supper Club, operated in partnership with the Northern-maire Resort in Three Lakes in Oneida County, Wisconsin. The exterior actually looked like a boat with a rounded bow and porthole windows. It was designed by Three Lakes resident Cy Williams. Williams was an architecture student at Notre Dame who went on to play for the Chicago Cubs (1912–17) and Philadelphia Phillies (1918–30). Williams died in April 1974 in Eagle River, Wisconsin. He was eighty-six.

- The Lark Supper Club in Tiffin, Iowa, opened in 1943 and burned down after a kitchen fire in 2000. The Lark was a meeting place for people en route to Iowa Hawkeyes basketball and football games, and it is a safe bet that actor Ashton Kutcher ate there since he is from outside of Tiffin (population 1,800).

- "Then we had the Ranch Supper Club in Swisher [twelve miles south of Cedar Rapids]," said Jeff Selzer, co-owner of the Ced-Rel Supper Club in Cedar Rapids. "That's now a church. They had an auction when the Ranch went out of business. The auctioneer called lazy Susans 'cake stands.' We bought the entire lot of 'cake stands,' about seventy-five of them."

The Pyramid of the Nile Supper club sits empty in Dodge County, Wisconsin.

- Pyramid of the Nile, near Beaver Dam in Dodge County, Wisconsin. The quirky supper club closed on New Year's Eve 2009 but you can still visit a website where meals are "fit for a Pharoah and His Queen." This supper club was really a forty-foot-tall pyramid in the middle of a Wisconsin cornfield. It opened in the 1960s as the Pyramid before becoming the Nile Club and then Pyramid of the Nile. The interior was accented with Egyptian columns, paintings, and sculptures.

  Unlike a Pharoah and His Queen, a lousy economy was blamed for the pyramid's demise.

  But the empty Egyptian-Wisconsin supper club still stands tall.

Jet-age architecture landed in the fields of Wisconsin in the form of the Gobbler Motel and Supper Club.

- The Gobbler Motel & Supper Club, Johnson Creek, Wisconsin, in the shadow of I-94. The Gobbler is larger than life now that it is dead. The Gobbler was created by an area turkey farmer, who designed the dining room in bright pink and pink shag carpeting. The shape of the dining room replicated a fat turkey. Several websites are devoted to the Jetsons-style supper club that opened in 1967. It featured a revolving bar reminiscent of the Carousel Bar at the Hotel Monteleone in New Orleans. But Johnson Creek is not New Orleans, and the Gobbler shut down in 2002. The supper club reopened for six months as the Round Stone Restaurant and Lounge, and then John's Rib House, but closed again for good in 2005.

    The Gobbler served turkey 365 days a year but also considered supper club staples like prime rib and seafood. The restaurant sat 350 people in the Lavender Room and the Gobbler Gallery. The circular bar was in the Royal Roost Cocktail Lounge. An adjacent motel featured waterbeds and newfangled eight-track machines.

    Current co-owner Marvin Havill, a local car dealer, is still trying to sell the supper club. The Gobbler restaurant equipment, furniture, and the petrified wood that used to line the supper club's fowl entryway were sold in a 2010 auction. Havill said the Gobbler is now just an empty building.

"The turkey farmer turned it over to his sons and his sons lost it for various reasons," Havill said from his home in Jefferson, Wisconsin, about seven miles from the site. "Then it turned into a Mexican restaurant. We purchased it in '95 and reopened it in '96 as the New Gobbler. We redid the whole place. But we were absentee owners, and that just doesn't work. We could have sold it many times over for other things than a nightclub, but the village won't tolerate that."

Tolerate what?

"Well, it could have been a Gentleman's Club many times over," he answered with a chuckle. "It's a perfect building for that. The building is in fine shape. There's twenty inches of poured concrete. It's like a bunker. There's walls inside of petrified wood. Quartz crystal. The outside is Mexican lava rock. It still has the revolving bar and it works.

"There is a big nostalgia thing with the Gobbler even though it is closed. It wasn't a Playboy Club, but similar to the atmosphere of a Playboy Club. The waitresses would have turkey feathers instead of a bunny tail. It has unique windows that were supposed to represent turkey eyes. Then there was the hotel up on the hill. It was a small-populated area but the Gobbler drew people from all over."

- Poole's Cuba Club, 3416 W. University Avenue, about a mile west of the present-day Smoky's Club in Madison, Wisconsin. Leonard "Smoky" Schmock was a bartender at the Cuba Club, which ran from 1946 to 1991. The one-level ranch-style supper club was burned down as part of a January 1992 fire drill for the Madison Fire Department.

  Smoky's son Tom said, "I may be disputed on this, but the Cuba Club invented the fish fry in Madison. They would have piles of lake perch in there on a Friday." The late Lyle Poole opened the club with the faraway name. His son Geoff now operates Pooley's sports bar, 5441 High Crossing Boulevard on the far east side of Madison.

"You know how the Cuba Club got its name?" Geoff asked. "Let's C U B A Customer of ours. But then over the years we'd get calls like, 'Is Fidel there?' and then they would hang up."

- The Melody Supper Club, Highway 47, two miles north of Appleton, Wisconsin. Names are always changing at some supper clubs. Bea and Elmer Poh bought the Green Lantern (established early 1930s) in 1943 and renamed it the Melody Supper Club, which became a legendary destination in the Appleton area. Bea and Elmer sold out in 1981, and a couple owners later the remodeled building still exists as the Legacy Supper Club (www.thelegacy-supperclub.com).

- The Tornado Steak House, 116 S. Hamilton near the state capitol in Madison, Wisconsin, is a timeless story in refitting a supper club. Longtime Madison residents remember the Tornado as Crandall's Supper Club, housed in a historic space that was built in 1873. Around 1909–10 the upstairs of the supper club was the offices of *LaFollette's Weekly*, which morphed into the *Progressive* magazine.

  In May 1965, the all-you-can-eat Friday night fish fry at Crandall's was $1.15, according to an ad in the *Wisconsin-State Journal*, back when newspapers were on newspaper.

  The Tornado opened in 1996. It is a popular dimly lit destination for Madison hipsters with excellent food. I've supped there a half dozen times and have never been disappointed (check out the grass-fed organic beef). But as New York Yankee Yogi Berra once quipped about the Saint Louis restaurant Ruggeri's, "Nobody goes there anymore. It is too crowded."

- Patterson's Supper Club, Sturgis, Michigan. This ranch house–styled supper club on 1104 W. Chicago Road served "traditional hospitality" a couple miles west of downtown Sturgis. Alice "Ma" Gibson was the longtime hostess, seating people in one of three large dining rooms. The first dining room was finished in black and gold lacquer with ample mirrors. The back room featured a big fireplace. Patterson's was torn down in 1985, according to Linda Winkens of the Sturgis Historical Society. "They had a wonderful buffet and hand-sized jumbo shrimp," she said. "I will never forget their open-faced chicken salad sandwich with a slice of cheese. A wonderful place."

- Welch's Embers, built on the site of the Ace of Clubs, which was destroyed by a 1958 fire in Madison, Wisconsin. Welch's was known for its majestic lobby chandelier that was imported from Germany. Welch's also had upstairs and downstairs kitchens.

- The Lake Club, 2840 Fox Bridge Road, Springfield, Illinois. Born in 1940 as a nightclub, closed in 1988, and burned down in 1992. Where there are politicians, there are long suppers and lots of fun. Located in the state's capital city, the Lake Club fit this bill. The hot spot's peak years were in the 1940s when acts like Bob Hope, Woody Herman, and Mickey Rooney appeared at the club while traveling Route 66 through Springfield. Gambling can be found in the distant roots of many old-school supper clubs, and the Lake Club was no different. Its downfall began during a December 1958 raid that shut the establishment down. The billiard tables were so large they had to be dismantled to get them out of the club, according to author Troy Taylor, who featured the Lake Club in his *Haunted Illinois* book.

Then, there is always lively debate on whether a supper club is really a supper club.

Pop culture students are evenly divided on the "supper club" status of the colorful Nye's Polanise Room, 112 E. Hennepin Avenue, in Minneapolis. I used to listen to Sweet Lou Snider sing "As Time Goes By" behind her piano at the popular bar–restaurant–polka lounge. (She retired in February 2011, ending a forty-year run.) I love Nye's, but I don't call it a supper club.

The original Nye's opened in 1950 in the spot that is now the adjacent polka bar. The bar served Tyskie beer, "The No. 1 Beer of Poland" then, and they still do today. In 2006 *Esquire* magazine named Nye's "The Best Bar in America."

Molly Stoddard, lead singer of the popular country-rock band Molly & the Hey-makers, is a resident of supper club–equipped Hayward, Wisconsin. "I think Nye's is a supper club," she said. "Nye's is one of those places that got embraced by the hip crowd. I used to go there in the 1980s with [lead guitarist] Andy Dee from my band. We went when it was still a little Polish neighborhood place. It truly felt like a supper club to me. Then it got embraced by the hip crowd and changed a bit. It's good. They changed with the times and they are going to survive because of it. They figured out how to hold onto it."

Supper Club Listing by State

Illinois

EAST DUBUQUE

Timmerman's Supper Club

Iowa

CEDAR RAPIDS

The Ced-Rel

The Lighthouse Inn Supper Club

DUBUQUE

Moracco

Michigan

DETROIT

Cliff Bell's

Minnesota

AVON

Fisher's Club

CLITHERALL

The Peak Supper Club

MINNEAPOLIS

Jax Café

Red Stag Supper Club

OTTERVILLE

The Otter Supper Club and Lodge

Wisconsin

BELOIT

The Butterfly Club

HANOVER

Ding-A-Ling Supper Club

HAYWARD

Turk's Inn and Sultan Room

LAKE DELTON

The Del-Bar

Ishnala

MADISON

Kavanaugh's Esquire Club

The Old Fashioned

Smoky's Club

RACINE

HobNob

SISTER BAY

Sister Bay Bowl

STURGEON BAY

The Mill

TOMAH

Mr. Ed's Tee Pee Supper Club

TREMPEALEAU

Sullivan's Supper Club

WISCONSIN DELLS

House of Embers

Photo Credits

1 **Turk's Inn and Sultan Room**
Dave Hoekstra, except page 5, Courtesy of Turk's Inn and Sultan Room

2 **The Ced-Rel**
Paul Natkin

3 **Sullivan's Supper Club**
Dave Hoekstra

4 **Jax Café**
Dave Hoekstra, except pages 44, 50, Courtesy of Jax Café

5 **Sister Bay Bowl**
Courtesy of Sister Bay Bowl, except photos on pages 66, 69, Dave Hoekstra

6 **Ishnala**
Dave Hoekstra

7 **HobNob**
Dave Hoekstra, except photos on pages 78, 80, 82, Courtesy of HobNob

8 **The Otter Supper Club and Lodge**
Dave Hoekstra

9 **Mr. Ed's Tee Pee Supper Club**
Dave Hoekstra

10 **House of Embers**
Paul Natkin, except page 118, courtesy of Mike Obois

11 **The Del-Bar**
Paul Natkin

12 **Ding-A-Ling Supper Club**
Paul Natkin

13 **Moracco**
Dave Hoekstra

14 **Smoky's Club**

Dave Hoekstra, except pages 152, 156 (bottom), 157, 159, Paul Natkin, and pages 153, 156 (center), 160, 162, courtesy of Smoky's

15 **Fisher's Club**

Dave Hoekstra, except pages 170, 171, courtesy of Fisher's Club

16 **Timmerman's Supper Club**

Paul Natkin

17 **The Mill**

Page 193, Ralph Valatka; 194, (top), 202, Dave Hoekstra; 194 (bottom), 196, courtesy of the Mill; 195, courtesy of James Cordier; 198, courtesy of the Petersilka family

18 **Kavanaugh's Esquire Club**

Dave Hoekstra

19 **The Lighthouse Inn Supper Club**

Paul Natkin, except pages 213, 214, Dave Hoekstra

20 **The Peak Supper Club**

Dave Hoekstra

21 **Red Stag Supper Club**

Courtesy of Red Stag Supper Club, except page 238, Dave Hoekstra

22 **Cliff Bell's**

Courtesy of Cliff Bell's, except pages 252, 253, Dave Hoekstra, and page 258, courtesy of Audrey McCrimmon Kolyer

23 **The Butterfly Club**

Paul Natkin

24 **The Old Fashioned**

Paul Natkin

Postscript

Dave Hoekstra, except page 277, Marv Havill

Acknowledgments

Much gratitude to Susan Betz, Rick Kogan, Paul Natkin, Kirby Nelson, and my empathetic editors Lisa Reardon and Michelle Schoob, who were careful with the knife. They made this a better book.

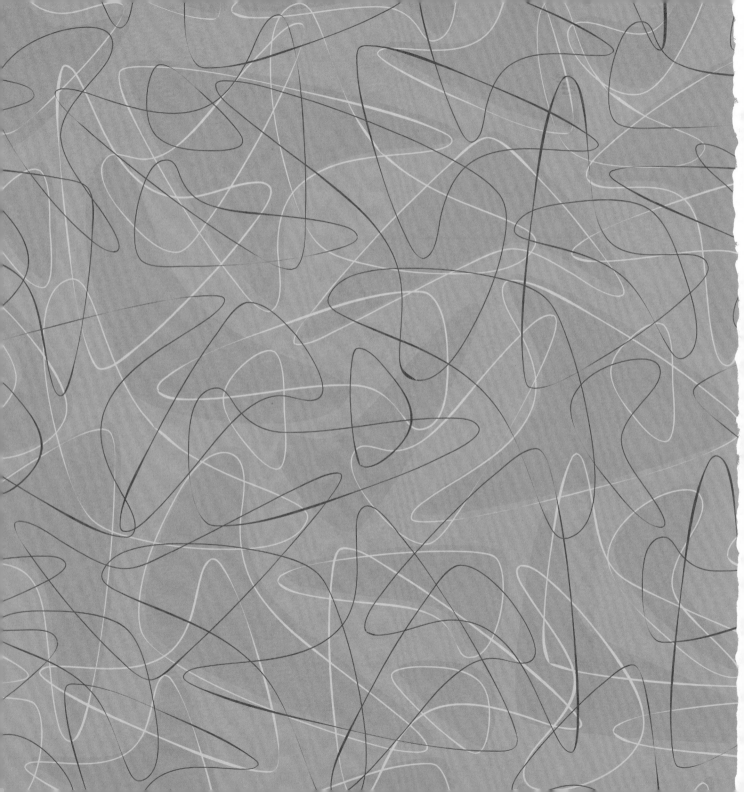